The Roosting Box

Also by Kristen den Hartog

Non-Fiction

The Cowkeeper's Wish: A Genealogical Journey
(with Tracy Kasaboski)

The Occupied Garden: A Family Memoir of War-Torn Holland
(with Tracy Kasaboski)

Fiction

And Me Among Them

Origin of Haloes

The Perpetual Ending

Water Wings

The ROOSTING BOX

REBUILDING THE BODY
AFTER THE FIRST WORLD WAR

KRISTEN DEN HARTOG

GOOSE LANE EDITIONS

Edited by Linda Pruessen.
Copy edited by Jess Shulman.
Cover and page design by Julie Scriver.
Cover image: Artificial left hand, Birmingham, England, 1914-1920. Science Museum, London. Attribution 4.0 International (CC BY 4.0)
Printed in Canada.
10 9 8 7 6 5 4 3 2 1

Library and Archives Canada Cataloguing in Publication

Title: The roosting box : rebuilding the body after the First World War / Kristen den Hartog.
Names: Den Hartog, Kristen, 1965- author.
Description: Includes bibliographical references and index.
Identifiers: Canadiana (print) 20230540813 | Canadiana (ebook) 20230540856 |
ISBN 9781773103266 (softcover) | ISBN 9781773103273 (EPUB)
Subjects: LCSH: Dominion Orthopaedic Hospital (Toronto, Ont.)—History—20th century. |
LCSH: World War, 1914-1918—Medical care—Ontario—Toronto—History—20th century. |
LCSH: War wounds—Treatment—Ontario—Toronto—History—20th century. |
LCSH: War wounds—Patients—Rehabilitation—Ontario—Toronto—History—20th century. |
LCSH: World War, 1914-1918—Veterans—Medical care—Ontario—Toronto—History—20th century. |
LCSH: Disabled veterans—Rehabilitation—Ontario—Toronto—History—20th century. |
LCSH: World War, 1914-1918—Social aspects—Canada.
Classification: LCC D629.C2 D46 2024 | DDC 940.4/7571—dc23

Goose Lane Editions acknowledges the generous support of the Government of Canada, the Canada Council for the Arts, and the Government of New Brunswick.

Goose Lane Editions is located on the unceded territory of the Wəlastəkwiyik whose ancestors along with the Mi'kmaq and Peskotomuhkati Nations signed Peace and Friendship Treaties with the British Crown in the 1700s.

Goose Lane Editions
500 Beaverbrook Court, Suite 330
Fredericton, New Brunswick
CANADA E3B 5X4
gooselane.com

MIX
Paper from
responsible sources
FSC
www.fsc.org
FSC® C103567

For my father, Jim den Hartog,
and for the *ghosts* visiting these pages:
poets who died in the First World War

"A hospital alone shows what war is."
—Erich Maria Remarque,
All Quiet on the Western Front

Contents

Author's Note

This book has been many years in the making. One day while reading about First World War veterans, I came upon a digitized booklet about Toronto's Christie Street Hospital, compiled in 1920 and containing lovely candid photographs of patients and staff as well as page after page of names. I was absolutely taken with this little book, and with the history of the hospital. Since I lived nearby, I began to walk frequently to the spot and tried to imagine the hospital as it was more than one hundred years ago. The original building no longer exists and has been replaced by a sprawling retirement complex. A plaque marking the spot is the only clue to the site's remarkable history.

When I realized I could match up the names in the booklet with digitized service records at Library and Archives Canada, my obsession truly began. As I started gathering information from more resources, it struck me that the hospital was like a village, containing people from all sorts of backgrounds who'd had different experiences of war. I saw how the hospital itself offered an unusual way of examining the First World War and reviving the stories of some of the people who had lived there. So while the hospital is at the centre of this book, the story travels off from that point in many directions—to battlefields, to small home-towns in Canada and abroad, into makeshift hospitals on the frontlines, and across the ocean on war ships. It moves backward and forward in time, always returning to the place (and the concept) of healing. Many societal changes happened during this period and are explored in these pages—I could have doubled the size of my book had I included more of them. But I wanted to write an intimate story more than a history book, with a focus on individual people, what they endured, and how it changed them. I read widely to understand those lives: old newspapers, histories, and official war diaries, but also memoirs, in which people attempted to describe the life-altering strangeness of four years of war. I read poetry too. When I realized how many poets had died in the war, leaving their words behind, I began to draw from their work and weave it into my own. Fragments of these poems appear in *italicized grey text*, . helping me tell the tale.

—KdH

A Factory

In a way it was a magical time, given that magic can be dark or bright or both at once. Men by the thousands travelled up into the clouds in flying machines. Submarines lurked below the surface of the water and the men inside fired torpedoes at the enemy just like toys come to life. Little figurines full of wishes and nightmares. The earth *throbbed with the measured tread of marching feet.* As soldiers on each side moved toward the other, *brambles clutched and clung to them like sorrowing hands.* And on the eve of a big battle, there were always those permeated with a strange *knowing that their feet had come to the end of the world.*

Throughout, the birds sang. Ornithologists-turned-soldiers observed them carefully as they moved through foreign territory. They reported back to their societies that magpies had turned up all across the Western Front, and even though the large trees they loved for nesting had gone from much of the terrain, they sought out crooks in the smaller trees that had made it through. The yellowhammer was abundant even in the most devastated regions, laying eggs patterned with indecipherable brown scribbles. Great flocks of starlings swelled and contracted in the skies, as before; they made their nests in the ruined houses of the countryside below, as if the space had been cleared just for them. *The little owls that call by night* kept calling.

Flying was new for humans, so birders who trained as pilots thrilled at the opportunity to see *where all the wandering birds had flown.* They soared through the sky in flimsy contraptions, no parachutes to slow their fall in emergencies. They observed the heights at which birds migrated, and jotted notes in their diaries about green plovers and jackdaws. It seemed that many birds changed age-old migration routes because of war; nearly all birds of passage had flown over France when they moved south, but now the thunder of weapons had inspired them to find alternate routes. And yet: quail moved through the long grasses that grew around trenches. Sparrows perched on the telegraph wires while top-secret messages buzzed beneath their feet. In their dazzling uniforms, golden orioles whistled and twittered at the firing line.

There were bluebirds too—nurses nicknamed for their white veils and blue dresses, though these were often muddy and blood-stained, reeking of sweat after a long shift tending wounds. The nurses didn't engage in battle, but they were receptacles for the stories that needed unloading when patients came under their care. Whispered horrors that might never be spoken of again.

Men lost legs and arms in that war. They lost eyes and noses. Because of technological advances in warfare, every part of the body was vulnerable to *superhuman inhumanities.* The soldiers lost so many pieces of themselves that the medical teams of the day were pushed to new and astonishing levels of invention, of intervention. Some of the grandest achievements were made by accident, and some of the most thoroughly planned procedures failed miserably. But there were always more men coming; more opportunities for improvement. Fresh starts with horrible wounds. As one surgeon put it, "Man's ability to repair, it would seem, must always lag a little behind his ability to destroy."[1]

Short, tall, soft, sinewy, too young, too old, brave, and terrified, they had joined Canadian battalions from cities and towns, from remote reserves in the North, and even American addresses. Many had been on a years-long journey, marching through devastated landscapes of felled trees and skeletal architecture. They had dug trenches and lived inside them with rats and other vermin. They had seen the bloated corpses of horses at roadsides, and stepped through battlefields littered with the bodies of fellow soldiers and friends. Sometimes they'd walked right over them because there was no alternative. Or they had lain there themselves, close to death, hoping to be rescued. Often their pockets held strange souvenirs—the brass nose caps from shells, a dead enemy's Iron Cross, a lost friend's cap badge.

How did it feel to return from war's travels to *all the world's small things*? To come home to a place that war had not physically reached, where the houses were still standing in neat rows behind carefully planted gardens, and the streetcars glided along more plentifully than before, picking up and dropping off on all the main thoroughfares? Toronto had bloomed in the soldiers' time away. It had paved roads and new bridges; its infrastructure had grown rather than crumbled like the grand old buildings of Europe. Its residents had seen green space fill up with soldiers' tents and watched troops march through the city's streets; they'd been caught up in the war effort, making munitions, acetone, and army blankets, knitting socks, and sending cakes overseas. But they knew a different conflict than those who'd gone to war. How did the returned begin to convey—or hide—what they'd been through? Writing as a prisoner of war, one man joked about his eventual reintegration: "All who knew me will experience a sad deception when once again I break upon their sight. I was never noted as an example of beauty.... [But] my features seem to have acquired a strangely villainous expression."[2]

The gassed, the glass-eyed, the amputees, the shell-shocked: these were among the returned. For those who'd remained at home, the wounded offered disturbing inklings of what had happened "over there." In a way they evoked the ghosts of the ones who'd died; they carried the missing home. Nurses and doctors returned with these wounded, and now, in the less frantic environment of a military hospital, they remained connected: the patients and the caregivers, psyches grafted by shared understanding or inescapable memory. By funny times too. Their story—one made up of many—is necessarily told in great loops and swirls, just like starlings moving in a single flock, making patterns that might be decoded. It returns, time and again, to the trodden ground of a hospital, for that is how the war unfolded, much of it fought on the same small patch of earth scarred by trenches and swollen with bodies.

By 1915, the steady return of wounded soldiers had already hinted at war's toll, and the Canadian government established a Military Hospitals Commission to requisition buildings that could be easily converted into temporary hospitals. All across the country, schools and hotels were transformed for caregiving; even a convent and a prison were used. Sometimes private donors offered their homes as convalescent hospitals: at a refuge for shell-shocked soldiers in Rideau Lakes, the host provided pianos, canoes, rowboats, fishing tackle, gramophones, and even an automobile to help the men get well again. In Toronto, the wealthy Massey family gave over its Jarvis Street mansion, Euclid Hall, as a home for incurable cases who could be wheeled out to the magic of the landscaped gardens, or into the music room for regular recitals. Toronto was an important medical centre from the beginning of the war. Military hospitals took over several school campuses and a Salvation Army training centre near Yonge and Davisville, which became known as the Davisville Military Hospital, was renovated to hold 450 beds for patients with orthopaedic wounds.

And still the men kept coming. By late 1917, the commission had put forward a controversial proposal to build a temporary hospital in High Park, a vast, tranquil property that had been donated to the city forty years earlier and had become a beloved refuge. The *Globe* predicted a "merry war" over the issue at Toronto City Council, and sure enough, aldermen and residents living nearest the park opposed the plan, stressing the park's importance as an urban oasis. Some feared High Park would develop an "unsavory name," since "wherever there was a soldiers' camp a certain undesirable class flocked."[3] One alderman claimed he'd give City Hall or even his own home for the wounded, but High Park was "a breathing space for the citizens,"[4] and must remain so. After much squabbling, the plan was abandoned, and the search for space went on. St. Andrew's College, a prestigious boys' school in the posh neighbourhood of Rosedale, was eventually taken over for temporary use, and a couple of apartment buildings were considered, but small rooms weren't ideal for a hospital. Something much more substantial was required as the men continued to pour home.

They moved over the *Atlantic's lazy swells* on floating hospitals that bore huge red crosses, and from there they were dispersed to institutions across the country as officials saw fit. Toronto received the greatest number. The men appeared on streetcars with crutches, eye patches, and empty sleeves where arms had been. In the company of nurses, they travelled in group outings to the Toronto Islands and the "breathing space" that was High Park, their presence emanating an aura of war.

In January 1918, the *Toronto Daily Star* reported that the Military Hospitals Commission had paid $450,000 for a site near Christie and Dupont streets in the city's west end. The National Cash Register factory was an L-shaped, one- and two-storey building that had just gone up there a few years earlier. The news marked a "radical departure" from the government's policy against the outright purchase of land. But the site, reported as seven acres with a modern building "very suitable for hospital purposes,"[5] was deemed so superior that it could be sold for a profit when it was no longer needed.

As with High Park, there was controversy. Some said Toronto was already overcrowded with wounded men, and that neglect of patients and inefficiency in the city's existing military hospitals was rampant. There was plenty of space for men in hospitals outside the city, which made the expenditure a dismaying waste of resources. Plus, the *Globe* reported, "the excitements of city life retarded rather than helped the return to health. Rural scenes and country air would be much more effective in assisting a return to the normal mind lost amid the rigors and shocks and scenes of war."[6] Advocates of the plan argued that smaller centres were lonely places for a returned soldier, and the big city was where the medical expertise was; the men would need vocational training and jobs, not to mention entertainment in their spare hours. And anyway, the purchase had been made now, and the hospital would go forward regardless of what its critics said.

Work on the building began with the war still raging. Charles McVicar, a fortyish doctor and lieutenant colonel, was chosen to head up the facility, which would be known as the Dominion Orthopaedic Hospital (DOH), and eventually the Christie Street Veterans' Hospital. McVicar was well regarded in both military and medical circles: as a young man he'd served as a soldier in the Boer War; in the current conflict, he'd helped organize the University of Toronto's overseas unit, No. 4 Canadian General Hospital, and had served with No. 4 on the Macedonian front and most recently in Basingstoke, Hampshire, at a newly built mental asylum taken over for military use. Basingstoke might have provided some inspiration for him now, for patients agreed it was "a fine institution,"[7] even when it was crowded. "We have a beautiful new ward," one man wrote to his sister "with the best of beds. There is a big recreation room with lounges & easy chairs, a library & reading room, and a waiting room."[8] The only downside, in this patient's view, was that Basingstoke, with a population of about twelve thousand, was "not much of a town—very dull." The same criticism would not arise in Toronto, where waves of immigration going back decades had diversified the population, and new infrastructure regularly altered the landscape. It was a growing city. By 1921, it held 500,000 people, second only to Montreal.

The National Cash Register factory moved its business to a new location, and the construction firm that had originally built the plant in 1913 was hired to convert it into a space suitable for convalescence, adding floors and a cluster of new buildings. Aside from the hospital itself, rising to four storeys with a fifth rooftop ward, the grounds would include a nurses' residence, an isolation building, a recreation lodge, and an artificial limb factory. The complex was to be finished that summer—1918—since beds for the wounded were badly needed, and there was much congestion at less than ideal spaces elsewhere. But by fall it was still not ready, and the men continued to come, with thousands more poised on the other shore. A surge in influenza cases added to the overcrowding, and tents were placed on the grounds of the Base

Hospital on Gerrard Street in order to accommodate the huge numbers
of sick patients. The *Star* reported one dying man's claim that "Canada
can well be ashamed of the way she has treated her men."[9] Despite the
dire situation, renovations lagged on well past armistice and into the
new year.

By January, when *cutting wind nipped to the bone*, two of the nursing
sisters who would work at the new hospital were on their way home
aboard the *Empress of Britain*. May Bastedo and Mabel Lucas had served
with Charles McVicar in Salonika and Basingstoke with the University
of Toronto group. Mabel had been in charge of the Basingstoke shell-
shock ward, and May had worked under her supervision. Now they
were returning to take up new duties at home, for though the war was
over, their work went on. Years later, Mabel recalled that the voyage was
exceptionally rough. "I don't think the captain thought we'd ever make
it.... I was seasick most of the time. I remember after two or three days,
I thought I'd try to get up. The boat lurched and threw me across the
cabin.... I'm sure I wept a bit. When we got to Halifax, the captain—he
had a big, heavy moustache—was just coated in ice. He had a sou'wester
on too, but he was a sheet of ice from being on the bridge."[10] According
to Mabel, the only person on board who wasn't sick on that trip was
May Bastedo.

It was similar when they'd crossed together back in 1915. For the
forthcoming adventure, May Bastedo had purchased a travel diary
emblazoned with gold letters that read "My Trip Abroad." A small compass was embedded in the cover, and May likely took keen interest in its
movements, for her diary entries and her letters home show her to be a
formidable traveller, eager for new experiences. On board the *Kildonan
Castle*, the ship that took the nurses from England to Salonika, May
wrote of venturing down to the bowels of the vessel "to see the engines
and the coal holes," and she recorded the number of furnaces and boil-
ers, and listed the different types of crew, from Marconi man to purser,
engineer to deck hand. The mail ship had only recently been converted
into a hospital ship and was painted white with a surrounding green
stripe and red crosses to make its designation obvious to the enemy. At
night, it was illuminated by green lights and red crosses blazing from
bow to stern. But there was little that could be done to fend off the

weather. The ship rose and dipped, wrestling the choppy waves. "We are in the trough of the sea," wrote May, "and rolling finely." At times the passage was so rough that the operating room table "ran around and smashed things up." The majority of the nurses were so unwell that they took to their berths, which May instinctively knew was the worst place to be. "If they would only come up it would be so much better." For May, there was much to see. Porpoises swam alongside the ship, and "little birds fly in and out, which shows we are not far from land." She gobbled her meals—"Soup, Fish, Macroni, Chicken, Pudding and Melon"—and noted passing between Spain and Africa. Most of the other nurses were anxious to be off the ship by the end of the journey, but May recognized her strengths and mused, "I'd like to stay on board and nurse on a hospital ship." She seems the sort of person you'd want close by during a war: tough and unshakable. Or "robust," as the doctor who performed her medical exam wrote when she enlisted in 1915, already forty-five years old.[11]

And yet, good nursing required different traits at different times. Mabel Lucas described the Basingstoke shell-shock ward where she and May Bastedo had worked as an exceptionally difficult posting, partly because she was younger than the other nurses and they resented the fact that she was in charge, but mostly because there was so little that could be done for the men. The patients had "a certain amount of medication," and they did needlework and other forms of occupational therapy to distract their troubled minds, but the nurses' chief duty was to create a quiet environment and keep the patients calm. One of the nurses—by process of elimination she had to have been May—"had a very harsh voice," according to Mabel. "She'd get the patients upset."

Though some specially schooled nurses had been recruited from asylums to deal with shell-shock patients, most nurses of this era had no training for treating patients with mental illness. They learned as they went, as they did with treating so many other war wounds. Often they found they were drawn to certain types of nursing more than others. One nurse remembered having a special talent for surgical nursing, but after the war "I didn't ever do it again....I just knew I couldn't....I had seen too many arms and legs lop into buckets."[12] Her brother's struggles with shell shock sparked a curiosity in psychiatric nursing, something she might never have considered had the war not happened. Over all, whatever their discipline, the women seem to have loved their work, "if it were only possible to forget its cause."[13]

In caring for the men, nurses and their helpers prepared huge supplies of dressings ahead of time, and then drew on those stores as they were needed, washing wounds and checking for gangrene. They dealt with fevers and hemorrhages and nightmares. They fed men who couldn't feed themselves, and wrote letters home to their families. This same task often fell to the nurses when a patient died and families had to be notified. And though all of it was draining, challenging work, it was invigorating, too. In their diaries and letters, nurses regularly wrote of the breathtaking landscape in the foreign countries they found themselves in, of the moon and the sunsets, of the local children selling them bundles of flowers. "To be near beauty," one nurse wrote, "does

Helen Fowlds, far left, and fellow nurses having "heaps of fun"
(Trent University Archives, Helen Marryat fonds, 69-001-6)

not mean to be away from horrors. They are mixed in a most chaotic mess all around us."[14]

Both the chaos and the work they'd been assigned were made more bearable by the presence of each other. Helen Fowlds, a nurse who worked at Christie Street with Mabel and May after the war, made frequent mentions in her letters and diaries of having "heaps of fun" with her nursing colleagues.[15] Some of these women continued to work together long after the conflict had ended, and remained friends for the rest of their lives. Together they had taken part in a life-altering experience, with highs and lows that were impossible to convey to those who'd not been through it themselves. "You see I know," one nurse wrote to her father from the front, "and you can only imagine."[16]

The bonds formed from war service offered more than comfort —they were power, too. A week before the new hospital on Christie Street opened, the city's artificial limb workers went on strike. The limb makers were mostly veterans themselves, and often amputees, so their jobs were not just a livelihood, but an emotional investment. The men were demanding that their industry be headed by a returned soldier rather than a government bureaucrat—someone who understood the particular needs of amputees—and that all jobs at limb-making factories go to veterans. They believed the government was trying to cut corners regarding the cost of prostheses, and implementing a system where "one sort of leg could be made as cheaply as another. Now that's a wrong idea," said one of the strikers. "There is a great difference between the various makes of legs and arms, and where one fitting may do for one sort of limb, another may take ten fittings to get it right."[17] The strike was just one tiny aspect of the social unrest rumbling through Canada after the war, in tandem with an angry influenza. The fight played out in the newspapers over the next ten days, and spread to factories in other cities, and the accounts that remain show not just the men's determination but their commitment to each other, and their growing awareness that they had to advocate for themselves as a unit—that *wherever and whenever soldiers met*, the war would always unite them. By the end, almost all of the demands of the limb workers were granted, and "a returned man" was put in charge.[18]

The day the DOH opened in the reconfigured cash register factory in February 1919, fifty men, mostly amputation cases, bumped across the wintry city in four Red Cross ambulances from the Davisville Military Hospital. They were cheered on like celebrities upon arriving. The press was there, snapping pictures of the event and recording colourful details. The publication *Hospital World* gushed about the new facility, having seen plenty of "dismal interiors" for convalescing men. "Thanks be! There are no dark corners or dingy wards." Every ward was "a veritable sunroom" with cream and white walls contrasted by rich oak doors. The fourth floor was "a Mecca for doctors who rejoice in modern scientific improvements," with a bright surgical theatre contrasted by several dark, mysterious rooms where the noisy work of x-rays took place, amazingly taking pictures of the inside of a body. Just above that level, "Nothing in the city can surpass the comprehensive view from the roof... [which] will be the favored spot in the summer time, and possibly will be as cool as the shores of the lake." The writer was especially impressed by the basement, which, in the days of the cash register factory, had had only three or four rooms. Now there were thirty, including the massive dining hall and a "wonderful vocational 'colony'" of workshops for leather craft, clay modelling, shoemaking, woodworking, and so on. Large windows meant that even this underground area was "splendidly lit."[19]

The *Star* likewise reported that the DOH was one of the finest hospitals of its kind on the continent, boasting dental, massage, and hydrotherapy facilities, a six-hundred-seat dining room, an auditorium, and a gymnasium with "every modern apparatus for the soldiers."[20] The place came "suddenly to life" with the presence of bluebird nurses and khaki-clad soldiers in the corridors, and the workmen and decorators finally gone. Sniffing out a story, the reporter came upon two "legless heroes" wheeling through the building. Both men were ready and waiting for artificial limbs, since production had slowed because of the strike. They had a good snoop around the DOH, but believed it was too big to ever be homey, the way Davisville was. Davisville was smaller than the DOH, and had what one of the men called "fraternal spirit," since it had already been functioning as a hospital for almost two years.[21] The first cohort had made a regretful farewell from there, and each day for the next while, fifty more would join them. Still others would come from different hospitals, and the newly returned from overseas. For now, the focus was on orthopaedic wounds, the most common injury, but many men had multiple issues: they'd lost a leg, but they'd lost an eye, too, and their lungs had been weakened by gas. In time, as more men healed at other hospitals, some of the smaller centres closed or reverted to pre-war status, and Christie Street—necessarily expert in so many areas—became the country's main care centre for wounded soldiers of all kinds.

Charles McVicar was well positioned to understand the various perspectives of the population at Christie Street. He *knew what suffering meant*, for as a doctor, he'd treated sick and wounded soldiers, but he'd also been in that position himself, when he'd fallen dangerously ill with enteric fever in the Boer War. He'd been a young man just beginning a career as a schoolteacher when he enlisted with the Canadian Mounted Rifles in 1901. His record states that he was a "fair rider" and a "good shot," and describes his temperament as "sanguine," a useful characteristic for a man who'd endure two wars.[22] But he almost didn't survive South Africa. Enteric fever, now known as typhoid, caused temperatures to soar and brought on headaches, vomiting, delirium, and sometimes death. Charles recovered, but telegraphs between officials and his mother at home in Ailsa Craig, Ontario, show that it was some weeks before he was well again. When he returned to Canada, he studied medicine. An article published in the *Exeter Advocate* details the town's elaborate celebration when he came home from war: "The village was gay with flags and bunting and a dense crowd thronged the waiting room and platform to welcome him." He was driven through town to the village square, where bagpipes played "Home Sweet Home," and a series of speeches and musical performances were delivered in his honour. Children were dressed in white outfits trimmed with real maple leaves and accents of red and blue. Townsfolk gave him a basket of flowers and a gold watch and chain "as a slight expression of the esteem in which he is held by them." Then came "a clear-toned, quiet reply in which he stated that he neither wished for nor merited such a welcome. He had not gone to South Africa for a purely patriotic spirt but from a desire to profit. He had gained financially and educationally and was again in as good health as ever."[23]

Charles McVicar, left, with Edward, Prince of Wales,
on his 1919 visit to Christie Street
(Courtesy John A. Vila and Elizabeth Vila Rogan)

Nearly twenty years later, he was overseeing the newly opened DOH, and leading prestigious visitors through the halls. Correspondence from the hospital's first months shows that he was also juggling problems with staffing quarters, roof leaks, telephone systems, insufficient stock pots and excessive breakage of kitchenware. He was pressing for a larger stage for the auditorium so that lavish performances could be put on for the patients, complete with dressing rooms for the performers. He seems to have understood that the *small skill of rhyming*, the joy of song and dance, was essential medicine for *sick hearts* and lonely veterans. A number of concert companies and theatres had offered to entertain at the DOH, and McVicar wanted better lighting, an orchestra pit, and a proper theatre curtain to complete the effect. Aside from his own requests to improve the hospital, he had to answer grumblings among patients too—or perhaps belly rumblings—and an accusation that "variety" was a concept unknown to the DOH kitchen staff. "They supply us with macaroni and cheese until I'm ashamed to look an Italian in the face," a patient told a *Star* reporter. "If the grub was prepared in a tasty and inviting manner we might stand for it—but it isn't."[24]

At the end of February, when McVicar led the governor general on a tour of the hospital, he must have hoped any unresolved obstacles would stay tucked tidily behind potted plants while the dignitary did his rounds, and that veterans would keep their grievances to themselves.

Otherwise known as Victor Cavendish, Duke of Devonshire, the governor general poked around the DOH for two hours while a reporter trailed along to record Cavendish's impressions. The duke witnessed "a bothersome leg fracture" being photographed in the x-ray room on the fourth floor, and he made a stop in the records room, where photos were stored showing wounds in various stages of the healing process. He paused at the dental clinic and "minutely questioned" the doctor there, and he peeked into a number of empty operating rooms, glimpsing thin, narrow beds ready for bodies. But when he was invited to see an operation in progress, he graciously declined. "Duke is sensitive," the *Star*'s caption reported. "The smell of ether is repelling to me," he explained. "I do not mind at having to go under an operation myself, but I cannot stand seeing others go under the knife."[25] What did Charles McVicar make of the gentleman's squeamishness, however tinged with bravado and compassion? What he'd seen in his years of service would surely curl the duke's tidy moustache.

Cavendish swept on through the massage unit, the hydrotherapy unit, and the electric treatment department, smiling and nodding and small-talking here and there, as governors general do. He saw the gymnasium, the many "curative workshops," the recreation rooms, and the culinary department where the macaroni and cheese was churned out, and announced he was "agreeably surprised with the great work underway for the refitting of returned wounded heroes." At one point he paused to speak with a sergeant named Walter Mackintosh, "on whose breast were ribbons showing the [Distinguished Service Order] and [the Military Cross]." When the duke asked where such prestigious medals had been won, Mackintosh answered, "At Courcelette, sir." The reporter waxed on about the duke's "deep interest," and how "the soldier told him of his deeds, which drew forth the highest commendation."

A couple of days after the article appeared, the *Star* printed a disgruntled reaction from the supposedly beribboned Mackintosh:

> I would like you to give this letter the same prominence
> as you gave my alleged interview with his Excellency the
> Governor General. In the first place, I have not the honour
> to be wearing the DSO or the MC. These decorations are
> for officers only. That statement alone has caused all kinds
> of chaff....[And] that guff you published about my recount-
> ing the deeds I was decorated for, bringing forth the
> highest commendation etc., was all rot. You should know
> that it is not done in the best society, and it makes
> a man feel very cheap when he has about a dozen or more
> asking you how you got the write-up.[26]

The ribbing from his fellow patients must have been thorough to prompt such a response. And yet the soldiers knew better than anyone that decorations didn't tell the full story, whether you had them or not. *For every deed rewarded, a hundred lives went down. Unknown, unsung, forgotten.* What issues would have filled the newspapers had the war not happened? The same month the DOH opened, the *Star* had begun a regular War Veterans' Department, featuring content of special interest to returned soldiers, but news related to the war still spilled over from the designated page to practically every other page of the paper. On the day that Mackintosh's complaint appeared, the *Star* carried articles about surgical miracles in wartime, the Paris Peace Conference, "Germany fighting for her soul," and the plight of children orphaned by war. There was also a back-to-civvies ad for a men's apparel shop that called itself "The Returned Man's Headquarters." The classified pages contained ads for babies needing adoption, as well as notices from returned soldiers looking for mates — "no objection to a widow." At the top of the page was a reminder that returned men searching for work could place ads in the paper for free. "Thousands of these men will be returning each month, and they have earned the right, by faithful service, to any position for which they may be fitted."[27] On a regular basis, the *Star* published the names of local men newly arrived at the coast from overseas. Even the times of their train arrivals in Toronto were given, so that loved ones could arrange to meet them.

In the tricky shadow light, war had ended, but its residue was everywhere, and would be for some time to come. Though the men and their caregivers were home now, they remained separate from the rest, if only psychologically. This was why the bond between them mattered so much and was really a part of the healing. At some point in those early months at the DOH, a book was planned to commemorate the place and its people, and hold them in time. The cover of this so-called *Illustrated Souvenir* features a nighttime rendition of the hospital, its four floors of windows aglow, and Red Cross ambulances pulling up in front of the building, headlights shining. Inside, page after page lists the names of patients and staff.[28]

There are statistics too: one list breaks down the number of patients by wound type, and another categorizes forms of entertainment and tallies the numbers who attended. There were 453 "movie shows" put on in the hospital's first year and a half, and almost as many concert parties and auto rides. But the bulk of the book is given over to a rich collection of images that brings the hospital's world to life. A cartoon depicts a man who's pulled his leg off to buff his shoe. Photographs show doctors at work on masks for facial reconstruction, and nurses gathering for a three-legged race. Many snapshots show men linking arms and leaning into each other in easy friendship. The book feels like a family album or a yearbook — a collection of memories meaningful enough for preservation. Charles McVicar poses in his office in the opening pages, oak-panelled walls behind him. Though he'll be gone from the hospital by 1921, embarking on another aspect of his career, for now the busyness of the place no doubt consumes him. His desk is littered with papers and his pen is in hand, ready to sign some request to a higher-up, or perhaps to draft the introduction for the book in which this picture appears. "It is much more interesting," he writes, "and less fatiguing, to recall past experiences by pictures, pen pictures, photographs or sketches than by a studied review of dull statistics or accurate figures. So we present this pictorial review of the activities and personalities of the DOH." Aware as he was that the book might leave out much and even fail in accuracy here and there, just like this one, the whimsical documentation of the hospital on Christie Street went forward, and remains a tangible thing, full of clues and mysteries, long after the people have gone.

OFFICERS, NURSING SISTERS AND PATIENTS D.O.H.

Page Fifteen

Officers, nursing sisters, and patients at the
Dominion Orthopaedic Hospital, *Illustrated Souvenir* [29]

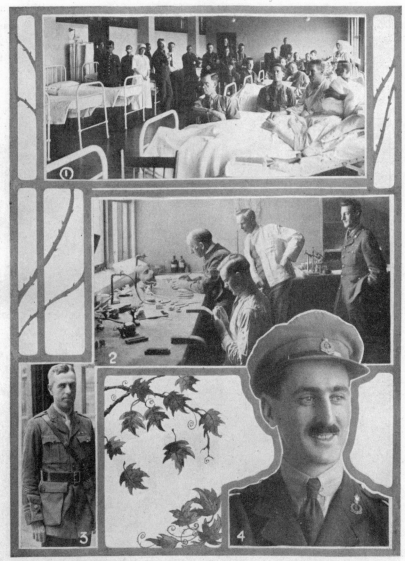

1. Facial Ward (326).   2. Dental Laboratory—Major A. H. L. Campbell, Capt. W. W. Thornton, Lieut. W. B. Gordon and Sgt. "Dan" Farrow.   3. Major J. Risdon.   4. Capt. Henderson.

Page Forty-seven

Staff and patients from the DOH facial unit, *Illustrated Souvenir*[30]

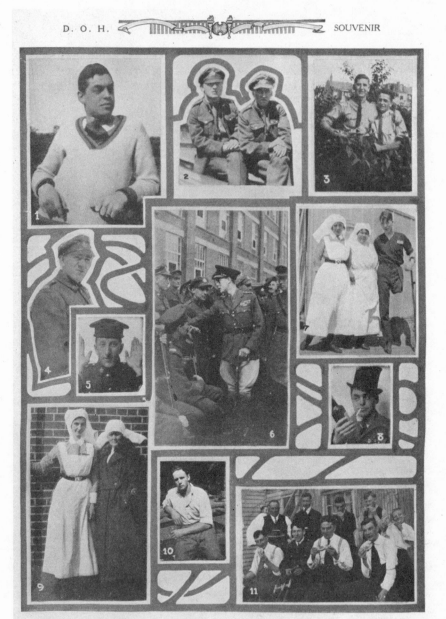

1. Charlie Partridge. 2. Keen and Friend. 3. J. Farrell and A. Manning. 4. "Jesse" James. 5. Chatfield. 6. H.R.H. Prince of Wales Greeting Boys on Front Lawn. 7. Nursing Sisters Jackson and Doig, Pte. Lowry. 8. Censored. 9. Nursing Sisters Croxford and Morris. 10. Pte. Black, M.P. 11. Watermelon Brigade.

Page Ninety-one

Patients and staff at the DOH, and the
Prince of Wales, centre, *Illustrated Souvenir*[31]

1. Two of the Original Roof Gang, Spr. C. Hamilton and Corp. R. G. Mills 2. Picnic Group at Grimsby Beach. 3. Frenchy at the Sports. 4. Corp. Gosling and Pte. A. McCracken. 5. George Payne. 6. Pte. J. A. McMaster. 7. Wesley Brennan and W. McKay. 8. Who said "Cook House?" Pte. J. Butler (C.A.M.C.). 9. Colin Barron, V.C.

Page Ninety-nine

DOH patients and staff, with Hamilton and Mills of the
Hamilton-Mills Weekly, top left, *Illustrated Souvenir*[32]

Legs

A panoramic picture taken in June 1919, the first summer of the hospital's existence, shows the men posing outdoors, in a long line several rows deep, in front of the main entrance.[1] At one edge of the image, the Ford Motor Company can be seen in the background, looming over a string of rail cars. A few patients who've remained inside the hospital peer through the windows. The curved headboards of their iron bed frames are visible, pillows propped against each. Charles McVicar sits in the centre of the photo, with officer-doctors on either side of him, but in spite of military rank and classism, this feels like a portrait of ordinary men. Almost all of the subjects in the front row are missing a leg, and pose with a pair of crutches. Behind them, arms rest in slings; sleeves hang empty. On either end, lending symmetry, men in wheelchairs have lost both legs. Not far from McVicar, one man cuddles a tiny puppy. Some of the men place a hand on the shoulder of the man in front, a touching gesture that contrasts with the mostly solemn expressions. Are the men bored? Tired? Hot? They seem to squint against a bright sun, but a sky in a century-old photograph can only appear grey and dreary. The men are wearing their uniforms, but they don't have the smart, crisp look apparent in so many military portraits. Much of the clothing is rumpled and ill-fitting. Hats askew, pocket flaps curling. The uniforms have seen action too.

The war had been over for less than a year, and since this was a military hospital, the practice of wearing anything other than regulation uniform was officially forbidden for patients, unless injuries made that impossible. Standing Orders reprinted in the *Illustrated Souvenir* state that, except in wards and the billiard room, jackets had to be worn fully buttoned, and though the book's photographs do show jackets open or removed, and hats tilted or altogether missing, it seems the rules were more or less followed, if sometimes sloppily. The men were accustomed to these clothes by now, and the uniforms emphasized their brotherhood and their collective experience at war. As in the army, a strict daily schedule was laid out: reveille at 7:00 a.m., beds made up by 7:20, breakfast at 7:30. Routine carried on through the day, and *a sun with light still in it* sank and rose again the next morning. Patients each had a little appointment book to carry with them, blue like a bluebird, and one of these, tattered and faded, appears tucked into the pages of a copy of the *Illustrated Souvenir*. The rules state that failure to produce the booklet, or to keep the appointments it contained, was tantamount to "Neglect to obey an order," a punishable offence soldiers surely knew well. But there were kind words in the booklet too — words of wisdom that had come from a speech by the Blind Trooper, a Boer War veteran and recruiter named Lorne Mulloy: "It is not necessarily the disabled soldier who is to be pitied, not the man who has lost an arm, or a leg, or been blinded, but the man who with all his limbs, his health and his strength, comes back with a piece of shrapnel in his moral backbone. Happiness is obtainable only through work — is possible only for a man who successfully finds his way back to productive activity. Self-mastery, self-reliance and purposeful self-direction are essentials on the part of the returned man himself for successful repatriation."[2]

Shortly after the DOH opened, Mulloy spoke at a veterans' banquet held at the Toronto Armories on University Avenue, a great fortress of a building that no longer exists. It had been used as a training facility in the Boer War and in the Great War, and would again be used for war purposes soon enough, but no one knew that when the men piled into the grand space to be honoured for their contribution in the war to end all wars. Dressed as soldiers, they were farmers and bricklayers and stock boys and tram conductors and factory workers and painters and gardeners and fishermen who might never have left their home-towns if not for the conflict. About fifty bluebirds—women like Mabel Lucas, May Bastedo, Helen Fowlds, and their colleagues—were there with them, sharing just a small portion of the limelight, but offering "a picturesque spot of color with their blue uniforms and large white caps."[3] Hundreds of volunteer waitresses served the men, wearing long white dresses and caps garnished with scarlet maple leaves. This was the first of several banquets, for there were too many veterans to host them all at once. Decorated tables stretched the length of the place, in rows laid out with military precision, and Canadian and allied flags fluttered as thousands joined in the celebrations, with their ladies watching from the galleries. Portraits of allied leaders hung on the walls, and a banner proclaimed "Toronto Welcomes Her Victorious Heroes. You Have Played Your Part, We Intend to Do Ours." With singing, boxing matches, and a plain but substantial feast, the night had "the 'pep' and action that the soldier boys wanted," according to the *Star*, and as Colonel Mulloy took the stage, in his uniform and his round dark glasses, the band played "Old Soldiers Never Die" (though of course that was not true—the old had died as easily as the young). The crowd let loose "a salvo of cheers," and then fell silent as Mulloy began to speak.

He announced he would break from his usual style of speech that night, and for the first time recount his own experiences on the battle-field, and his shaky return to civilian life. In the fall of 1899 he'd been a young school principal in a village near Ottawa, never imagining that one year later he'd find himself fighting a war in South Africa, a Canadian Dragoon firing on the enemy at close range. He was shot in the head and, once in hospital, the bravery he'd summoned in battle

abandoned him when he realized his wounds had caused permanent
blindness. "For four days, I was the yellowest coward who ever came
down the pike." He no longer wanted to live, and couldn't bear to
imagine what his life would be like when he returned home. "Finally I
was forced to take my shivering soul by the nape of the neck and make it
face the future in the only manly way. The moment I made that decision
I found happiness and relief. I had won the first round in the fight for
self-mastery."[4]

For many of the men at the DOH, things lost would never be won
back now, but such hopelessness was not the focus at veterans' banquets,
or in the pieces printed on the veterans' page in the *Toronto Daily Star*. A
week after the banquet, the *Star* reported that the pensions office near
Yonge and King streets was overrun with enquiries, keeping sixty clerks
busy from nine to five. There were those who needn't have bothered
standing in line, for Ottawa had issued a reminder that no pensions
would be granted to men suffering from shell shock. A government bulletin made it clear: "The condition arising from shell shock is likely one
to clear up at any moment under proper treatment and environment....
Give a man who has lost his nerve and spirit through shell shock sufficient [money] to live upon and what is more natural than that he should
sink into a chronic state of invalidism? There would be no incentive to
pull himself together. On the other hand if a desire is kindled to begin
life anew, a goal is set for the patient."[5]

Doctors who'd experienced the front apparently agreed. One
claimed to have seen very few actual cases of shell shock, but plenty of
"shell smashes." Another said these men must be trained back to sanity,
and be responsible for themselves. If assured an income, said a third,
the men might "lean back" and make no attempt to get better. The doctors agreed that the number of shell-shock cases were fewer now than in
1916 and 1917, and some turned out to be "absolute fakes."[6]

At Christie Street—and all over the country—there were men who'd
suffered both shock and smashes, such as Private Charles Harrowsmith
of the 3rd Battalion (Toronto Regiment). Charles was born in Chertsey,
Surrey, in 1887, the son of a furniture dealer, and was destined to a
life in furniture dealing himself, judging by the occupation given on
the 1911 English census. But he must have wanted something different,

because shortly after that time, he and his wife, Julia, and their two small children emigrated to Canada, settling in a tiny house on McCaul Street in Toronto. The roughcast houses along this stretch of McCaul, just north of Queen Street, had rippled tarpaper roofs, crooked doors and windows, and outhouses that took up much of the tiny space in the muddy back yards. They backed on to other houses just like them on neighbouring streets. There was a Chinese laundry across the way, and St. Patrick's Market to the south, and pretty St. George the Martyr Church to the north, across from the public baths. A few blocks west was the notorious slum then known as The Ward, so perhaps the lifestyle was a step down for the Harrowsmiths, who came from a middle-class rather than a working-class background. Charles found a job at the National Cash Register factory, long before war turned it into a hospital.

His service record says that he was five foot six, with dark brown hair, blue eyes, and a fair complexion, but a photograph of him in uniform in the pages of the DOH's *Illustrated Souvenir* reveals more: a handsome, gentle-looking fellow with soulful eyes, head tipped slightly to the side. Family lore says that he was a cheerful if not terribly responsible man who liked to spend time at the pub. He enlisted in July 1915 and left for England in March of the following year, finally arriving in the Ypres Salient in June, just after the Battle of Mount Sorrel. The Ypres region in western Belgium was a key location throughout the war, deemed "salient" in military terms because it bulged out into enemy territory, making the troops there more vulnerable. The elevated, wooded portion at Mount Sorrel overlooked the city of Ypres and the German trenches, and when Charles arrived it had just been lost and mostly won back again, leaving the landscape ripped through from shelling, and drenched from heavy rains. Along with about 125 new men, Charles joined soldiers who had just come through that brutal battle. The recapture of the hill had meant fighting in the dark, in wind and rain, and afterward dealing with the bodies, or the pieces of bodies, and the shell holes that constantly filled with water; the soggy, churned-up mud was less than ideal for repairing the trenches. Charles had missed the action, but the stories the men told, and the physical evidence left behind, must have given him some idea of what he was in for: *the scream of shrapnel, and the whining wail of bullets drenching the earth as with a hail.*

He and the others had been sent to replace the dead and the wounded, but war was a leaky well—much of what poured in was lost as quickly.

The humdrum entries in the unit's official war diary show that the next weeks were quiet.[7] Summer was spent undergoing the usual training, having kits inspected and helmets tested, and there were sometimes baseball games to relieve boredom and tension and incorporate a bit of exercise. One entry notes "Baths," which must have felt delicious for so many filthy bodies, though the event was followed by "Lecture on sanitation." July 1 was Dominion Day, and though the war diary notes only "Holiday. Weather fine," in fact the deadly Battle of the Somme had begun in France, and Canadian troops would soon make their way to join it.

By August, they were moving south through France, and their *blistered feet, sore backs, and soldier's cramp* were eased by the sights and smells of a pretty countryside as yet untouched by war. They passed old châteaux nestled in the woods, and homes with red clay rooftops baking in the sun. The medical corps travelled south too, and one diarist among them later recalled that the pleasant march was an "interlude between Ypres and the Somme.... The sun came out, and we had brilliant August weather, with the light in a strong blaze travelling from field to field. France disclosed to us all its dignity, beauty, and richness."[8]

The men were in place in the trenches by the end of the month and ready to take part in the battle. All through the first week of September, the 3rd Battalion war diary notes daily numbers of killed and wounded, and it was sometime in here that Charles Harrowsmith succumbed to any combination of exhaustion, shell shock, concussion, trench fever, enteritis, asthma, and gas poisoning, depending on which note you read in his file. One small scribble says he was "buried in Sept '16" following a shell explosion, and that diarrhea started two days later.[9] He was first treated in France, and rejoined his unit after about a week, but following that *mouthful of earth* and all the organisms it contained, his health continued to decline. By October he was so unwell that he was invalided to England.

What was it like to be buried alive? To believe that death was the earth encasing you? The lucky ones were rescued, and lived to remember being sealed in the darkness with *a thousand fears*. One Australian

soldier, buried at the Somme like Charles that October, later described
what had happened to him:

> The earth was too soft to make the usual holes to shelter
> in, so our resting quarters consisted of what were known
> as "shell-slits." They were made by digging out from the
> side or back of the trench far enough and wide enough
> for a man to lie down; these slits were about five or six feet
> deep, the bottom being about level with the bottom of the
> trench. They were a fairly efficient shelter from shell-fire
> unless they got a direct hit, and I had chosen one of them
> for my headquarters. I intended to lie down and have a
> short rest and the Sergeant Major was to call me if anything
> happened.... I had just sat down at the end of it and was
> leaning back against the mud wall when a salvo of shells
> landed near. I glanced up to try and locate the bursts by the
> flying mud, when I noticed that the whole side of the shell-
> slit was falling in. The bursts had apparently been close
> enough to loosen the soft earth. It struck me in the act of
> rising and completely buried me. The weight on my tin hat
> pressed down irresistibly and forced my chin into my chest.
> After struggling a little I found that it only settled the earth
> closer round me. The brim of the hat kept the earth out of
> my nose but the weight gradually forced it further down on
> my head, the head band gradually travelling down my nose
> and taking the skin with it. The plate of my teeth had jolted
> out of position and was jammed across my mouth, keeping
> it slightly open, so that I soon found the end would not
> come for want of fresh air—I could breathe. Then the real-
> ization came of what was gradually but surely ending things.
> The soft earth at first yielded slightly to my struggles, but
> was slowly settling down and compressing under the weight
> above, so that the movement of my ribs was becoming more
> and more constricted. It was as though an iron band were
> tightening round my chest and preventing any movement.
> Then I heard the Sergeant Major speaking, and calling me,

as though he were a long way off. He went again, apparently
to ask the sentries in the firing line if they had seen me. He
soon came back and I heard him say, "Good God, I believe
the man's buried! Come here two men with shovels. Now
gently—don't maim him." At last the terrible weight was
relieved.[10]

There's no mention in Charles Harrowsmith's record of how he was
excavated, like a human archaeological treasure, or if anyone else was
buried with him in the smothering earth. His illnesses continued into
1917, but eventually he was deemed well again, and as per regulations,
entered a convalescent camp and then joined his reserve unit to undergo
a process of "hardening" that would prepare him for a return to the
battlefield. By the summer of 1918, he was back with the 3rd Battalion
on the Western Front. August 4 marked the four-year anniversary of
Britain's entry into the war, and newspapers and war diaries carried
the speech made by British Army General Douglas Haig, thanking the
troops for their bravery and resolution thus far, but also reminding
them that more would be asked of them. Four days later, the Battle of
Amiens began, and on that first day, *the air was loud with death.* Canadian
forces suffered four thousand casualties, and Charles, with gunshot
wounds in his thigh, hip, hand, and arm, was just one of many listed as
dangerously ill. He was taken from the battlefield by stretcher bearers
and given over to medical care, where someone had the nasty job of
quickly separating men into three categories: those with minor wounds,
those with severe but survivable wounds like his, and the hopeless, upon
whom no time could be wasted. A steady flow of casualties streamed in.
The battle would last four more days, and would come to be seen as the
beginning of the end of the war, but Charles Harrowsmith's small and
devastating place in it was finished.

Back home, the *Star* reported that Toronto casualties were mounting, and each day the paper carried pictures of men who'd died or
been wounded. It was down to *Chance's strange arithmetic* whether a man
returned home or joined *the lost ones scattered wide.* A notice on August 16
headed "Wounded Second Time" featured a picture of Charles in civilian clothes, wearing the same sorrowful look evident in his military

portrait. "The wife of Pte. C.T. Harrowsmith, 32 McCaul Street, has received word that her husband has been dangerously wounded.... Over a year ago he was sent to England to recuperate from the effects of shell shock. He has been overseas for two and a half years.... Before enlisting he was employed by the National Cash Register Co."[11]

It would take time before he arrived at his old workplace as a patient. Those first steps saw him moved through the evacuation chain that served the wounded and rapidly delivered them from the front through various stages of care. Evacuation was designed to happen quickly, with stretcher bearers collecting the men from the field, and perhaps pouring iodine into the wounds before carrying them to a field ambulance unit, a mobile medical station that could be quickly packed up and moved to a different place as battle locales shifted. Then patients were treated just enough to prepare them for transfer to a casualty clearing station, a larger, facility where men could receive more extensive treatment. But here, too, the goal was expediency, and patients were soon moved to base hospitals — "stationary hospitals" often set up in schools or hotels, or the larger "general hospitals" that were better equipped for long-term care. Next, if necessary, the men went to England and home. The reason for the urgency was twofold: emotionally, the sight of the injured was bad for the morale of the other soldiers; and pragmatically, space was needed for the subsequent wounded coming in.

Things slowed down once Charles reached England, and it was June 1919 when he was invalided back to Canada and admitted to the DOH. Summer was in full swing in Toronto, with bright *green grass and bursting trees*, and birds chirping in leafy branches. His arrival by ambulance, with all the other men admitted that day, was in sharp contrast to his earlier comings and goings in work clothes, toting a packed lunch made by Julia. Did he know ahead of time that the NCR was now a hospital? As the ambulance pulled up, he would have recognized the bones of the factory, for though it had grown in height, its plain, boxy, L-shaped design had not been altered. It still looked across to a tannery, and sat directly north of the railway, though in recent years an underpass had been dug so that trains could roar overhead without slowing or endangering traffic on Christie Street, whether pedestrians, the horses and buggies that still travelled the city, or the motor cars that had become more frequent sights. Due south of the tracks and the hospital, the Ford Motor Company had opened a show room and factory around the same time the underpass had been dug, "giving Toronto and vicinity the most 'up to date' motor service in the world."[12] Black Model Ts gleamed in the windows of the main floor showroom, and up above, the cars were assembled on site. The area around the hospital hummed with industry that had been lured by the railway. In Ford's case, a spur line enabled product to be delivered right to the factory doors, as with the tannery across Christie. The same had been true of the NCR, though the line disappeared with the renovation, and the men were brought from Union Station by ambulance. It must have seemed a strange dream for Charles Harrowsmith to be wheeled into the building—for he was still not walking—and to find the rooms filled with fellow soldiers, and not a cash register in sight. Once there'd been the constant whir of machinery worked by able-bodied men in aprons and suspenders piecing together "up-to-date Cash Registers which quicken service, stop mistakes, satisfy customers, and increase profits."[13] Now it was the men themselves who needed assembling.

Charles Harrowsmith's wounds combined to render a grave disability. Notes from the DOH medical staff specify that he had suffered a "through and through wound" that had opened his bladder, and long after it had healed, "he goes frequently; about once every ¾ hour during day and 3 times during night." Though the urine was normal, the muscle power controlling it was impaired. The multiple injuries to his right hip, thigh, abdomen, right forearm, and hand continued to plague him. A long, lacerated wound had destroyed the flexor muscles of his forearm, which affected his elbow, wrist, and fingers. His hip had been so thoroughly damaged that only a few degrees of movement was possible, and caused a great deal of pain. His knee, ankle, and sciatic nerve were all affected, which meant that "functionally his leg is almost useless." When he did begin walking, he wore specially made boots, and used a crutch designed to accommodate his ruined fingers. But pressure ulcers developed on his Achilles tendon and were slow to heal, and all kinds of other challenges loomed. The staff wrote that he "can sit down only with difficulty because of the fixation of the hip. Cannot reach foot. Cannot dress himself. . . . amputation of his right leg has been suggested as an improvement on his present condition, but patient does not desire this."

Harrowsmith spent a year in the hospital on Christie Street, and it was not long after his discharge that he and his young family moved back to England. The bulk of their new life in Canada had been eaten up by war, so they'd never quite settled here, and they missed friends and relatives back home. From Charles's great-granddaughter, the story goes that Charles didn't work upon his return, and spent much of his time in bed or in the pub. He was affable but unreliable, and Julia was severe—but it's difficult to say whether Charles's war experience played into this dynamic, and what direction their lives might have taken had the war not happened. The 1939 census places them in Chertsey, Surrey, where they'd begun, and a 1944 announcement in the *Surrey Advertiser* reveals Charles's death at age fifty-eight. "Mr. Harrowsmith was a native of Chertsey," the obituary reads, "...during the last war [he] served in the Canadian Army in France, where he was badly wounded, and it was only with difficulty that he was able to get about."[14] So the injuries bothered him for the rest of his life. Would he have fared better had he shaken his reluctance and accepted the doctors' advice?

Most men didn't find themselves in the position of choosing; an amputation happened because it had to. The term comes from the Latin *amputare*— *ambi*, about or around, and *putare*, to prune—which sounds more like gardening than a harrowing surgical procedure. The words don't begin to capture the trauma of amputation, even now, with all our wondrous surgical advances, though, yes, we have come a long way. In a manual for surgeons dated 1721, the author advises that the patient be given a block of wood to bite down on during the operation. "Cut quick with a crooked knife before covering the stump with the remaining skin." If the wound was only a flesh wound, it should be bathed in brandy, but if it went deeper, "to the nervous parts," then camphor, sugar candy, and myrrh should be dissolved into it.[15] More than a century passed before Western medicine understood the powerful benefits of gases as anaesthesia, and then a little more time still before carbolic acid was used as an antiseptic. Despite those crucial advances, amputation in the First World War, especially on the frontlines, was a risky operation, often performed in less than ideal circumstances, without the proper supplies or an adequate level of hygiene. The war's notorious *mud, four miles deep*, cultivated and rich with horse manure, meant that "practically every wound is heavily infected," according to the British bacteriologist Almroth Wright, who tried to convince the establishment of the importance of thorough cleansing of wounds.[16] The potential for gangrene lurked harmlessly in farmers' fields, but if driven deep into a body, where antiseptic couldn't reach it, it came dangerously alive. As the Christie Street nurse Mabel Lucas put it, "You know, you can smell the gangrene."[17]

In his 1918 book *The Doctor in War*, Woods Hutchinson wrote:

> When a group of these gas-producing bacteria in the soil are blown on a piece of shell deep into the human body they find themselves in clover. The fragments of the tissues which have been torn and crushed and mangled out of all vitality by the shells furnish dead animal matter for them to grow upon. They are deeply enough buried to be freed from the thing they hate most — the oxygen of the air; and the warmth of the body "forces" them like a hot-house. The result is that after about forty-eight hours, the edges of the wound begin to swell up and turn outward or backward, making it open. The discharge from the wound almost stops, and its cut surface takes on a curious half-jellified, half-mummified sort of look; then the whole wounded limb begins to swell up and distend in the most extraordinary fashion, turning, as it does so, first an ashy white and then a greenish color. This is because the tissues are being literally blown out with the gas, and on pressing the finger down on this balloon-like swell-ing, a distinct crackling or tiny bubbling sensation can be felt. The gas and the swelling extend on up over the surface of the body, bloating it, and distorting its shape; the patient begins to complain, not so much of pain as of a sense of great restlessness and depression and dread of what is coming next. His face is white and pinched, his lips bluish, his eyes widely distended and "all pupil," his

temperature, instead of rising, goes steadily down, down,
and unless something can be done to stop the terrible
march death ends the scene within forty-eight hours,
sometimes within twenty-four of the first appearance
of gas in the tissues.[18]

William Wishart knew all about gas gangrene. In December 1915 in
Belgium, he'd been carrying rations just behind the front line when he
was struck by a machine-gun bullet. The bullet entered his inner left leg,
just above the knee, and exited eight inches higher. Though it seemed
promising that the bone had not been injured, there were difficulties
with his recovery from the beginning. In England, doctors tried stimu-
lating the leg with electrotherapy, but "could get no reaction below knee
by faradic current that patient could stand. He was very nervous & upset
& shouted loudly." To galvanism, a gentler form of electrotherapy, "the
calf muscles reacted sluggishly." By the end of the month, he could move
his toes, which seemed a positive development, but within a week he had
constant pain in his foot and "a rather hard pulsating tumour" could
be felt at the site of the entry wound. A splint had almost straightened
his leg by this point, but the whooshing sound coming from inside the
wound—a vascular murmur called a "bruit"—was a bad sign. Within
a few days the murmur could be heard by stethoscope over the whole
thigh, and though there was no pain now, William could feel a "bursting
sensation" in the knee. Next the discoloration began, first over the knee
cap, and then on down the calf and ankle and over the top of the foot.
At the end of January, the leg was amputated at mid-thigh. [19]

Despite the difficulties, William Wishart seems to have been a model
patient. His stump healed nicely and he wore his artificial limb without too much discomfort, walking well without a cane. By the time he
returned to Canada, the Davisville Military Hospital had opened on
Yonge Street, and William's training as a woodworker got him a job in
the limb factory there. His record says he assisted at "limb parades" too,
and was having a special limb made for demonstration purposes. By the
end of 1917, he was in charge of these parades, held to show the men
how to put on the leg and move with grace and ease. William's work
continued when orthopaedic patients were moved to grander quarters

at Christie Street, and he was probably a familiar face to Charles Harrowsmith and other men with leg wounds.

The limb parades might have been frustrating to watch for men with bigger challenges in using their prostheses. Jack Hoar was among the first patients admitted to the DOH in February 1919, and had come with the other orthopaedic patients from Davisville. He was a dark-haired, blue-eyed Irish American whose roots showed in his tattoos: a bald eagle and a shamrock. In June 1917, just after the Americans officially joined the war, Hoar filled out a draft registration card in his hometown of LaSalle, Illinois, not far from Chicago. But he must have been swept up by a Canadian recruitment wave, for late in August he travelled north to Toronto to enlist with Princess Patricia's Canadian Light Infantry, along with a number of other Americans. The lies that enabled his enlistment are easily uncovered now: the Canadian Army could recruit Britons living in the US, but American citizens risked losing their citizenship if they joined another country's armed forces, so Hoar's service record says he was born in Kerry, Ireland, when in fact he was born in LaSalle. He called himself "Harton" rather than "Hoar," added five years to his age, and said his parents were both deceased, though in fact his father was still living.[20]

But what prompted the move, when Hoar's own country was actively gathering soldiers? On August 14, two weeks before he joined the Canadian forces, an Illinois newspaper advertised a presentation by "Scrappy Jerry Hanley" of the Princess Pats, telling of "war in all its grimness. Not a censored newspaper story, but as it actually exists.... The sergeant's talk will stir you as nothing ever has before."[21] Gerald Hanley had enlisted in the war's earliest days, and fought in the 1915 battle at Frezenberg Ridge, where the Princess Pats lost hundreds of men—killed, wounded, or driven mad by shell shock. Hanley's service record reveals that when a shell exploded behind him, it blew him out of the trench, and he was picked up unconscious and taken to a casualty clearing station, where he remained—"partly out of his mind"—for a week, before being moved on to military hospitals in France and then England.[22] He suffered fainting spells, memory lapses, and severe headaches, and the sound of gunfire brought on fresh attacks of extreme nervousness and anxiety. He was sent home "with permission to do some recruiting," and from here on, it seems, he travelled around telling the story of "the slaughtering of 'Princess Pat's' Canadian regiment," as it was billed in the papers.[23] That the story, accompanied by film footage of fighting in the trenches, drew men in rather than repelled them is in itself telling. One Illinois paper credited Hanley with inspiring 150 men to serve.

In Canada, Jack Hoar trained with the other new recruits at Camp Borden, just north of Toronto, and in September made out the soldier's routine, basic will—that *sacred scrap of paper*—leaving all of his worldly possessions to a cousin. The will was witnessed by two fellow Americans who'd enlisted at the same time—Van Buren Whetsel, a fifteen-year-old Pennsylvanian who'd claimed to be an eighteen-year-old Montrealer, and Richard Wilkie, a Chicago man who'd said he was born in Collingwood, Ontario.[24] Jack was the first of the three to leave for England, arriving in Liverpool in October, and finally joining his unit on the Western Front in April 1918, that changeable time of year when the weather alternates between dull and cold and gloriously warm and sunny. Occasionally snow still fell from a grey sky and briefly masked the ruined countryside, like a fresh white bandage for a wound. For Jack and others new to the front, the landscape must have held some ominous glimmer as the men marched through it in a long column, loaded down with everything deemed necessary. Devastation surrounded them as they moved toward the fighting: *a village sacked; a town in raging flame*; heaps of bricks and furniture; shattered glass and broken crockery; demolished bridges and gaping craters where who-knows-what used to be; felled trees and upturned gardens that continued to push out new shoots from a tangle of decay. It was spring, and *the pink blossoms that had slept for a year were waking*.

By now the Pats had fought at Vimy Ridge and Passchendaele, and were engaged in skirmishes at Avion, France. But just two weeks in, Jack was struck by a high-explosive shell, and both legs were badly wounded. Dangerously ill, with his ear drums punctured from the din of the explosion, he began his journey through the evacuation chain, first to a field ambulance unit situated in a once grand and now crumbling French château. The shelling continued while he was there, and the ambulance's war diary says that patients were held deep in the cellar

of the château's brewery, out of further danger. He was assessed and
bandaged, and moved on to the nearest casualty clearing station almost
one hundred kilometres away at Aubigny. The trip over rutted roads
must have been excruciating, with his ears ringing and bleeding, and
pain ripping through his wounds. At Aubigny, a doctor determined that
the left leg was fractured in four places between the knee and ankle,
and had to come off immediately. The right had shrapnel embedded
beneath the knee cap, but might be saved. Following his operation,
Jack was sent on another painful journey to No. 7 Canadian General
Hospital, the Queen's University unit then situated at Étaples, which
received more than three hundred patients that day alone; some four
hundred had come the day before. Here the doctor saw that gangrene
had set in, and both legs were badly infected. The left was re-amputated
and the right was removed. These would not be his last amputations as
doctors continued to chase the infection that spread through him.

Medical teams were now practised in all sorts of procedures that had
been rare only a few years earlier. Dr. George Kidd, a Kingston anatomy
professor, was working at No. 7 during Jack's time there. He may even
have been the doctor who performed the amputations. Kidd's wife, a
nurse named Lula, was also in Étaples, and so was Ruby Cornett, the
nurse who'd soon marry George's doctor-cousin. It was likely one of
these three who collected several albums of photographs eventually
deposited at Library and Archives Canada under the surname Kidd,
and depicting the wards and the grounds, the "Chinamen" labourers,
the patients, and the staff. One album, labelled "Some War Wounds
1914–1918," is entirely made up of photographs of injuries, and presents
a vivid, near-wordless account of what doctors and nurses dealt with on a
daily basis: bubbling mustard gas burns, toes eaten away by trench foot,
a face melted from an ammunition dump explosion, and legs darkly
mottled and split open by gas gangrene. Another photo shows severed
legs spilling out of a bucket, ready to be carted to the incinerator.[25] The
haphazard piling of them fits with what Elsie Tranter, an Australian
nurse stationed at Étaples, wrote in her diary in 1917: "Today I had
to assist at ten amputations, one after another. It is frightfully nerve-
wracking work. I seem to hear that wretched saw at work whenever I try
to sleep. We see the most ghastly wounds and are all day long inhaling

the odour of gas gangrene. How these boys suffer! This war is absolute hell."[26]

The final photograph in the war wounds album shows a patient reclining in a wheelchair, propped up by pillows and dressed in a rumpled hospital gown. Both legs have been amputated and the stumps are wrapped thickly in soft white bandages. The photograph isn't dated, and the man is not named, but there is a tempting likeness to Jack Hoar: high forehead, pointed brows, full face, similar wounds. He holds a cigarette aloft and looks at the camera with the confident, challenging gaze that appears in other photographs.

By mid-May Jack was still recovering at No. 7. *The long grasses swirled in the spring breeze; buttercups and mignonettes* and bluebells were pushing up all around, sending out sweet fragrances. The Kidd photographs show patients resting outdoors beneath flowery parasols, and a make-shift greenhouse surrounded by wooden boxes of seedlings sprouting. There's an image of girls from the village selling fruit, and local women laying out nets to dry. Étaples was a fishing village near the coast in northern France, an achingly beautiful spot that had long attracted artists chasing the *saffron streaks* that sunsets made in the sky, the fishing boats resting on sparkling water, and the bustle of market day. Long before he found fame as a member of the Group of Seven, A.Y. Jackson had painted here, drawn by the sand dunes and the pine trees. "France was a wonderful place in 1907," he later recalled. "You never thought about war....I think those were the happiest days of my life."[27] He returned to paint again in 1912, and then as a wounded soldier in 1916, by which time the artists, for the most part, had gone, and the area had been transformed into a "Land of Hospitals." It was some time after this that A.Y. Jackson's war duties shifted, and he was brought on as an official war artist for the Canadian government, painting twisted landscapes: night skies lit by poisonous gases, forests devastated by shellfire.

Along with No. 7, where Jack Hoar lay, there were some twenty other hospitals in Étaples, staffed with Canadian, Australian, English, Scottish, and New Zealand medical personnel. There were also training camps, segregation camps, prisoners' detention centres, a supply depot, a railway station, a mortuary, and a cemetery whose borders continually expanded. Several photographs record groups of "lady drivers" who

Wounded soldiers knitting at No. 7 Canadian General Hospital
in Étaples, France (Library and Archives Canada / PA-149304)

wore smart uniforms with ties and caps, and transported the wounded
to ships that would take them to England. Essentially Étaples was a
thriving military centre, with thousands traipsing through on a regular
basis, and the village sitting right next door. The size of the camp, and
the scope of work that went on there, made it a tempting target for the
enemy, and also what the poet Wilfred Owen called "A vast, dreadful
encampment.... It seemed neither France nor England, but a kind of
paddock where the beasts are kept a few days before the shambles."[28]

Gravely wounded, Jack was not one of those soldiers just passing
through. And there were others like him, unable to move or be moved
because of their injuries. A fractured femur was one of the most common
wounds, so prevalent by this time that there were whole wards of men
grouped together for specific treatment, their limbs raised and strapped
into place to let the healing begin. One of the Kidd photographs shows
two such patients at No. 7, relaxing in their beds. A long beam runs the
length of each bed, and their wounded legs are tied there so they'll stay
elevated. The photograph suggests staff went to great lengths to make
patients comfortable. The men are propped up on pillows, knitting.

Between the beds sits a tall vase filled with grasses and leafy branches, probably gathered by the nurses on a stroll off-hours. Some pretty fabric trims a folding screen at the edge of the photo, and a birdcage hangs from one of the beams. Canadian nurse Mabel Clint wrote that she and her colleagues developed a reputation for making their surroundings cozy, "though the English army nurses were inclined to think we didn't know there was a war on."[29]

Despite the ambience, war was close at Étaples. As patients drifted off to sleep at night, the booming and rattling in the distance made its way into nightmares; those who laid awake might see sparks of light brightening a black sky. A man might comfort himself that he was out of it for now, and may not ever need to go back, but the terrifying truth was that war could still come and find him. On May 19, at about 10:30 p.m., German planes soared over Étaples and released their bombs. The thundering explosions must have especially alarmed Jack Hoar and the fractured femur patients who couldn't run for cover. The first sweep of bombs set fires blazing, which illuminated the site for the next set of planes to roar through and cause yet more damage.

Elsie Collis, a nursing sister stationed at No. 1 Canadian General Hospital, wrote in her diary that before the raid it had been "a beautiful night—as light as day," and that she'd heard guns in the distance but had thought nothing of it. A little later she had just arrived at the kitchen door when the bombs began to fall. She and several others crouched on the kitchen floor, watching the fires through the window and listening to the ammunition and the sounds of people calling out. "It was dreadful.... The windows all fell in, dishes kept breaking, the plaster wall fell in in places. We were sure the next one would hit us."[30] Elsie survived the night, but three of her fellow nurses at No. 1 died. The raid lasted two hours and tore through the entire camp, taking nurses, orderlies, officers, patients, and civilians too. Footage of a mass funeral days later captured a parade of men in teams of four, just like the stretcher bearers, carrying coffins to the cemetery, and laying them in side by side. A striking panoramic photograph from one of the funeral processions stretched across the top of the *Daily Mirror*, showing Canadian nurses in their dark capes and fluttering white veils, passing rows of crosses as they made their way to the burial site.

Sometime after the event, an observation balloon rose like a giant
bloated bird and photographed the devastation at Étaples. Painters
painted it too, though the images were nothing like the quaint pictures
Étaples had once inspired. British artist Austin Spare's painting *Étaples
After the Great Raid* shows a row of huts reduced to framework, sitting
empty beneath a blue sky. The ground is littered with broken pieces of
wooden siding blown from the huts, and a severed arm rests almost cam-
ouflaged amid the debris. A man lies in the foreground, his uniform
streaked with blood, his young face grey with death.

The Kidd photographs can't bring us the colours of that day—the
soft spring sky, the bloodstains, the mud-coloured clothing, and the
drab grey of the shattered buildings—but the ruin is plain in each shot:
one image shows a group of about thirty men and a few women moving
through the mess, pausing to look at the camera with a collective expression of resignation. Not posing, not one of them smiling like the men
convalescing under parasols or the lady drivers proud in their caps and
ties. Shoulders slump; hands are stuffed in pockets. A line of huts forms
the backdrop, roofs open to the sky, timbers leaning this way and that.
Some of the men stand on a hill of rubble that will have to be cleared
away in short order, for despite the photograph conveying a pause, there
is no time for moping over *mad catastrophes*. The rubble spread through
the camp and beyond, into the old village, where someone ventured to
photograph the houses that had been destroyed.

The clean up must have been near unbearable, given that thousands
at Étaples had already been wounded before the strike happened. A
member of a field ambulance team wrote in his diary that he'd been
assigned to a night burial party, "trying to clean things up after
raid....An awful job."[31] Newspapers on the home fronts reported the
"Étaples outrage" and described the attacks as "simple murder" since it
was against the rules of war to bomb hospitals.[32] But Étaples was much
more than a hospital base, which led to criticism of the fact that so many
of these facilities had been placed near legitimate military targets. If
the plan had been to protect the wider camp by using the hospitals as a
shield, it had been a tragic failure.

One wonders what Jack Hoar made of the disaster. It must have
seemed as if the battlefield had come to his place of convalescence,

as if the further he got from the fighting, the more obvious it became that he would never escape it. The war diary for No. 7 notes that nine of its patients died the night of the raid, and that more attacks followed through May and June. Jack's record leaves out these broader details beyond his personal injuries and treatment, however much they might have affected his state of mind and his physical recovery. By early June, his condition was amended from dangerously ill to severely ill, and he was sent to England, where his stumps were amputated further. A curious symptom developed following surgery: his right arm and shoulder were paralyzed.

There were probably other bizarre symptoms too — the "phantom limb" sensation by which amputees detected the presence of the missing piece, and perhaps questioned their own sanity. The term was first coined by Silas Weir Mitchell, an American Civil War doctor who'd claimed that "Nearly every man who loses a limb carries about with him a constant or inconstant phantom of the missing member, a sensory ghost of that much of himself... faintly felt at times, but ready to be called up to his perception by a blow, a touch, or a change of wind."[33] Today, 150 years later, no real cure has been found. And following re-amputations, the missing piece is even more likely to burn or throb or tingle. It might feel as if it's been set on fire or plunged into freezing or boiling water. Pain stabs through it, or sometimes it just exists, seeming as tangible as the remaining parts, but all the more startling because it can no longer be seen. One British doctor wrote about a man whose leg was amputated and re-amputated in 1916, and twenty years later he was still experiencing so much pain in his missing left foot that he sometimes contemplated suicide. A cordotomy was performed, essentially disabling the spinal cord's pain routes to the limb, and for a while the patient felt better. He was still aware of the missing part, but it didn't hurt anymore, and he could live with the strange sensation. Soon enough, though, the agonizing pain returned, and the treatment was deemed a failure.

When Jack Hoar left England for Canada on board the hospital ship *Neuralia* at the end of October in 1918, the war was still playing out, but bit by bit as he crossed the ocean it died away. A man died too, a day into the journey—a tuberculosis patient who suffered a sudden hemorrhage and was given to the sea, leaving the ship one soul lighter when it docked in Halifax on November 10, a day before armistice. The sea had accepted thousands of war's cast-offs, little offerings like this man, tipped in alone, but also shiploads of men and women floating to or from the fighting. They were down there still, and fish swam through a coral reef of cabin doorways and broken portholes, making the ruins a part of their environment the way birds did with bombed-out buildings and trees split in half.

By the time Jack arrived in Toronto, *peace had settled on the world*, and the city was still reeling from exuberant celebrations that even the influenza pandemic couldn't dampen. The *Star* reported that there'd been enough noise for Berlin to hear "the roar of triumph" when news of the armistice came in. "It mattered not that the glorious tidings came in the wee small hours. The shrill call of the newsboys, the deep tones of the church bells, and the strident shrieks of the sirens got Toronto out of bed quicker than any alarm clocks ever accomplished the task." The city was in a "delirium of joy" for the next twenty-four hours. People made their way in droves to the heart of the city. They packed street-cars beyond capacity, even climbing onto the roofs, but eventually the streetcars stopped running because the drivers wanted to take part in the celebrations too. The sidewalks filled with people forming makeshift parades, and for musical accompaniment, they used tin cans and coal scuttles, "any old thing capable of making a racket." There were proper brass bands, too, as well as buglers and pipers, and the frenzied party went on through the day and into the night, "a seething, surging mass of celebrators intent on enjoying themselves to the utmost.... Suffice it to say that Toronto cheered itself into silence after an orgy of pleasure lasting fully 24 hours."[34]

This frenzy is what the photographs of that time show too—in Paris and London and New York, people dancing in the streets, the masses cheering. But there were other reactions: exhaustion and disbelief; a profound sense of loss; a sadness for *a world grown old and cold and weary*. A British officer claimed that, for men still at the front, "it was one of the flattest moments of their lives. They just couldn't comprehend it…and there was nothing, no joy." For another man, recovering in a hospital in London, "There was a sense of unreality about it. As though we had entered into another world and hadn't got our bearings." A Nottingham man, already home from the Western Front, didn't go to the celebrations in the city's market square. "I do remember—for some reason or other—inexplicable, especially in so young a chap as myself, I felt sad—I had a feeling of sadness. And I did remember all those chaps who'd never come back."[35]

On November 13, 1918, Jack Hoar was driven up Yonge Street and entered Davisville Military Hospital, where he continued his convalescence through the winter, until moving to Christie Street in February. Notes in his record show that his stumps were still shrinking at this time—a natural process as the limbs recover from amputation—and he was sent to Hart House at the University of Toronto for a daily exercise regimen that would help ready his legs for prostheses. The DOH was still finding its own legs in these early months, and since 1917, Hart House had provided physical rehabilitation to soldiers. Eventually these facilities would move to Christie Street, but for now, wounded bodies were heated, soaked, exercised, massaged, and essentially re-educated at Hart House, all in the name of "reclaiming the maimed."[36]

Physical therapy was still a new and developing field in 1919, fed, like so much else, by the circumstances of war. Photographs from the time show men wearing great fan-like protractors measuring the angle of a shoulder joint, and tiny ones measuring the flexion of a finger. They worked at simple paper-crumpling exercises, or used finger treadmills and wrist and ankle circumductors and pulley weights for all the parts of a person—all to coax compromised bodies back to their original way of being, or as close to that as possible. Veterans like William Wishart, who'd been through the rehabilitation process of conditioning his

A soldier undergoing rehabilitation in Hart House
(University of Toronto Archives, Hart House fonds, 2011-4-33MS)

stumps and learning to use his artificial legs, passed on their knowledge
to others with similar injuries.

Before the war, artificial limbs had been made as needed, on a small
scale, by specialty craftsmen. Now the government funded mass production. Legs came in pre-determined sizes like footwear, and then
were adjusted to fit the individual. Men with money could pay for more
sophisticated limbs from other sources, but the literature of Jack Hoar's
era raved about the marvellous prostheses soldiers received from the government. They were "the very best arms and legs yet devised anywhere
in the world," provided free, along with specialty boots and splints and
braces, and any adjustments required at any time.[37] The legs were made
from two varieties of light-weight willow, and on average they weighed
seven to nine pounds—much lighter, many noted, than the actual leg
of an average man. But it was one thing to lift a thirteen-pound limb

that was part of the body you'd been born with, and that contained its own workings to assist in the chore, and another thing entirely to lift a seven-pound lifeless one strapped on after the fact. For his postwar armour, Jack Hoar needed two new legs—double the load to carry, plus the huge adjustment of walking without an actual part of his body touching the ground. By March, final measurements had been taken and the new legs had been ordered. By late April he had them, and was attending regular classes to learn to use them.

Not surprisingly, his double amputation doubled his challenges. The right stump measured eight inches below the perineum; the left stump was just a couple of inches longer, and so easier to manoeuvre. He was fortunate to have full movement of his hip joints, but since both amputations had been done above the knee, achieving a sense of balance with the new legs was all the more difficult. His stumps were fitted into the "buckets" made for them, with the thighs encased in leather that laced closed like a boot shaft. The contraptions attached either to a belt that wrapped around his waist, or to braces that extended over his shoulders. Wearing the gear was awkward enough; moving with it was another challenge. To practise, Jack was suspended with a belt under his arms that was attached to an overhead trolley, and bit by bit he gained confidence and ability as he stepped along. But even by the end of his stay at the DOH, many months later, the legs were far from marvellous. They'd been traded in for a second pair, but there was no improvement. "Art. legs are only fairly satisfactory," one of the doctors wrote in his file, "but can use them very well considering his disability."

He managed well without them, too. In June—around the time the panoramic picture was taken of the patients of the DOH, with Jack in a three-wheeled chair at one end of the image—the Great War Veterans' Association, precursor to the Canadian Legion, put on a picnic and track meet at Scarborough Beach, a popular amusement park east of the city, on the shores of Lake Ontario. "One of the most novel competitions of the afternoon was an event for legless soldiers in invalid chairs," the *Globe* reported.[38] Propelling his wheels forward in a flurry, Jack came a close second to the winner, who beat him by "half a chair, so to speak," as the crowd cheered them on. And then in September, DOH patients were taken to the High Park swimming baths, and a *Star* reporter watched Jack repeatedly climb the thirty-foot ladder, stepping with his stumps and pulling with his powerful arms, then diving into the tank. "It requires considerable nerve for even an average swimmer to perform this feat," the reporter wrote, "so that Hoar's performance is all the more extraordinary."[39]

What a feeling of freedom it must have given him: first the determined climb, and then the exhilaration before diving, looking down from that great height; the sheer joy of soaring birdlike through the air with no cumbersome attachments, no stiff willow legs, no leather cinching his thighs, no belts or straps bound to his torso. A *swimmer into cleanness leaping.* Just himself, the air, the water—and the satisfaction of accomplishing something that could easily intimidate an unaltered body.

The *Illustrated Souvenir* contains several photographs of Jack Hoar. One, which must have been taken that summer, is particularly striking. He sits on a beam at the water's edge next to another double amputee —the third-place winner in the wheelchair race. Both are wet from a swim, with hair slicked back. They wear swimsuits that cover the upper body in the fashion of the day, but also extend down around the lower limbs. The second man folds his muscular arms across his chest and

looks off to the left, a straight spine assisting his balance, while beside him, Jack straddles the beam and stares into the lens with an almost-smile and a look of determination.

Jack Hoar, left, with fellow leg patient, *Illustrated Souvenir*[40]

There is no attempt to hide the limbs, not by the photographer or his subjects, and in fact the image exudes strength, pride, and resilience. The photograph and the newspaper accounts, small as they are, suggest this was a period of profound accomplishment in Jack's life; that he was absorbing the government's message about "what every disabled soldier should know.... there is no such word as 'impossible' in his dictionary."[41] He may well have believed this, for a time, since in the specialized environment of the hospital on Christie Street—with fellow veterans and other patients like him, with daily exercise therapy and picnics and sporting events that proved his prowess—he seems to have thrived. But a hospital, in some ways, is like a roosting box: a communal space that provides ideal but temporary shelter for vulnerable beings. Soon Jack Hoar would take flight, and enter his darkest times.

It was early December 1919 when he left the hospital. His trip south differed vastly from his trip north two and a half years earlier. In those *young green days*, he would have been full of anticipation, his imaginings of war based on what he'd seen and heard from others, or perhaps from the footage shown at Scrappy Gerald Hanley's recruiting event. Now, returning, he was a changed man for all he'd witnessed and experienced. Surely all the soldiers were changed to some degree, for even if they had not been physically altered, they had probably killed, or seen friends killed. Jack bore the physical evidence of his service. Forever into his future, anyone who saw him would immediately think: soldier; casualty of war. Did his face change, too, like the POW who worried he'd acquired a "strangely villainous expression"?[42] Did the expression in Jack's hospital photographs—a look of defiance, determination, conviction—come after the wounding? Or was it there already, and part of what drew him north in the first place?

There is something of Ernest Hemingway in Jack Hoar's look, though that may just be trivia fooling the eye. Like Jack, Ernest Hemingway received severe shrapnel wounds to both legs in 1918. After the war, he was also an American in Toronto, writing for the *Star*. He later observed,

"When you go to war as a boy, you have a great illusion of immortality. Other people get killed; not you. . . . Then when you are badly wounded the first time you lose that illusion and you know it can happen to you. After being severely wounded two weeks before my nineteenth birthday I had a bad time until I figured out that nothing could happen to me that had not happened to all men before me. Whatever I had to do men had always done. If they had done it then I could do it too and the best thing was not to worry about it."[43] Hemingway hadn't endured what Jack had, but in the years to come it would be apparent that he knew something of demons.

The report drawn up on Jack's condition at the time of his discharge stated that his once-paralyzed arm and shoulder had slowly improved, and though the arm could be swung freely in all directions, it was markedly weaker than it should be, and the shoulder gave out "a dry crepitus," cracking and popping as it turned. He sometimes felt a sharp pain if he rested on that shoulder for too long, and changes in weather made it ache. If the weight of his whole body was borne on his right arm, he could not depend on it. Perhaps more frustrating, his tinnitus had not let up since the day he'd been wounded, and while the report noted an operation was recommended and could very likely fix the problem, there was no doubt some dismay on Jack's part upon hearing this news. The report summarized his response: "This condition has existed ever since he was wounded, he has frequently been to the NTE spec., and operative treatment has not been mentioned until now. Two good jobs have already been lost to him through having to wait for completion of artificial legs, and now he has reached the stage where he can leave Hospital and accept an important position he feels that he must refuse further treatment of Nose, Throat and Ear condition which should have been done while waiting for his legs."

And so it was that Jack began his journey home. There's nothing in his record to tell us about his trip, or who accompanied him, but by March 1920 he'd married Catherine (also called Kitty and Katie) Menrath, and they settled into an apartment with two small rooms. Catherine had been born in Hungary in 1897, and had emigrated with her family as a small child. Chicago at that time had received an influx of Hungarian immigrants, and throughout Catherine's childhood, the

Menraths lived among others of similar background, listing German as their mother tongue when the census takers came around. During the war they'd likely experienced anti-German sentiment, and seen businesses and street names changed if deemed politically inappropriate. In the neighbourhood where the Menraths lived, the *Chicago Tribune* reported on two "American girls with Irish pep" painting over the sign for Hamburg Street so that it read Victory Place. "As long as we are going after the Germans," one of the girls said, "let us go after their names."[44]

Catherine's background didn't deter Jack Hoar. Their romance had started before Jack had enlisted, and resumed when he returned. Jack worried he'd be a burden to her, but Catherine loved him, the story goes, and insisted they get married. Though Jack worked for a while, the job required him to stand for long periods on his artificial legs, so he suffered pain and infections and quit before long. He looked for other work, but couldn't find anything, and Catherine became the sole provider. By September he'd sunk into depression, and one day when his wife was away from the apartment, he killed himself.

There were several articles written about Jack's death, but it's hard to know which parts of them are truthful, since all contain errors of some kind, as well as condescending and melodramatic language. His body was discovered by the rooming house's landlady, and beside it, apparently, was a letter from the Canadian government. The day after he died, the *Washington Times* reported it this way:

> Every morning John Hoar's wife wheeled his chair to the front window, so that the sun could warm his body, or what was left of it. For a burst of *minenwerfer* in a shell hole on the Somme, almost in the shadow of the Cathedral of Amiens, had shot off John's two legs. He had joined the Princess Pat regiment in Canada before America had decided to go in. John's wife would kiss him and tweak his nose and kiss him once more and hurry down for the elevator to go down to the State street department store where she worked. They lived in two small rooms in a light housekeeping apartment. Theirs had been what one might call a war romance. They were engaged before John went away on the great

adventure. He was sent home last March a helpless bit of war debris. Catherine Menrath, loving him even more, insisted they be married, and they were. She went to work. "But I don't feel it's right. I'm selfish, Kitty," he used to protest. "You're working your fingers off for me. I'm no good now. Just like a baby, I am." She did not pay any attention; she loved him. But yesterday, while she was away at work, John was handed a letter by his landlord. The letter made John more helpless than ever. The Canadian government authorities at Ottawa, said the letter, had decided to stop his disability allowance of $85 a month. The $85 had helped a lot, too, because Kitty could not make very much. John got out his war medals, his MM, his DCM, his Croix de Guerre. He smiled grimly. Last night his wife went out for a visit with her mother. John thought of Vimy Ridge, when the Canucks blew up a whole mountainside of Germans; he thought of shell holes and the yellow Flanders mud and boys sitting around drinking vin blanc and singing. Then he thought of his Kitty working there downtown, and he looked at the letter again—and turned on the gas. The police found his body this morning.[45]

Did the writer of this article feel any reluctance in inserting himself so intimately into Jack Hoar's last moments? There were other fictions too. The *Butte Daily Bulletin* wrote that:

John Hoar lived in a wheelchair after the war. He had fought in the Princess Pat regiment and lost both legs. Catherine Menrath, to whom he had been affianced before he went away, insisted on marrying him after he was smashed up. She worked to support him. But the other day, when she was at work, a letter came, saying the Canadian government had stopped his $85 a month disability allowance. Hoar's thoughts went back to Vimy Ridge and torn men and the noise inside a man's skull when he goes over the top—and he remembered the story of the sergeant

leading the charge of American marines across the open
oat fields against the machine guns, crying: "Come on, you
——! Do you want to live forever?" He remembered, too,
the gentlemen's agreement between the armies that the
general staffs of both sides must be left untouched in the
bombardments, and that nobody on either side must fire on
the iron mines of the other, said iron mines being busy producing raw material for munitions. He fingered his croix de
guerre: there was a queer glint now on its metal. Then Hoar
looked at the Canadian letter again and thought of his wife
working patiently for him. And all these thoughts, flooding
in together, were too much. There was only one way out. He
took it. He turned on the gas.[46]

Did Catherine, or others who loved Jack Hoar, ever read these
accounts? Someone in the Canadian government did, for in short order
an official statement was released, and published in the *Globe.*

This man was in receipt of a 100 percent pension of $75
per month. He was suffering from amputation of both legs
below the thigh and had been fitted with artificial legs.
The artificial legs are reported as having been fairly satisfactory. During the period of accommodation to become
accustomed to artificial limbs he was granted additional
helplessness allowance of $250 per annum.... This period
expired on June 12 last. The Ottawa letter referred to...was
one to explain to Hoar the law as regards this special allowance for helplessness during the period of accommodation
such as is required in becoming accustomed to artificial
limbs. His full disability pension was continued as hereto-
fore, and no intimation was given to him that it would be
cut off.[47]

The article went on to say that Hoar had enlisted in Toronto with
the Princess Pats on August 29, 1917, was discharged on December 12,
1919, and—despite the descriptions of him in his last moments with

his Distinguished Conduct Medal, his Military Medal, and his Croix de Guerre — had not received any decorations.

However many errors and embellishments the articles about his death contained, one thing remained true and irreversible: Jack Hoar had died by his own hand. He was far from the only one. There are countless stories about suicides of returned men. One was seized with melancholia and another "worried about everything." An amputee was "a great sufferer from neurasthenia," a desolate farmer had "awful experiences" in the war, and another man left a note that said, "I cannot stand the war pains any longer."[48] A few months before Jack's death, a Toronto veteran cut his own throat with a razor. The army's Circumstances of Casualty record attributes his death to a "mental condition developed on service." Anguish is sometimes contagious. Two days later, his wife died of "shock due to husband committing suicide," and their death records appear side by side in the ledger. They left a daughter not quite six years old. On through the 1920s and then the '30s, papers continued to report suicides of veterans aching with an *old war-pain* that came on so strongly they believed it would be *easy to be dead*. Even in peace time, the casualties kept mounting.

The news of Jack Hoar's death must have saddened the doctors and nurses who'd treated him at Christie Street, and Charles McVicar, who'd written in the *Illustrated Souvenir* of the hospital's "eternal vigilance" regarding the men's mental and physical healing process. "Each case has been so persistently followed up that each patient has felt that he was treated as an individual. Every effort has been made to rid the disabled man of bad influences coincident with forced idleness. At the same time that he has been fitted with an artificial appliance, he has been quietly but constantly presented with the prospect of his altered outlook on life, so that the process of adaptation to further environment might be less irksome.... We have the strongest faith in the returned men as individual future citizens — if they are kept free from patronage and pity."

What the patients made of Jack's death is still more intriguing. Given the accusations about his pension and the articles in the news, they would certainly have heard how he'd died. And they seem to have been concerned about their own futures, and wary of government promises. A week after Jack's death, a new patient newspaper called the *Hamilton-Mills Weekly* included a jokey little poem that implies this sense of worry:

> Twinkle, twinkle, little pension
> wealth beyond my comprehension,
> How I've planned what I would do
> And the things I'd buy with you.
> Started out with fourty "per"
> Didn't get me very far.
> Now they've cut it down to ten
> Called me up for board again.
> Twinkle, twinkle, in the distance
> Gravest fears for your existence.[49]

So what was it like for Jack's fellow soldier-patients to read about the challenges he'd faced, and for those still anticipating their release to learn that he had *left the world*? His wheelchair-race rivals and the man seated next to him in a matching swimsuit were up against a battle he ultimately found insurmountable. Many with no limbs missing had probably watched him pull himself up the ladder to the diving board at High Park, and had thought, as he twirled off, *I could never do that.* For all the patients, and the veterans already settled in at home, working to get back to normal, what was it like to know a fellow survivor had chosen to die?

Van Buren Whetsel, the teenager who'd witnessed Jack Hoar's will back in the early days when they came up from the States to join the Canadian army, had been wounded just before the war ended, and was also a patient at the DOH, still there when Jack left in December. One leg had been amputated, and the other just barely saved, so he was very nearly in the same situation as Jack Hoar. He'd arrived in July 1919, so he doesn't appear in the panoramic photograph that includes Jack and so many others, but his sense of camaraderie with his fellow soldiers stayed with him all of his life, if we are to believe a 1950 newspaper account looking back on Whetsel's war service, his wounding at Cambrai, and his eventual return to the US, "happy to be home but saddened by the thoughts of his buddies who were sleeping in 'Flanders' Fields.'"

When he'd first begun to wear civilian clothes again, he'd decided that a constant part of his attire would be a simple black tie with "solemn significance," acknowledging the ones who'd *risked and lost*. Decades later, he'd held to his promise, and still sported the tie every day, "as a symbol of loyalty to his fallen comrades."[50]

Did Jack Hoar stand out in Van Buren Whetsel's memory? A fellow American; an amputee; a Princess Pat? Whetsel's daughter, MaryAnn, born during the Second World War, says her father rarely spoke about the war, but that "his service in the army defined his life ever after." A framed letter from King George V, thanking him for his service, hung on the wall in their home. The letter was a facsimile of a handwritten document, and had a personal look and tone — *The Queen and I wish you God speed*. The return address corner was stamped "A message to you from the King," and many soldiers and their families may well have believed King George had written to them directly. Van Buren Whetsel's letter was composed specifically for men who'd been wounded, and wished him "a safe return to the happiness and joy of home life with an early restoration to health."[51] The healing, however, was slow. For the rest of his life he got around on crutches, and his artificial leg hung unused in the garage. MaryAnn remembers that a pantleg and a shoe had been professionally painted on to the prosthesis, but for Van it didn't make the device any more appealing.

The family story says that Van lay in a ditch for three days before being rescued, and during that time, his mother back in Pennsylvania saw a cross form on the wall of his bedroom. It was a little like the visions soldiers had at the front—impossible moments where a dead brother appeared to guide you to safety; where hands pushed through the mud "seeming to beckon to you"[52]; where you came face-to-face with *the enemy you killed*. That the soldiers' magical thinking extended also to families far from battle shows the war's great reach into ordinary lives.

Arms

In the first year of the hospital's existence, someone took a photograph from the rooftop. The hospital itself is not in the frame, only the desolate space to the north of it, with Christie Street appearing as a lonely dirt road. One little house sits on a plot of barren land in the centre of the frame, a string holding a row of laundry. There were four such houses here when the cash register factory dominated the spot, and in the 1919 photo you can still see the rectangles where these homes sat, like scars on a body. The single remaining house is a rented working-man's dwelling, made of wood, with rickety additions that give the property a makeshift look. Lumber litters the yard, and some of these wood planks have been placed end to end around the perimeter of the home, the way duckboards formed walkways in trenches and through muddy terrain at the front. Enlarging the photograph reveals a cluster of houses on the Davenport horizon, but between the house and that main street two hundred metres away, the scene is sleepy.

A cow grazes in a field; a figure walks south along Christie toward the hospital; a child dashes across the street. At the house itself, a woman stands near one end of the laundry line, hanging out or bringing in the wash, and a man sits on the porch, behind a railing, facing the camera that takes his picture. The family who lives here moved from an address a little south, razed when the cash register factory was built, and here they'll remain for years to come, neighbours of the returned men and their caregivers, of a hospital quickly growing into its own small village, with outbuildings popping up on the site. The front of the house faces the hospital rather than the street, so the neighbours are like an audience watching the comings and goings of ambulances, top-hatted politicians, royalty, army bigwigs, silent screen stars, and also the "ward aides" who teach soldiers crafts as part of their healing.

In these early days of occupational therapy, the work these women did was an integral part of a man's overall care at Christie Street, and his eventual reintegration into society. Months after the war had ended, soldiers kept returning, hoping to *find old things old, and know the things they knew*, but for many it was impossible to pick up where they'd left off. In the record of a railway man who'd lost an eye, an exasperated doctor has filled in a form on his behalf. "Can the former trade or occupation be resumed?" the form asked. "No," the doctor wrote, "railroad men need at least two eyes."[1] If a man had built houses, felled trees, raised livestock, caught lobster, or played violin, he might never do so again, and how that reality affected his quality of life and his sense of usefulness, not to mention the country's economy, were the great new conundrums. The three-part approach to rehabilitation—overseen by the specially created Department of Soldiers' Civil Re-establishment (DSCR)—involved bedside occupational therapy in the form of crafts, then workshop activity that required more strength and agility, and finally job training that happened out in the community.

In the early part of the war, women skilled in various types of crafts volunteered to do beadwork, embroidery, basketry, etching, clay modelling, and so on at soldiers' bedsides, but by the end of the war, the work was so obviously successful that it had become an official and essential job.[2] Women studied occupational therapy at the University of Toronto and McGill, and wore official, recognizable uniforms: long, green linen

Ward aides, or the "girls in green," with Herbert Haultain,
who started the occupational therapy program at U of T
(University of Toronto Archives, Herbert Edward Terrick Haultain fonds, 2011-21-1MS)

dresses and smart white hats or veils. Skill with crafts wasn't necessary
for entry into the program. Rather, according to the DSCR's own
description, "She must be of the very best type, well educated, and must
possess a personality which is bound to please, together with a healthy
constitution. It is desirable that she should be between the ages of 25
and 35, have unlimited patience, be intelligent, and not too emotional.
She must be prepared to meet all kinds of difficulties and all kinds of
treatment. The work is very hard. This is largely due to the mental strain
to which these workers are subjected."[3]

The men benefited from their work, but the women did too: Gertrude
Pringle, writing for *Maclean's*, praised the "girls in green" not just for
their contribution to soldiers' rehabilitation but to women's place in
the working world. "Out of the strain and stress of the war," she wrote,
"there has sprung up in Canada a remarkable movement, which is now

pointing the way to a new profession for educated women." The path was not smooth at first. Staff at military hospitals were already overworked, and anything new and different interrupted routines and annoyed doctors and nurses who didn't initially see the benefits to their patients. "It was a difficult situation for the girls," wrote Pringle, "going daily to work where they were not wanted, and knowing that they were considered in the way with their raffia, their beads and their clay littering up the neat wards."[4]

Fairly quickly, though, the power of craft became obvious: the man with missing fingers learned dexterity; the shell-shocked man learned tranquility; the blind man honed his sense of touch as he built his creations, and though he'd never see what he'd made, how brilliant to *construct* something as a means of healing from so much destruction — to stitch, string, mould, weave, paint, paste, and knit in order to put things together after such a painful time in history. The activities alleviated boredom and anxiety, boosted confidence, and readied men for the next step in "civil reintegration." At Christie Street, that meant workshops that taught carpentry, printing, metal work, and more.

The DSCR produced pamphlets and posters that underscored the importance of this process, and put on lantern-slide presentations that showed how the men attained "Victory Over Wounds.... Come and see how our wounded defenders win back the strength and skill that make their future safe." The images showed them raising chickens and painting houses, engaged in electrical work or plucking fruit from a tree. The promise was that if a veteran couldn't get rid of a disability, he could "acquire a new ability to offset it," but he must "help them to help him." Another poster showed a man with an artificial arm working a drill press, and featured the caption, "Once a soldier, always a man."[5]

There was a mounting sense that the war had meant more than *a little set-back* for its participants; that something owed might never be repayable. One man wounded at Vimy Ridge made the news for his refusal to pay taxes. "I have lost an arm at the front," he declared. "I have paid all the taxes I am going to pay."[6] Increasingly, the men were advocating for themselves, and for each other. A private in the DOH wrote anonymously to the *Star* to deplore "the sense of coldness or stand-offishness put out to [soldiers] by the average passer-by or citizen of Toronto.... if

there is a cause the soldiers should know of it. . . . My plea is for a greater
sense of comradeship from the civilians to the soldiers, who have been
for so long a time estranged from civilization; for the breaking down
of the wall of false human reserve that we all suffer from more or less,
and it is easier for the man in civil life to start doing this than for the
man in uniform. . . . I speak for the man with few or any home ties, or
who is far away from home and who for the time being is 'mentally
rotting,' . . . awaiting his discharge or the healing of his wounds, as the
case may be."[7]

The papers carried reminders to Torontonians to give up their seats
for veterans, who could ride free on local transit, and to show them
courtesy and respect at every opportunity. In March, just a month after
the hospital opened, two men on crutches boarded the College streetcar, and were annoyed enough by their experience to contact the *Star*,
which reported: "No one considered themselves under sufficient obli-
gation to offer these palpably disabled men a seat. It remained for two
returned men, themselves partly disabled, to rise and urge their less
fortunate comrades to take their seats. It would be interesting to know
if ever the people of Toronto will awaken to a fuller realization of their
debt to those who have fought, bled and been disabled in France on
their behalf."[8]

The same page of the paper carried an interview with Dr. Frederick
Starr, who encouraged tolerance on the part of both the general public
and the returned men as soldiers went about settling into normal life.
The average soldier came home "somewhat abnormal," he said, and
would likely be restless for some time to come, therefore it was essential
that the public sympathize with his situation and that he himself "be
decently patient and do his part."[9] Starr claimed that during their service overseas, Canadian soldiers had behaved in an exemplary fashion,
and if the men continued to exhibit such self-respect and discipline at
home in peace time, the return to civilian life would go smoothly.

To some at the DOH, this must have sparked conflicting memories,
for there are many stories of rowdiness and drunkenness, and even
outright riot among Canadian soldiers: a taking-up of arms against the
establishment. The very day Dr. Starr was quoted, on March 4, 1919,
rioting broke out at Kinmel Camp in Wales, where some seventeen

thousand Canadian troops were stationed in cramped, adverse conditions, waiting to be repatriated. The men were frustrated by how long it was taking for them to get home, and a rumour had spread that ships meant for their own transport had instead been loaded with American soldiers, so the men at Kinmel would have to wait longer still. Getting such huge numbers of people home after the war was a logistical nightmare, and the men were angry, as well as anxious to see their families and find good jobs. They knew the first to return would have the best opportunities. Disgruntlement among large groups can be a powerful force, and that evening fires were lit, the officers' mess was looted, and rioters wielded rifles and makeshift weapons, such as razors strapped to broom handles. There was a weird resurgence of *the old war-joy*. Though twenty of the men initially leading the attacks were subdued and confined, their fellow rioters broke in and freed them, and the frenzy spun into the next day, gathering up some one thousand soldiers. One of the men interviewed at the inquiry the following month said, "It was just like going over the top."[10] *The breathless rush; the charge; the tingling thrill.* As on the battlefield, there were casualties: five men died, adding to the scores who'd already perished at Kinmel Camp, mostly from the recent influenza epidemic. The event was played down in Canadian papers, which reported that "the English papers made it appear a lot worse than it was,"[11] but details travelled home with the men who'd witnessed it, and whose repatriation was expedited following the scandal.

Arwood Fortner was a new patient at the DOH at the time of the riot, and the stories of Kinmel might have reminded him of his first days as a soldier in Berlin, Ontario, a place, as its name suggests, heavily populated by people of German ancestry.[12] The group who'd long ago named the community had been Mennonites who'd migrated from Pennsylvania in the early 1800s, establishing churches and schools, and European immigrants had subsequently come because of language and cultural connections that further intensified with their presence. German roots went so deep in Berlin that, in the 1890s, a bronze bust of Kaiser Wilhelm I was placed in Victoria Park, honouring the residents' attachment to their homeland. The unveiling was a great celebration that drew German Canadians from far and near. One speaker predicted that the memorial would be "a constant emblem of peace and unity in our adopted land.... We do not wish to establish a sectional state in this land," he clarified. "We will remain loyal and true to the land in which we have found a home and livelihood. We do not wish, however, to forget our mother tongue; we wish to nourish and cultivate our German language, our German song in church and school and the family and societies. We do this on the principle that a man who does not honor his native land and origin, his forefathers, the language and literature as well as the customs of his people cannot be a good citizen of the land in which he resides."[13]

A statue of Queen Victoria joined the bust of Wilhelm in 1911, and the two together were stately figures in Berlin's park, he in his ceremonial spiked helmet and military garb, and she with her crown and sceptre, a lion at her base. They were both grandparents of Kaiser Wilhelm II, ruler of Germany when war began in 1914.

In August of that year, when the war was a few weeks old, the treasured bust of Wilhelm I vanished overnight. The bronze queen stood by in silence as the town hunted for the Kaiser. The lake was dragged, and townspeople were questioned, but no clues surfaced until a woman living close to the park said she'd heard a huge splash at about two a.m., as if something heavy had been dropped into the water from a great height. The searchers dragged the lake again, this time closer to the bridge, and the old Kaiser was pulled dripping from the depths. A photo shows him with his rescuers: three spindly teenage boys in swimsuits and two clothed men stand in a rowboat and pose with the prized possession. All wear solemn expressions, Kaiser included, as they look at the camera. It's as if they understand that the Kaiser's dunking was more of an omen than a prank, and that their community hovers on the brink of enormous change. The Kaiser was tucked away for safekeeping at the Concordia Club, home of the German choral society, but he would appear again before long.

Late in 1915, recruitment began for the community's own overseas battalion, the 118th. The fighting was more than a year old, and it was obvious, now, that the war would not be won quickly. The growing numbers of dead and wounded made recruitment a challenging task. Posters went up around town, and notices appeared in the local paper. There were the usual recruitment rallies and military parades through the streets, as well as visits to homes and workplaces to encourage fit young men to enlist, but numbers grew slowly. This was true elsewhere in Canada at this time, but in Berlin, the high numbers of German Canadians coloured the issue. There was also a portion of Mennonites in the community who wouldn't enlist for pacifist reasons. Some of the earliest men to join the battalion had actually been recruited in Toronto, and they had a crude understanding of Berlin's German heritage when they arrived in town, presuming German names meant enemy loyalties. The soldiers' constant harassment of those who hadn't enlisted only caused more friction in a community that was already divided and wary.

Arwood Fortner's mother had German roots, and his then-girlfriend, Florence Rickert, was descended from the original Pennsylvanian migrants. Arwood hadn't been raised in Berlin, as Florence had, but he worked there now, at the new Dominion Tire Plant, which hoped to capitalize on the growing popularity of motor vehicles. His older brother William was among the early local enlisters in December 1915, so maybe it was this that convinced Arwood to join a couple of months later, when tensions were escalating. Whatever his motivation, Arwood signed on with the 118th Battalion on February 7, 1916, and in Toronto, that same month, another brother, Edwin, joined a different battalion.

Shortly before Arwood's enlistment, the Parliament Building in Ottawa had gone up in flames, and there were rumours that this and other factory fires had been deliberately set by so-called enemy aliens. Worried about traitors in its midst, Berlin City Council was pushing the federal government for a register of enemy aliens, and the general unrest in the community sparked the curiosity of a *Star* reporter, who travelled to the city to assess the situation himself. Over the course of a three-day stay, he decided it would be unfair to characterize Berlin and the areas around it as "hot-beds of German sympathy." He hadn't heard German spoken in the streets, nor seen German flags being sold, as some had suggested; but he did say that the first generation of immigrants were more outspoken than the newer arrivals. "They feel at liberty to say what they please, being Canadians, even in defence or praise of Germany."[14]

In the hotel where he was staying, one of the porters spoke only German, while the manager of the cigar store was of English stock. "The

German and the Englishman play pool together every evening. The
Englishman teaches the German his language, and the German gives a
nightly example of German efficiency in pool. They are pals....Yet, the
118th Battalion calls vainly for recruits."[15]

On February 15, a group of soldiers and civilians vandalized the
Concordia Club, smashing furniture and setting fire to flags and sheet
music. They seized the Kaiser bust stored there after its mysterious
tumble into the lake, and paraded through the streets with it. They
smacked it and spat on it, and back at the barracks, they used it for
target practice. The hooligan behaviour continued the next day, when
soldiers posed for a group shot, about fifty of them rising up in a pyramid so that two stood waving flags from the pedestal where the Kaiser
had once sat. Berlin was in turmoil. In March, an outspoken minister who questioned anti-German propaganda was beaten, and in July,
another German club was raided and ransacked.

What did Arwood Fortner think of the actions of his fellow soldiers?
Was he with them or against them, or caught somewhere between?
Records of the 118th Battalion are a rich resource of letters regarding
desertions and transgressions, but of Arwood there is only a small mention of a request to marry: "He became engaged to Florence Rickert
last fall," his superior wrote, "and this young lady is now apparently
in such a condition as to necessitate marriage, although I believe the
child will not be born for some time. The girl belongs to a respectable
family and Pte. Fortner is a good soldier. Since he is prepared to thus
treat his fiancée honorably, I recommend that permission be granted
him to [marry] on the understanding that separation allowance will be
allowed him."[16]

Florence and Arwood were married in early May of that year, shortly
before a referendum was held to propose changing the name of the
community. Berlin had been Berlin for a century, and within the city
there was strong resistance against a change. The "no" campaign placed
a lengthy notice in the local paper, lamenting the fact that such a "vexed
question" was being put to the population at a time when other communities were postponing elections and important municipal matters
so that the focus could remain solely on the defence of the British
Empire. "We are told that if we do not change the name BERLIN, our

manufacturers will have to close down and the grass grow in the streets of our city. [Yet] To-day our manufacturers are nearly all busier than they have ever before been." But since the vote was going ahead, the "no" side urged people to take part. "To vote Yes would be to plead guilty to the stigma of disloyalty, which these agitators are trying to fasten upon you and your city. Show your confidence in the city of BERLIN and the loyalty of the people by going to the polls on Friday next, the nineteenth, and voting NO!"[17]

The turnout was small, and the "yes" side won by a narrow margin. By the time Arwood had made his way to London, Ontario, for training, name suggestions had begun to come in from across the country. Some were inspired by the city's manufacturing base—Industria and Factoria—and others by patriotism—Prince Edward and Empire. But it was Kitchener that won, having been hastily added to the list after Lord Kitchener's death that June, when his battleship struck a German mine.

By January 1917, Arwood had crossed the sea, and by February, he was in France. His brother William, flat-footed, had stayed behind in Canada, but Edwin would soon join him at the front, where they would witness for themselves *the freezing trench* and *the silver call* of the bugle announcing reveille, mealtimes, and the happy arrival of letters. Arwood must have awaited news of his new baby girl, and photos that would reveal how quickly she grew and changed. But his lot was similar to that of millions of young men: soldiering age was also the typical age for starting a family.

Once the ground thawed, there was danger traversing this landscape even when the guns were silent, for if a man fell from the duckboard path, the mud could swallow him up. Years afterward, a soldier with the 10th Battalion recalled falling in, the soup sloshing around him. Another man stopped and tried to pull him out, and very quickly the line was "bunching up" behind him, making the whole group more vulnerable. Someone further back called out to just leave him there—"it was better to lose one man than a dozen"[18]—but the rescuer pulled hard, and the mud released the man, cold, drenched, and filthy. It was a regular occurrence to save a life, or to take one, so everyone simply carried on, at least to the next obstacle.

Somewhere in a long line like this was Arwood Fortner of Berlin-turned-Kitchener, tire-finisher-turned-soldier, and new father of a baby girl. He picked his way over the *sodden plains*, carrying the heavy load of all of his belongings: his weapons and ammunition, his various layers of clothing, his rations and the dishes he ate from, his tools for digging trenches and cutting wire, his gas mask and his steel helmet. The load added more than sixty pounds to his slight weight of 115, and if it was pouring rain, all of it was heavier still. But the kit was a bag of tricks and a treasure trove too—it had everything he needed to survive, plus pockets for letters from home, and photographs that carried him elsewhere. At Passchendaele he smelled *death stinking in the nostril* but by now the smell was ordinary to him, and he could probably dismiss it, or even laugh it off, whatever was necessary in the moment, for these were among the skills a soldier acquired, like standing waist-deep in cold brown water, like burning lice from the seams of your clothing, like sleeping with your boots on, and pushing a bayonet through another man's body, feeling the breath come out of him. The smell of death that has happened already is different from the smell of death in progress, but he'd have known that smell too, and the sounds that came with it. At Passchendaele he endured days of *spitting shrapnel and shrieking steel*, and all the while men fell around him. If he wondered when his own time might come, on November 6, he got his answer.

His record states, "While advancing in open...a shell burst near him killing 4 and wounding him." Jagged bits of shrapnel pierced his arms and hip, and were painstakingly removed at the casualty clearing station, which was overrun with injured men. His record also tells us "wounds were very painful and he was quite badly knocked out," which must have given him some relief, not just from the physical anguish but from the reality of the other four deaths. Were they men he knew and would always remember? Or men who happened to be near him in the chaos? These were the sorts of horrors that turned men "dazed and stupid" and set them trembling from head to toe, "rather like a jelly shaking,"[19] according to a British inquiry on shell shock undertaken after the war. Footage filmed in France in 1917 shows one such man among a stream of walking wounded heading away from battle.[20] The men have bandaged eyes and chins, or arms in slings. Paper tags attached to jacket buttons state their injury, allowing for easier sorting once they arrive at the next level of medical care. Some walk alone and others in pairs or groups, talking and smoking cigarettes. As a cluster of men moves out of the frame, the trembling man is revealed, walking with a tall friend. When the friend stops to swig water from a gasoline can being shared at the side of the road, the trembling man stops too, but doesn't partake. He stands alone on the opposite side of the road, looking lost and bewildered, holding a quaking hand in front of his body; the other arm dangles at his side. A man passes and looks back at him, as if to say, "Come on, you can walk with me," but he stands in place as the others file by, so many in number; *the crowding souls a-hustling from the field.* When the tall man finishes his drink, he motions to the trembling man, and touches his arm, and they move on together. The tall man moves with confidence, and appears to chat easily to his friend, and the shocked man seems thankful to be near him.

At Passchendaele there were more than 500,000 casualties, if you count — though we so rarely do — the people on both sides as one number. Contested ground was won at huge cost, only to be lost again later, making the deaths and injuries even more tragic. Arthur LaPointe, who served with the 22nd Battalion, later remembered the "bare, terribly scarred plain, over which a cataclysm seemed to have passed. It was as if life could never return to these killing fields."[21] *No earthly hand could make it look the same.* Will Bird, who served with the 42nd Battalion and later became a writer, remembered a similar place: "a nightmare never to be forgotten." And yet when he returned to the area thirteen years later, he found new homes built in the style of those that had been shattered, new churches erected as exact replicas of those destroyed. The old German pillboxes — concrete fortifications wedged brutally into the land — were now in use as tool sheds and chicken coops, and farmers told him the earth here was richer than before, "'the best land I have ever seen.'" From a hilltop once under German control, Bird viewed the salient and saw it had become "a great saucer of green"[22] at odds with the destruction he remembered. It seemed incredible to him that such destruction had ever occurred.

Arwood Fortner had physical reminders of Passchendaele that would stay with him forever. He'd left a tooth behind, and his hearing was badly damaged in both ears. There were grievous injuries to his hands and arms, and it was these that doctors puzzled over once he reached England. His service record contains numerous photographs of his *failing hands*, doodled on with inky dots and stripes that denote varying degrees of sensation. Each of the photographs is dated, and there are diagrams, too, that show the right hand wearing such an array of patterns and borders that it resembles a battlefield map. Notes in the record say Arwood experienced paralysis, and that even when this cleared up, he couldn't grip properly or stretch all of his fingers out of a tight curl. Nine scars showed where the fragments had entered his body. But he'd been luckier than his younger brother Edwin. While Arwood recovered in England, Edwin died of wounds in France.

Arwood returned to Canada, and via hospitals in Guelph and Whitby, eventually made his way to the DOH, where he was admitted shortly after it opened. He was there that summer day a photographer visited and took candid photographs of the patients and staff, and though he isn't immediately apparent in the panoramic image, a single full-length

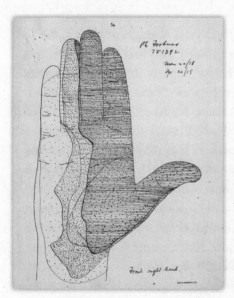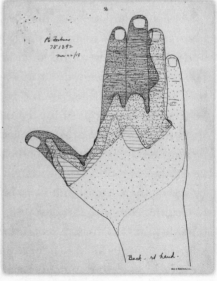

Service record diagram of Arwood Fortner's hand

(Military file: Fortner, Arwood, Regimental no. 751392 © Government of Canada.

Reproduced with the permission of Library and Archives Canada (2023).

Source: Library and Archives Canada/RG 150, Accession 1992-93/166, B3221-S100)

portrait appears in the *Illustrated Souvenir*. It carries the caption "Pte. Art Fortner" and shows him with his uniform properly buttoned and his shoes shined. He remained at the DOH for more than a year and a half, and his record gives a Toronto address for his wife, too, so perhaps Florence moved from Kitchener to Toronto to be close to him. He was discharged in the fall of 1920, three years after the Battle of Passchendaele. His wounds were not as grave as those of many others, but his recovery was long, and when he left the hospital, he still had a weak grip and flexion deformity.

When the 1921 census was taken the following spring, he and Florence were still living in Toronto, with three small children. Arwood was a salesman. His curled fingers probably prevented him from doing his old job at the tire factory, but he was only one of many who needed to learn new skills now, and to reinsert himself into the regular world after his life-altering time away. These were no easy tasks for the body or the mind. In a sense, the distant enemy convalescing in Germany was a *strange friend* because he understood the *undone years* in ways loved ones at home could not.

Arwood had been at Christie Street long enough to have come to know many of the men. He was there when Jack Hoar left for Chicago, and when the news of his suicide broke; he was there when Charles Harrowsmith arrived and also when he was discharged, limping, but with his leg still attached; and he was there when young Van Buren Whetsel, still not out of his teens, made his way to a girl he'd marry in Winnipeg. Some of the other patients had married nurses during Arwood's stay, and he'd probably seen those romances blossoming, or heard the rumours. As time went by and consolidation became practical, he'd seen the hospital shift from focusing solely on orthopaedic patients to treating men with facial wounds and tuberculosis. Increasingly, from outside and in, Christie seemed more like a home for veterans than a hospital, and a place where their experiences had context. Though Arwood is alone and unexpressive in his photograph at the DOH, other images in the *Illustrated Souvenir* suggest an intimacy among the Christie Street boys, as they came to be known. "Brothers in arms" embrace or lean into each other for group photos; they grin and gobble watermelon together; two "in a tuneful mood" pose with mandolins.

Often the armless and the legless remain so in these photos, and it's hard to say whether they aren't wearing their prostheses because they don't have them yet or because they find the limbs uncomfortable. Both long waits and poor fits are frequently mentioned in service records. Many men were like Van Buren Whetsel and never adjusted to the limbs they received; they simply went without and learned to do things differently. The arms, it seems, were especially cumbersome, though they didn't look that way in the rehabilitation posters that showed how men who were "Down and Out" could become "Up and In Again."[23] In 1918, the Military Hospitals Commission gave dubious high praise to the arms it offered to Canadian soldiers. "At the present time the Commission issues an artificial arm with a working hook which is capable of holding a knife, fork, or pen, and by which a man can dress himself, eat or write as well as with his own hand." It was known as a "utility hook," among other names, but the cruder attachment could be removed and replaced by a gloved hand with a workable thumb. "With this dress hand a man can hold an umbrella or a valise, or carry his coat on his arm comfortably."[24]

Dr. R. Tait McKenzie, a pioneer in physiotherapy, categorized the prettier, less useful hand as "ornamental for Sunday." In his 1918 book *Reclaiming the Maimed*, he advised that the types of prostheses issued should depend on the occupation chosen. Then, day by day, the man should practise, increasing his hours with the device as he went along. In McKenzie's view, a clamp design that could grip a tool was good for heavy work, and a simpler hook was best for light work. One common design was the Dorrance hook—a split hook that could be pinched closed by way of cords that extended up the arm and across the back to wrap around the opposite shoulder. The man shrugged his shoulder to open or close the hooks. The Carnes arm, an American-designed mechanical arm with movable fingers, "is seldom used except by an expert."[25]

But who was an expert if not a man with a missing arm? As the *Star* put it, "No man...can be so interested in the quest for an artificial arm that will be the best possible substitute for the real thing as the man who has himself lost an arm and every day and hour feels the loss of it."[26] Edgar Spear was one such fellow. In 1917, during the Battle of Hill 70 in Belgium, he'd lost his right arm and several fingers on his left hand. In June 1919, in connection with the DSCR, the Vancouver veteran finished up an extensive tour of Canadian military hospitals, vocational departments, and limb factories, and found there was lots of room for improvement. He sent a statement to the *Star* outlining his concerns and stressing that soldiers should have more say in what type of prosthesis they received. Spear was a member of the Vancouver Amputation Club, precursor to the War Amps, and his recent tour had convinced him that time, money, and material were being wasted, and that men were receiving limbs "entirely inadequate to their needs."[27] He disagreed with the government's policy not to offer limbs made by private firms, and believed that while a utility hook or clamp was a good choice for labourers, it was of little use to men doing office work. The gloved-hand attachment was indeed "ornamental," even though it had a movable thumb; many soldiers complained that the thumb spring was weak and the thumb not long enough to be helpful. "If the fingers were movable, much more use could be derived from the hand." In Spear's view, "If the Government has no arm or cannot have a suitable arm manufactured they should permit the introduction of private arms to the men whose living to a great extent depends upon having a suitable limb."

The following week, the *Star* printed a rebuttal from R.W. Coulthard of the DSCR. Despite claims in the government's own literature about the wonders of the prostheses it offered, Coulthard felt it "advisable to make clear to the uninformed that, unfortunately, no arm yet produced can replace the functions of the lost limb in any but a crude manner and minor degree. And it is undoubtedly due to this deplorable circumstance that dissatisfaction often is engendered in the minds of those whose misfortune it is to be deprived of the use of the arm or arms."[28] Coulthard insisted that the experts were "wide awake" to the latest developments, and offered "the sanest and most practical devices. The cost has been a secondary consideration, as it is well understood that the returned soldier is entitled to the best." He disagreed with Spear that men should be allowed to select devices from private firms, and said that standardization was one of the great features of using government-run factories. Only with standardization could the government continually repair and update limbs for men all across the country in the years to come. It meant that a man could get his arm in Toronto or Winnipeg, for instance, then move to Calgary or Halifax, and easily have adjustments made if need be. Up until recently, the government had offered mechanical arms manufactured in the United States, but when questioned about their opinion of these limbs, only two out of forty-five wearers found them useful. "One of these, it has since transpired, is an employe of the manufacturer in question, and the other one has applied for our own Government arm to replace the mechanical contrivance of which he formerly expressed approval." Most of the men found that artificial hands with mechanical fingers were "a source of great annoyance."

The record of Walter Dunn, an arm patient with Arwood Fortner at Christie Street, shows his dissatisfaction with the prosthesis he was given. He'd been wounded at Arras and had his left arm amputated

A soldier undergoing rehabilitation in Hart House
(University of Toronto Archives, Hart House fonds, 2011-4-34MS)

just below the elbow, and then further up due to gangrene, the skin stitched closed with silkworm thread and horse hair. He'd been fitted for a new arm, but a tender spot on the scar of his stump bothered him, and he couldn't wear the arm for more than half an hour without the pain being too much. He was given regular massage and hydrotherapy, and a small opening was cut into the leather of the prosthesis to relieve the pressure, but the pain continued. One doctor wrote in his file, referencing the latest model offered by the government: "He now wishes a Starr Arm, which I feel is more a whim on his part than a real need."[29]

The Starr Arm—also known as the Canada Arm—had an elbow joint that could be shifted into different positions using pull cords that extended from the attachment and wrapped across the man's back, looping over the opposite shoulder; as with the Dorrance hook, when the man shrugged his shoulder, he manipulated the arm. Walter's record shows that he received a Starr Arm, and that he attended classes to help him learn to use it. Shortly after this, in December 1919, he was ready to leave Christie Street, with "satisfactory dress and working arms." Doctors acknowledged his previous occupation as a hotel porter could not be resumed "on account of amputation," and by March 1920 he'd found a job as an elevator operator at the Dominion Bank Building at King and Yonge, an elegant, twelve-storey tower—a skyscraper in those days—that had gone up the year the war began. If the job wasn't fancy, the setting was, with Corinthian columns and gold-leaf accents, and Walter probably felt, settled with his wife and daughter not far from Arwood Fortner in the city's east end, that there were calmer days ahead.

Arwood and Walter had enlisted on the same day—February 7, 1916 —though Walter had begun his war journey in Montreal, and travelled overseas with a Quebec regiment. There wasn't much enthusiasm for "England's war" in Quebec, but Walter was from Liverpool, and may have felt a strong allegiance. He'd been in Canada for almost twenty years, having arrived in 1898 with a ship full of British "home children"—children who'd been orphaned or abandoned, or whose parents were simply too poor to care for them. The home child program had been in place since the 1860s, and would continue until the 1930s; many of the men who served in both wars had come to Canada this way.

The passenger list for the *Numidian* shows eleven-year-old Walter and his sister Maria, just nine, leaving Liverpool that September in the care of the Liverpool Catholic Children's Protection Society, and bound for Miss Agnes Brennan's home on St. Thomas Street in Montreal. They were the two oldest children of Walter Dunn, a dock labourer, and Margaret Shearon, a hawker. The fact that Margaret worked, and at such a lowly occupation, selling her wares in the street, implies the family lived in poverty. Walter Sr.'s job suggests the same. Dock labourers loaded and unloaded ships, and moved the goods around. The work was casual and uncertain, and in 1891, the Dunns were living in one room just a short walk from the docks, the *Numidian*'s point of departure when the children left for Canada. What caused this to come about can be guessed at. The children weren't orphaned, and they were probably not abandoned, since baptism records show that more children were born to the couple before and after Walter and Maria moved away. So it was likely just dire poverty that led to the elder ones parting from their parents and siblings. According to the *Liverpool Mercury*, kids in the society's care went to "happy homes in Canada...[and] would otherwise have probably floated into the criminal classes of the city, thereby becoming a burden on the ratepayers."[30]

Just a few years before Walter and Maria's arrival at Agnes Brennan's receiving home, the *True Witness and Catholic Chronicle* described it as a large, plain brick building, with "an appearance of neatness and scrupulous cleanliness which would do credit to a Dutch housewife."[31] It was newly opened then, and had space for more than fifty children. As for Miss Brennan herself, there was apparently "no more suitable lady...to fill the position of superintendent." Records suggest most children were placed quickly, but even if their circumstances had improved, many of them must have longed to return home. An 1899 article reported on a "young wanderer" who'd made his way to Ottawa, unhappy in his latest placement. It was late January, and when police found him on the streets, they put him in jail to keep him out of the bitter cold. At age fifteen, he'd been in Canada about four years and had lived with ten different families, but had run away from each of them. When he was sent back to Miss Brennan's home, she reported that she had a low opinion of him, and that he told "the same story for every place . . . people always shouted at him for nothing."[32]

In that hasting time when the war began, many men who'd been home children hurried to enlist so that they could see their families back in England again. Walter Dunn, though, seems to have completely lost touch with his parents in Liverpool. Asked on an Army form if his mother and father were alive, the answer was "does not know." Was Walter curious to find them when he enlisted? Or was he moved to join up because of the posters he saw around Montreal? One showed a soldier on the battlefields, wondering "Why don't they come?" He stands looking forlorn as bombs burst behind him. A cloud of smoke drifts from his rifle and displays a picture of a hockey game, with a massive crowd cheering on the players. "Why be a mere spectator here when you should play a mans part in the real game overseas? Join the 148th Battalion." Another poster picked up on the same theme: a man lounges in a chair, with a newspaper spread on his lap. He's holding a pipe, from which a cloud of smoke drifts, and this time the image in the cloud is the first poster repeated: the soldier and the rifle and the cloud that shows the hockey game. "Why don't I go?" the man asks himself. "The 148th Battalion needs me."[33]

In October 1916, Walter left for England on board the *Laconia*, by day looking out on endless water, and by night floating beneath *the vasty distance where the stars shine blue.* The *Laconia* was an ocean liner converted for war use. A few months after Walter's voyage, the ship was torpedoed and sunk off the coast of Ireland, one of many harrowing messages that surviving the war was sometimes just a matter of luck and timing. Despite the dangers of sea travel, Walter made it safely to Liverpool. As the city came into view from a distance, he would have seen that a magnificent new building had gone up, graced with two enormous birds that stood high on the uppermost domes, their backs to each other. One watched over the sea to ensure ships arrived safely, and the other watched over the people of the city below. The Liver Birds, as they were known, were mythical creatures deeply rooted in Liverpool's history, and symbolic of the city itself. The copper renditions on top of the Royal Liver Building resembled cormorants: with long necks and sturdy bodies, they stood on guard with their wings spread wide. They hadn't seen Walter and Maria leaving, but they were here on Walter's return, as the city swelled with soldiers and war workers.

The birds were a powerful symbol of home and pride and security and history, the sorts of messages clung to even more fervently in wartime, and it was a strange twist that the figures had been designed by a German-born sculptor long before the war began. Carl Bernard Bartels had come to England with his wife in the 1880s, and his beautiful designs of the Liver Birds had outshone other proposals in a 1908 competition. The building and its striking birds had been completed a few years later, when Liverpool's German population—many of them bakers, shoemakers, and butchers—lived in relative harmony with the rest. But with war, Bartels was one of thousands of "enemy aliens" interned on the Isle of Man as a prisoner of war, separated from his wife and children.

When Walter Dunn arrived in Liverpool, the city had a different atmosphere to the one he had known as a child. With so many men at war, women were driving buses and sweeping the streets. They were delivering the mail and filling fuses in munitions factories. For all he knew, his mother and his sisters were among them. He wasn't in Liverpool long, but he'd return soon enough: after a week in France, in December 1916, he fell in a trench and fractured his ankle. Just before Christmas the Montreal *Gazette* reported that his wife, Blanche, had been informed he'd been sent to hospital in Liverpool. It was the kind of injury many men who were *sick of the conflict* hoped for: a "Blighty wound," not fatal or devastating in a long-term way, but serious enough to get you invalided to England, and well out of the war zone.

Like the "puttees" soldiers wore to wrap their lower legs (which stemmed from the Hindi word *patti*, for "bandage"), "Blighty" was a term that had roots in India—it came from *vilayati*, the Urdu word for "foreigner," as in the British themselves during the time of the British Raj. In essence, to Britons, it had come to mean "home," or England, but the war expanded the definition further and brought the word into widespread use. One British soldier wrote to his parents that "I have as nice a little Blighty wound as you could wish to see. It is a bullet in the calf of my leg, which came out against my ankle bone." Another, less jovial, wrote that "The shell fire is terrible, and the dead stink horribly. If we hang on there will not be many of us left....I have given up hopes of getting out without a hit, but am living in hopes of a Blighty wound."[34]

The word turned up in wartime songs and poems, and in skits at the music hall. By the time Walter Dunn tripped in the trenches, there was a *Blighty* magazine circulating, filled with drawings and writings by men from the front, and promising "Every Copy Sold Sends Three to the Trenches." The Christmas 1916 edition featured soldiers peering out from among sand bags, and staring with shock at a newly delivered offering: a bomb dressed up like a Christmas pudding. The issue contained jokes and cartoons about rats and gas masks — all the bizarre elements of a soldier's ordinary world — but there was serious content too: in the "Comrades' Column," men could inquire about fellow soldiers who'd gone missing, or request information about how a friend had died.[35]

Walter spent eight months recovering in England, enough time to find family and to reacquaint himself with his childhood home, but his service record doesn't reveal such intimacies. If he was corresponding with Blanche and getting news from Montreal during this period, he'd have learned that his sister Maria had married into the French Canadian family who'd taken her in as their adoptive daughter, and that fury was burbling over the issue of conscription in Quebec. The army desperately needed more troops to replace the huge losses suffered so far, but as the consequences of war intensified, enthusiasm for volunteering waned. In the government's view, the only option left for getting more men overseas was to force them to go. To bolster support for conscription, Prime Minister Robert Borden expanded the voter base for the election that followed in December. Overseas soldiers could vote — including "status Indians," though only while they remained part of the army — and so could women serving as nurses. And at home, women related to men serving overseas — their mothers, sisters, wives, and daughters — were also granted a voice, while conscientious objectors and so-called enemy aliens were not.

Photographs from the period show convalescing soldiers outside a Toronto hospital, posing with their canes and slings in front of messages chalked on a brick wall: *Slackers beware of the green eye monster conscription.... Your time has come at last.* Their expressions—smirks and defiant stares—hint at how they voted.[36]

For women like Blanche and Maria, and the nurses overseas, the opportunity to vote for the first time came with paternalistic warnings. When Major Andrew Macphail of the Canadian Army Medical Corps addressed a group of women in Montreal shortly before the election, he told them, "Far be it from me to offer you any counsel," but then went on at length about how they should vote and why. "Now ladies,...You have become tangled up in political life, but...keep in mind that it is for the soldier you are voting and not for yourselves, and that upon how you vote will depend the future of this Canadian army." Their own liberties were also at stake, he told them, and their choices in this particular election could "determine whether this temporary right of voting is to be continued."[37] Robert Borden won the election, but the policy of conscription divided the country and had lasting repercussions.

Walter had returned to the front by the time the election was held, and rejoined his battalion after the horrific losses at Passchendaele. From then until the time he was wounded, he was back in the thick of it, travelling through France with his fellow soldiers as the seasons changed, and attacking the enemy when those orders came through. Often the marches from one place to another were long, which was hard on his ankle even though the break was deemed healed. His record says that anything more than a few miles was difficult, especially in damp weather. In April, the rainy season, he was charged with drunkenness in the field, and awarded fourteen days' Field Punishment No. 1, which meant that, for up to two hours each day, he'd be on public display, strapped to a fixed object, and left to endure extreme discomfort, inclement weather, and the stares and taunts of anyone who passed by. If his nose ran, or if his uniform was *verminously busy* against his skin, he couldn't respond. If it poured rain he got soaked and shivered.

Again, though, timing was everything. In 1916, there'd been a public outcry when one in a group of Liverpool soldiers was said to have died during the punishment. The men had been "tied by the neck, waist, hands and feet" for losing their gas helmets in a marsh—one can visualize them sinking in the thick mud, just the way men did. Some deemed the punishment extreme and barbaric, and likened it to "crucifixion,"

for often the arms and legs were spread wide.[38] Others maintained the
punishment was essential, and an excellent deterrent since troops on
the move didn't travel with portable prisons. One officer wrote, "What
are we...going to do with our 'hard cases' when they get drunk on service and advise the provost-marshal and his assistants to go to blazes?"[39]
Civilians expressed their dismay about "degrading, cruel punishments"
in letters to newspapers, and suggested they did more harm than good,
since men often came out of the ordeal broken, and went forward
"poisoned in mind."[40] The War Office's answer to the uproar was to
clarify in a bulletin how Field Punishment No. 1 should be administered
in order to make it safe but effective. An illustration accompanied the
bulletin, showing a soldier so bound, tied to a fence.

> The soldier must be attached so as to be standing firmly on
> his feet, which if tied, must not be more than twelve inches
> apart, and it must be possible for him to move each foot at
> least three inches. If he is tied round the body there must
> be no restriction of his breathing. If his arms or wrists are
> tied, there must be six inches of play between them and
> the fixed object. His arms must hang either by the side of
> his body or behind his back....Irons should be used when
> available, but straps or ropes may be used in lieu of them
> when necessary. Any straps or ropes used for this purpose
> must be of sufficient width that they inflict no bodily harm,
> and leave no permanent mark on the offender.[41]

The permanent mark, of course, might not be visible. If the punishment was meant to deter others, and also one's self, it didn't work
for Walter Dunn. Late in August, he was sentenced again, this time for
insolence to a superior officer. The battalion was near Arras by then,
and had been on the move all month. The days were hot, and *through
the sunny flowers the bee wings droned.* The war diary records weeks of
tramping from one place to the next, usually in the wee hours, and
of bivouacking in the woods upon arrival. At times they must have felt
half dead for want of sleep, though it was beautiful, too, to *talk and walk
with trees,* and to sleep under *the old star-eaten blanket of the sky.* The day

of Walter's insolence was the first in a long while spent resting "in comfortable billets," but only until seven p.m., when the battalion marched again.[42] Enemy aircraft buzzed above them, but they reached their destination by midnight without sustaining any casualties. Was it during this period that Walter endured his punishment? And what had he done to receive it? His case doesn't appear in the thousands of pages of archival documents that detail the charges against Canadian soldiers in the First World War, but another man from the same battalion was sentenced to sixty days because he'd been ordered to carry an officer's equipment, and had answered, "I refuse to carry anybody's equipment but my own."[43]

The day after the note in Walter's record, the battalion marched again, and prepared to go back into battle. Summer was drawing to a close so the days were shorter and *twilight glimmered into night* more quickly. The men were on the move in the darkness, though it rained heavily, according to the war diary, "[and] this and the enemy Shell Gas encountered made marching very difficult." In the ensuing days of fighting, Walter received a through-and-through arm wound that was treated at the casualty clearing station, but it turned gangrenous the next day, and the limb was amputated before he was sent to England. From there he moved through a number of different hospitals, ending in Liverpool, where he'd begun, and eventually sailing to Canada with the Liver Birds behind him.

On the day of Walter's discharge from Christie Street—December 6, 1919—patients were treated to a show by the legendary Julia Marlowe and her dashing husband, E.H. Sothern. The couple were famous for their Shakespearean performances, and had just charmed the audience at the Royal Alexandra Theatre with a magnificent rendition of *Twelfth Night*. Julia was in her mid-fifties by this point, but "She is still twenty-five in appearance," raved one critic, "with something of the finished art that comes of restraint and omission with two-score years and ten."[44] At the DOH, accompanied by other performers, they put on a show specially choreographed for returned soldiers, acting out skits, telling stories, and singing. One performer imitated the sound of a bugle for several of the songs, making the army calls that each man remembered well, and that would always, no doubt, *stop his heart and hold his breath* and send him back to his war days.

In the section reserved for war veterans' coverage, the *Star* reported that "Soldiers forget pain when fair Julia comes," and that the new stage settings — renovations requested by Charles McVicar months earlier — "were opened on an auspicious occasion."[45] Cots had been moved into the theatre so that bedridden patients could enjoy the show, and once the performance had ended, Julia and the rest of the entourage stayed a while to visit with the men.

Jack Hoar, Charles Harrowsmith, and Van Buren Whetsel were likely all in the audience that day, along with hundreds of other patients and the nurses, doctors, and staff who made up the DOH. Just days before Julia Marlowe's show, more than one hundred men had come from Hôpital Sainte-Anne near Montreal, where they'd been undergoing treatment for facial wounds. They were arriving as Walter Dunn was leaving to join Blanche and daughter Elsie and resume civilian life. Elsie was seven now, so Walter had missed much of her childhood. Sometime during the war, or shortly after, Elsie and Blanche had moved from Montreal to Toronto, to a small house on Gamble Avenue, just a short walk from the wilderness of the Don Valley, with its branching elms and draping willows. Eastern bluebirds landed there during spring migration, and swallows lived in holes in the riverbank, but by the time Walter had arrived, the Bloor Street Viaduct stretched across it, connecting the east side of the city to the west. Photos of the bridge in its early years show it laden with cars and pedestrians during rush hour, and it must have been this route that Walter followed when he found work as an elevator operator downtown.

It was mid-March, his second day on the job, when tragedy struck. Blanche was also working at a job downtown, and Elsie had finished setting the table in anticipation of her parents' arrival, and had gone out to play. A neighbour — a boy of eleven — was gathered with his friends, playing with a rifle when Elsie walked past. Perhaps they were planning an excursion into the woods of the Don Valley, or had just come from there. The boy lifted the rifle and the gun went off, and a bullet flew into Elsie's chest. He ran to her, picked her up, and carried her to a shop nearby, but she was dead already. Walter and Blanche might have been making their way home across the towering viaduct just then, *not knowing how the day had gone.*

A coroner's inquest found that the boy knew the rifle was loaded, but that it was in poor condition; a bullet lodged inside it had previously failed to discharge. The boy's brother and father also testified, and said that they'd laid the barrel of the gun in a fire several times, trying to "clean it out." The coroner deemed the death accidental, but hoped it would awaken local authorities to the prevalence of boys playing with guns in the woods of the Don Valley. It was impossible to walk among the trees there, he said, without "shots from rifles in the hands of boys...falling about pedestrians."[46]

Were guns a growing problem after the war ended? Were young boys more drawn to them than they had been before because of the stories they'd heard of great battles and the veterans who now lived among them? The policy of gathering national statistics on crime and on cause of death in Canada was in its infancy in 1920, and was patchy at best for many decades. What is obvious, though, is that war had a profound impact on children, who dressed up as soldiers and nurses and saw themselves reflected in the government's ample propaganda material. One recruitment poster showed a girl sitting on her father's knee, asking "Daddy, what did YOU do in the Great War?" Children's sweet faces often featured in posters that encouraged people to buy Victory Bonds to raise money for the war. The Toronto branch of the Canadian Patriotic Fund distributed lapel pins to kids whose fathers were fighting, showing a uniformed man wielding a bayoneted rifle, and bearing the slogan "My Dad is at the Front."[47] Younger children knew nothing other than war, and older children studied it from patriotic texts at school, and felt the changes in their own lives—absent fathers, worried mothers. At home, they grew vegetable gardens, conserved food, and sent packages overseas. Little girls learned to knit so that they, like their mothers, could make the distinct "fairy click of women's needles" that resulted in warm socks shipped off to the front.[48] Boys played with soldier figurines as well as model tanks, submarines, zeppelins, and fighter planes. Department store windows displayed extravagant battle scenes, and the shops sold board games and puzzles themed around war. The *child of circumstance* could not help but be affected. Even after the war had ended, newspapers printed children's letters to Santa, expressing wishes for a toy machine gun, a Red Cross truck, bullets, and a child-sized soldier's uniform.

There is a record of Elsie Dunn's interment in Toronto's St. John's Norway Cemetery: Section 7, Range 15, Grave 13. She lies alone in *a little grave that has no name.* Either a stone was too costly, or Walter was simply sick of death, having seen so many laid to rest where *the earth was soft for flowers.*

Spines

The panoramic photograph taken at Christie Street in June 1919 includes more than two hundred subjects, which means that every time you look at it, you notice something new: a train in the background; a pyramid of crutches; a puppy small enough to be held in a soldier's hand. What isn't obvious—what can only be known by turning to other sources—is that these men make up only a fraction of the hospital's population at this time. Hundreds more remain inside the building, bedridden, not well enough or unwilling to be part of the portrait. Though the men who do take part are posing, the mood seems relaxed and even happy, suggesting *war is good when the stress is past*. At the far left of the image, well behind the intended subjects, a man in uniform runs toward the group with his hand raised, as if not wanting to be forgotten in the shot. Two women sit with a soldier in one of the windows, leaning out and watching the portrait form.

The women are dressed in civilian clothes, so perhaps they are sisters or wives or girlfriends, or the volunteer visitors that newspapers urged to come. Further along, vines climb up the brick columns.

Although it doesn't appear so, the men would have stood in horse-shoe formation to pose for this photograph, so that the people on each end were closer to the photographer than the people in the middle. The rotating panoramic camera—a Cirkut—moved in an arc as it took the picture, so that each person would appear in proper proportion in the final image, seeming to straighten out the line. But the process left clues behind: the building itself appears curved in contrast, as does the sidewalk that follows its border. The clues remind us that things are not always as they seem; that history and its documents can fool the most careful observer.

What is clear is that most of the men are well turned out for this photograph, just as they would be when the Prince of Wales visited a couple of months later, as part of a two-month Royal Tour of Canada. In anticipation of this grand event, a memo was sent ahead of time to ensure the men would be properly dressed, with caps on and jackets buttoned, and standard issue puttees neatly wrapping their lower legs. For bedridden patients, "uniformity of appearance and dress should be obtained,"[1] and the men must be freshly shaved with tidy haircuts. Someone special was coming, and they needed to look their best.

From Britain's perspective, the prince likewise had to impress. The official reason for his tour was to thank Commonwealth countries for their wartime contributions, but there were tactical reasons too. War had seen *idols tumble down*, and with the fall of three great monarchies, there was a new awareness of the wisdom of forging bonds with ordinary people. Canada as a country had swagger now, and confidence. After its key role overseas, there was a growing feeling of independence and national pride. At the same time, pockets of bitterness existed over the enormous losses incurred in a conflict fought, some said, for Britain.

None in the royal family was better suited as a reminder of the monarchy's vitality than Edward, who was young and stylish, and had already proven his ability to connect with Canadian soldiers. Born in 1894, he was a contemporary of many of the soldiers, and in October 1918, he'd joined Canadian troops in France, and taken a great liking to them.

He'd found their accents "so catching" that he'd written to his mistress to say he might return home speaking just like them. They were "good fellows in their own rough way," he told her, "& we owe them a big debt of gratitude, though they are conceited devils & they are always rubbing it in that they are Canadian & not 'Imperial Troops,' as they call British troops in a rather disdainful way which annoys me a lot!!"[2] He was still with the Canadians in November, when the war ended, and for many he became a legendary figure woven into their own extraordinary experiences. Soldiers remembered seeing him ride by on a bicycle or on horseback, or munching a sandwich on the side of the road. They told stories of his incognito trips into danger zones, of his fondness for Canadian slang and all the latest popular songs. "He whistled solos for us," one veteran recalled, "and he can whistle better than the average man." Another remembered groping around for a match to light a cigarette, when a man leaned in gallantly and flicked his lighter; afterwards a mate hissed, "*That was the Prince of Wales!*"[3]

Edward's presence at the front had defined the public's impression of him, and across the country there was great excitement about the arrival of "the people's prince." The press called him "a shy lad of delicate physique" who'd emerged from the conflict as "a bronzed young warrior who had found real manhood"—though photographs match the first description better.[4] His lovesick letters to his mistress, full of baby talk and nasty aspersions, reveal another layer. "I had to read a couple of addresses in French this morning," he wrote to her from Quebec, "what a strain, though these French Canadians like it…they are a rotten narrow-minded crowd who haven't played the game at all during the war & never do!!"[5]

But the Canadian public read the newspapers rather than his letters, and it seems they couldn't get enough coverage of the prince's visit. When Toronto's mayor brought him to view the Bloor Street Viaduct and saw that he liked the design, the mayor suggested naming the bridge the Prince Edward, and the prince concurred. Caught up in the royal fervour, the *Star* dipped back in time to 1860, and wrote about the visit of Edward's grandfather, an earlier Prince of Wales, and how that dashing figure had captivated two Toronto sisters, now the mother and aunt of Christie Street nurse May Bastedo. The women—old ladies by

1919—remembered dancing near the prince at the Old Crystal Palace, and giving their skirts an extra twirl, "that they might brush against his princely person."[6] One saved a feather that had somehow parted from his hat, the other the program from that special evening, and the *Star* ran portraits of the sisters as elegant young women in the finery of their youth. It's hard to imagine that May—who'd worn muddy rubber boots and a sou'wester and fared choppy ocean crossings with a cast-iron stomach, who'd endured dysentery outbreaks and air raids and shell-shock wards—would have been equally starstruck. But she and many other nurses were due to receive awards during the prince's visit.

On the day of his speech at the National Exhibition Grounds in Toronto, the *Star* reported that "sixty thousand people rose on tiptoe and shouted their throats raw" when the prince appeared before them. "I am glad there is not any 'No-Man's Land' between us to-day," he told them, and they roared their appreciation.[7] There were men and staff from the DOH in the crowd, and from other military hospitals too, but the prince also visited Christie Street in person for a more intimate time with the patients, especially those whose injuries prevented them from leaving the hospital.

It was a bright spot in days that rolled by at the *same old steady pace*. He was due to arrive at 11 a.m. that day, and according to the *Star*, "As early as nine o'clock, little knots of men, women and children commenced gathering, and when the 'up' patients were paraded on the lawn at ten-thirty, Christie street was simply a mass of glad and eager faces."[8] Right at eleven, the prince's open-top motorcar rolled up to the main entrance, and accompanied by Charles McVicar, he immediately began greeting the double amputees, gripping their hands and asking where they'd been wounded and how they were doing now. Jack Hoar must have been among this group. In just a couple of weeks, he would fly from the diving board at High Park.

Photographs convey the prince looking at ease on this visit, and chatting casually with the men. With McVicar and the rest of his entourage, he rode the elevator to the specially constructed rooftop ward, where nine patients were receiving heliotherapy, the so-called sunlight cure for spinal tuberculosis, or Pott's Disease. TB was an all-too common sickness, caused by bacteria inhaled into the lungs; sometimes the infection

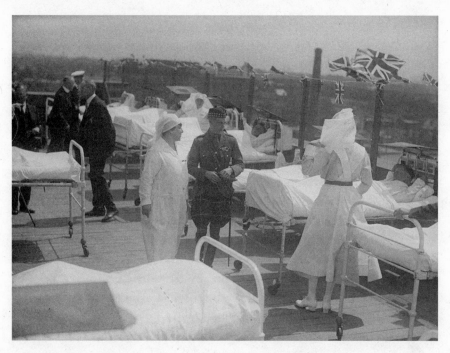

The Prince of Wales, nurses, and patients on Christie Street's roof ward, on a
1927 visit to the hospital (City of Toronto Archives, Fonds 1266, Item 11137)

spread further, carried by the blood to other parts of the body—the
heart, the brain, the kidneys, the bones. As part of their treatment,
the men rested outdoors, flat on their backs, soaking up the sun's rays,
and nurses recorded the number of hours of exposure they received
each day. Each had a small round mirror positioned in front of his face
so he could see the goings-on from different angles without exerting
himself. The prince stopped at each of the nine beds and spoke to the
men individually. Cecil "Fish" Hamilton, who'd served as a sapper with
the Royal Engineers until he'd fallen ill at Passchendaele, had some of
his cartoons and sketches by his bedside, and the prince admired them,
and laughed at the army humour they portrayed. Perhaps it encouraged
Fish: after more than a year of bed rest, he and his fellow tuberculosis
patient Robert Mills would begin publishing the *Hamilton-Mills Weekly*,
poking fun at hospital life with Fish's sketches and Robert's tongue-in-
cheek editorials.

Cameras clicked and followed the prince as he travelled through the rest of the hospital. The wards were spotless, and the floors gleamed. Even in the occupational therapy room, where the "up patients" did beadwork and wove baskets, everything was in its place. "We've been cleaning up and getting ready for him for about three years now," one man joked. Vases of flowers brightened each ward, and the nurses were so immaculately turned out that they would have impressed "the strictest of regimental sergeant-majors."[9]

A photograph of the prince's departure shows police officers holding back a sea of hatted men and women, and a straw bowler raised above the rest in farewell. The press's cameras stand on tripods, and curious little children squeeze together at the front of the crowd. One teenage boy cups a hand around his open mouth and calls out to the prince. What he shouts has been lost to time, but the prince appears to have heard him, and turns to look. If the boy ever saw the photograph, what a souvenir it must have been, enriched by his own personal anecdote. What the *Star* tells us offers a broader perspective, and records the prince's last words to the patients gathered on the lawn:

> "I cannot adequately express my distress at seeing so many of you incapacitated and badly wounded. But I can congratulate you, and offer my deepest sympathy for all your suffering. It has been an intense delight for me to visit you this morning, and I shall carry away with me a very happy memory of our meeting. Some of you I know I have met before. Good bye!" ... Unostentatiously slipping into his motor, he left with a smile and wave of his hand amidst an uproar of cheering which Christie street hospital may never again witness.[10]

The Royal Tour continued into the autumn, taking the prince all the way west and back again. As his train headed toward Lake Louise, through some of the country's most majestic landscape, he wrote to his mistress, "I've got thoroughly bitten with Canada & its possibilities, it's the place for a man, particularly after the great war, & if I wasn't P. of W. well, I guess I'd stay here quite a while!!"[11]

The roof ward was one of the marvels of the DOH, under the direction of a young doctor named Robert Inkerman Harris, who arrived at the newly opened hospital from Davisville with a gaggle of "war wrecks" wasting away from tuberculosis.[12] Harris had suffered from tuberculosis as a child, and that old memory apparently fuelled his curiosity about the disease. In the early 1900s, tuberculosis was the leading cause of death for Canadians between the ages of fifteen and forty-five, spreading insidiously via the tiny droplets of coughs and sneezes. Because it was so common, the army did screen for TB during medical checkups of potential soldiers, but only by a physical examination and queries about family history of the disease, and not by x-ray of the lungs. X-rays, still rarely used at the beginning of the war, were really the best way to confirm the presence of tuberculosis, so the absence of these tests meant that many men entered service with a dormant infection that was at great risk of worsening in awful living conditions. Soldiers were frequently exhausted and rundown; they lived in close quarters that were often cold and damp and impossible to keep clean. When the disease entered the secondary phase, it also spread to others more readily, and so tuberculosis brought down many men on all sides of the war.

The large numbers of soldiers who contracted the disease gave doctors the chance to expand on medical theories already underway. Absolute bed rest, usually for years, was a standard form of treatment. With Pott's Disease, the infection attacked the spine, depriving it of nutrients and gradually causing the bone to degrade. Early clues to the spread were back pain, night sweats, fever, and a general feeling of weakness and unease. For some patients, the illness caused permanent deformity and neurological issues; for others, the degradation was so severe that the vertebrae collapsed into a spinal cord injury. At Christie Street, bone-grafting operations to try to reverse spinal deformities were often necessary, and plaster jackets or casts encasing the torso helped to ensure the body was resting in the right position as it healed. Harris employed these methods, but he was most intrigued by encouraging reports by Auguste Rollier, a doctor attempting to attack the disease with sunlight in the Swiss Alps. Though Rollier apparently believed "only the kind of sunlight found on mountains would do the trick," Harris was keen to try heliotherapy in Toronto.[13] With the help of funds raised by the Parkdale Women's Patriotic Association, "a little tin shanty"[14] was erected on the hospital's roof, and by the spring of 1919, the men were in place, receiving the sun's blessings.

Exposure happened gradually. Naked, with only a towel covering their genitals, the men received sunshine for twenty to thirty minutes on the first day, adding another fifteen minutes each subsequent day. Once they were well tanned, the men could lie in the sun all day, being turned carefully so their backs and fronts got equal exposure, just like chickens roasting. Between each May and October, weather permitting, they were "sun worshippers,"[15] spending upwards of five hundred hours of the year this way, a number Harris thought surprisingly high, given that the hospital was situated in a smoky, industrial part of the city, right beside the railway tracks. In fact, sometimes the sun was too intense, and the heat, on a building with a gravel roof, proved excessive. Little canopies were devised to keep a patient's head shaded, when necessary, and "smoked glasses" cut the glare that could otherwise cause conjunctivitis.[16] The patients were delivered cool drinks, and electric fans sent a gentle, delicious breeze over their basking limbs and torsos. These details—shades, refreshments, and breezy sunshine—form a picture of tropical paradise when compared with chewed-up battlefields and *the cluttered trench*. Photographs suggest that other patients visited the rooftop too, just because it was a pleasant place to be, and no doubt it was cooler on hot summer nights as well. In such an environment, the men's spirits rose and their skin bronzed. Their bodies filled out, too, on a plentiful diet rich in milk and eggs. So encouraging were the results that new patients were regularly added to the "rooftop garden," as the men called it, tended there by the nurses nicknamed "roses."[17] The nurses were nothing quite so delicate, of course. They were more like the backbone of the hospital. But nicknames flourished in the garden: one of the men, an Acadian named Edward Chaisson, whom everyone called Frenchy, played the fiddle to pass the hours; another, Edmund "Chappie" Chapman, made up stories about the pigeons who visited, giving them not just names but "human virtues and failings"[18]; "Big Chief"[19] was the predictable nickname for John Spaniel, an Ojibwe hunter and trapper from a tiny island in Lake Pogamasing north of Sudbury, but John's wardmates may not have known that his grandfather, uncles, and father actually had been chiefs of the Spanish River First Nation.

The name Spaniel—other relatives used Espagnol, Espagnole, and Espaniel—stemmed from the late 1700s, when a Spanish-speaking trader had married an Anishinaabe woman, John's great-grandmother. In time there was a Spanish River, a town called Spanish, and a town called Espanola. The son of the Spanish trader—known to government officials as Chief Espagnole—was awarded medals for his loyalty to the British in both the War of American Independence and the War of 1812. So John Spaniel of "Pogma," as it's called in his attestation papers, was not the first in his family to offer wartime support to the occupiers.[20] His father, Louis, ran the Lake Pogamasing Hudson's Bay Company post from the 1860s to the 1880s, and over time, with the arrival of the railway and an increasing number of white prospectors—hunters and trappers who "kill and destroy all they can," he became an outspoken advocate for the people of the region.[21] "The trappers have stolen all of our beaver," he wrote to the Department of Indian Affairs in 1884. "All of my old people who used to hunt near here are in great need.... They all join me in asking you to help us."[22] What he was looking for was an agreement that would protect the land, the animals, and the people, and allow them to continue a way of life in harmony with the environment and the non-Indigenous population. And years later, in 1905, he must have hoped he was getting it with the signing of the James Bay Treaty. Government-appointed commissioners travelled with their entourage throughout the region that summer and the next, by train and canoe, and presented the agreement to Cree and Ojibwe communities. Written in English, the terms were nonnegotiable, and explained by missionaries or HBC officials. But there seems little doubt, now, that the oral promises recorded in one of the commissioner's diaries—"it was explained to them that they could hunt and fish as of old" and that "the land was theirs forever"[23]—did not accurately reflect the written document, which opened Ontario's north for "settlement, immigration, trade, travel, mining, lumbering and other such purposes," and gave some of the community members in attendance a lump-sum payment of eight dollars.[24]

(left) John Spaniel's father, Chief Louis Espagnol, at the signing of the
James Bay Treaty (Canada. Dept. of Interior, Library and Archives Canad, PA, 043561);
(right) John Spaniel in uniform (Courtesy Armand Garnet Ruffo)

The day the treaty was signed, John's father Louis was photographed
outside the HBC post at Biscotasing, wearing a buckskin suit made by
John's mother, Sarah, as well as his father's impressive old military
medals, surely a sign of his awareness of the historic connection between
the two sides; a symbol of loyalty and support. Louis is surrounded by the
people of his community, little children and the elderly alike. Perhaps
his son John is in the crowd, for he'd have been sixteen then, and old
enough to understand the concerns his father had tried to address.

Louis had died by the time John enlisted a decade later, at Frood,
just outside of Sudbury. It was spring 1916 when he joined the 159th
Battalion, though he was soon transferred to the 119th and then the
52nd. All three battalions recruited from northern Ontario, and so

included a number of Indigenous soldiers. In the early days of the war, the government had been reluctant to actively recruit Indigenous men, but as the months wore on and the need for soldiers grew, attitudes changed. And as in other demographics, men joined for a variety of reasons: steady money, a sense of duty or adventure, the fact that friends or brothers were serving, or that ancestors had fought in earlier wars.

What called John Spaniel to Frood that day is not known, but a family story says his brother Joe had joined up the previous year and was killed overseas. A photo said to be of Joe shows him in 1915, in uniform before leaving Canada. He's not smiling, but there's a brightness in his eyes that suggests he's prepared for the challenge ahead, whatever it might hold. He looks fit and healthy, and poses against a leafy background by the CPR line between Chapleau and Sudbury, his rifle in hand, ammunition pouches fastened to the wide leather belt of his uniform. Little else is known of Joe—how he died, or how his loved ones took the news—but the family album shows John, slimmer, and with a serious expression, posing for his own soldier portrait.

John's record tells us that in 1916 he was five foot nine, with black hair, black eyes, and a dark complexion. He had just turned twenty-seven when he enlisted, though he looks boyish in the image. The contrast between this photo and the ones that appear in the *Illustrated Souvenir* is stark, though only a handful of years had passed.[25] In his rooftop bed, he looks old and tired. He leans back into a pillow, eyes smiling, blankets pulled up under his chin.

John was in France shortly before the war ended, and suffered a gunshot wound in his back. He was admitted to hospital but must have healed well because he was discharged two weeks later, and though the injury is mentioned several times in his record, there is little detail about it. A couple of months after that, in December 1918, John was diagnosed with appendicitis. Doctors in France operated, draining an abscess on the appendix but not removing the organ itself. By the summer of 1919, when he'd returned to Canada, the area still hadn't healed, and doctors noted in his file that "patient an Indian...looks suspicious of TB," though he'd been in good health before becoming a soldier. His file shows he was admitted to the "roof garden" for heliotherapy under Robert Inkerman Harris's care, and that he continued to suffer for some time. His "very fibrous" appendix was removed, along with another mass of tissue "about the size of a hazelnut," and his eventual diagnosis was tubercular appendicitis, pulmonary tuberculosis, and tubercular peritonitis, all deemed to have been contracted in France. Thirty years on, his cause of death in Espanola in April 1958 was listed as "intestinal obstruction due to old gunshot wound (war service)," but when the pension board reviewed the claim by his widow, it found "no evidence that this veteran ever had a gunshot wound during service and there is no evidence to associate the cause of death with service."[26]

John and his family were trappers and guides, so during that royal visit of 1919, he would have heard that the Prince of Wales was scheduled to travel through Biscotasing on his trip across Canada, with hopes of shooting a moose. Maybe the news reminded him of a great old photo from back home—his sister Margaret, dressed up in fine clothes, wearing a pretty hat and sitting on top of a felled bull moose, their mother beside her, crouched on the forest floor. He stood next to them, his hand resting on the moose's antler. With expert skills honed from years of hunting in the Canadian bush, Indigenous men often became valued snipers at war. And yet when they returned home, they were frequently denied benefits received by non-Indigenous veterans.

Partly as a reaction to this unequal treatment, a League of Indians was formed at the end of the war, and held its first convention in Sault Ste. Marie during the royal visit. It was hoped that if First Nations from across Ontario and the West joined forces, age-old concerns about all kinds of Indigenous rights would stand a better chance of being heard. The constitution drawn up by the league covered a wide range of issues, from public education and self-determination to improved medical care to stop the vicious spread of tuberculosis in their communities. The prince was passing through Sault Ste. Marie at the time of the convention, and his presence there, and the accompanying media, must have seemed a golden opportunity for the league, but the request to read an address to him, outlining Indigenous inequalities, was refused by government officials because "all Indian addresses to the monarchy must pass through Canada's hands first."[27]

John Spaniel with his mother and sister (Courtesy Armand Garnet Ruffo)

Ironically, the next stop on the prince's tour—a three-day fishing trip up the Nipigon River—was briefly jeopardized by the convention. Two in a team of highly skilled Ojibwe guides hired to lead the fishing expedition were chiefs who'd gone to Sault Ste. Marie to attend the League's convention, and wouldn't be able to make it to Nipigon in time to start the planned journey. But since his visit to the Sault coincided with theirs, it was arranged that the chiefs could travel with him on the royal train to Nipigon—as long as they rode in the baggage car.

As well as these two chiefs, some forty Indigenous guides had been brought in for the fishing expedition, "the best within 200 miles" and "all of them cunning in camp life and the secrets of stream and wood."[28] Together with the prince, "seeming anxious...in knickerbockers," they set off along the sparkling river, which was in some places serene and in others wild with the rushing current. For the prince, it was a magical trip, far from the "ordinary kind in which he stood on the rear platform of his train, accepted the greetings of leading citizens and kissed the

hand of some ancient lady who had danced with his grandfather."[29]
His attendants paddled him around, caught speckled trout for him,
cleaned and cooked it, fed it to him, and generally kept him safe and
comfortable in the wilderness until the royal train whisked him off to
his next destination.

The day before the prince visited the hospital in August and chortled
over Fish Hamilton's cartoons, a Scotsman named Thomas Ronaldson[30]
joined Chief, Chappie, Fish, Frenchy, and the other sun worshippers on
the roof ward. It must have been something to receive a prince on his
first full day at the hospital, but Ronaldson, by now, was accustomed to
unusual experiences. A sergeant with the Winnipeg Rifles, he'd gone
overseas with the first contingent in October 1914, and upon arrival on
the opposite shore, had taken the opportunity to travel to Edinburgh
to visit his parents and siblings. He'd only left Scotland for Canada a
year or so earlier, so if there were happy surprises connected to war's
outbreak, the chance to see his family again was surely one of them. And
yet newspapers report a dark turn in the visit. Early on his last day, his
family was accompanying him by tram to catch the breakfast train back
to London. Each was probably anticipating a difficult goodbye when
Tom's father suddenly became violently ill, and died on board as the
tram reached the station. It was a grim beginning to Tom's war career.
Even if his stay was extended to attend the funeral, it must have been
hard to leave when the time came.

By April 1915, Tom was fighting in Belgium, in the Second Battle of
Ypres. It was the time of year that *the kind old sun wakes the seeds,* but the
city of Ypres was in ruins. The Germans waited until the weather conditions were just right to release a hissing poison—chlorine gas—from
thousands of canisters set up along the front line. The wind carried
it toward their enemies: *thick green light, as under a green sea.* Algerian
troops were hardest hit in this first assault, *guttering, choking, drowning;*
Canadians were the next targets.

A British pilot had a bird's-eye view of the first attack from his airplane and watched "this yellow wall moving quite slowly towards our lines. We hadn't any idea what it was."[31] As loose and free as an enormous pollen cloud, the mist advanced over the battlefield, wisps of it snaking down into the trenches, searching out every nook and crevice, every mouth and nostril. The men choked and gasped for breath, falling to the ground and writhing in pain as the gas permeated their lungs and filled them with fluid. Even if there were *no wounds, and no blood was shed, the poison gas had done its work*. Men who'd been wounded were down on the ground already, all the more vulnerable to the fumes that sank around them. When the Canadians were gassed, a medical officer who recognized the substance ran along calling to the men to wet handkerchiefs or bandages and press them to their mouths and noses to mitigate the fumes, for the soldiers at that time carried no other form of protection from this startling lethal weapon.

"Our eyes were streaming with water and with pain," one soldier remembered. *Yelling out and stumbling*, the men tried to help each other. They wrapped bandages around each other's eyes, and whoever could still see led the way, with ten or twelve others behind him, each with a hand on the shoulder of the man in front. "You could see lines and lines and lines of [them] going back with roller bandages round their eyes, going back towards Ypres."[32]

Tom Ronaldson was not among the men finding their way to doctors and nurses. He'd been badly gassed, according to his record, and captured by the enemy, along with some 1,400 other Canadian soldiers. At first he was declared missing—surely an agonizing time for family and friends—but after two weeks, *The Scotsman* reported that his mother had had news of his whereabouts: "Information has been received in Edinburgh that Sergeant Thomas S. Ronaldson, 8th Battalion, 1st Canadians, has been made prisoner of war, and is now at Münster."[33] Details were probably slight, and delivered on a card that each prisoner was given after being captured. "I am a prisoner of war in Germany," the cards declared, with spaces for name, rank, and regiment. The soldier indicated whether he was "sound," "ill," or "wounded," and on the flipside, entered the recipient's details. There were instructions to "Fill this card up immediately!" and to "Write plainly!" and "Address carefully!" but there was no space for a personal message of any kind.[34]

Letters would be allowed, though — frequently or infrequently depending on the camp. Tom's fellow officer Sergeant William Alldritt, captured at the same time, wrote a four-page letter to his girlfriend shortly after being taken prisoner, lamenting the fact that the battalion had been "badly smashed.... The sights and sounds of those days will live in my memory forever. I was fortunate enough to escape all shells and bullets, though I had dozens of narrow squeaks. . . . Now I am down in Germany as a prisoner of war. They are treating us quite well and our main trouble is that we *are* prisoners. I cannot write again for two weeks and I am only allowed this much space."[35]

At Münster there were photographic postcards printed, so the men could send missives home just as if they were on holiday. *Don't fret or worry over me. I am as right as I could be.* The scenes featured prisoners arriving by train, or standing in line with their food bowls. Some of the images were hand-tinted, and showed the contrast of khaki with vibrant red and blue French uniforms, and with the multi-coloured kilts of Scottish and Scotch Canadian regiments. A souvenir photograph album from another Winnipeg Rifles man held at the camp contains images of Algerian, Indian, Moroccan, Russian, British, French, and Canadian prisoners, with one picture labelled "14 Different Nationalities."

With so many men from so many places, communication was challenging in a prisoner of war camp. In German, these were known as *kriegsgefangenlager: krieg* for war, *gefangen* for prisoners, and *lager* for camp. Thrown in together, the men created a "Lager Lingo" that was a "go-as-you-please tongue" for which the grammar was as basic as the spelling. "There are no rules, and therefore no exceptions," one prisoner wrote in the camp's newspaper. "The fine (and superfluous) distinctions of past, present, and future are ignored, and there are no irregular verbs to trouble about.... Many of us can swear in [the Lager Lingo]. That is the final test that proves a man can really master a language...!"[36]

Given the "cosmopolitan crowd of *gefangen*,"[37] it isn't a wonder that articles about "Types" would feature in the camp newspaper, turning a group into a single man, and emphasizing his peculiarities. One of these describes the Canadian soldier as "pre-eminently a Canadian" no matter where he'd been born.

He extols Canadian life on every possible occasion, without
boasting and without false shame....As befits a dweller
in regions of great distances, where conditions are not
always friendly, he is hospitable, and ever-ready to lend a
helping hand....In versatility [the Canadian] gives place
to no man. He has learned the happy knack of shifting for
himself—of making the best of conditions which others
would find intolerable—and he contrives to turn the most
unlikely objects to useful ends. Give him a piece of wire and
he will turn you out a pair of pincers; a bully beef tin, and
he will arrange you a coffee pot....No one can accuse the
Canadian of militarism. He is no lover of ceremony and routine, and the formalities of discipline irk him. He chuckles
over the story of the General who, legend states, found it
necessary to caution his men, on the eve of some ceremony,
not to address him as "Bill" during the proceedings, and he
approves of the state of feeling exemplified by the narrative.
He is essentially democratic, and but little concerned with
distinction of rank.[38]

Whether Tom Ronaldson fit the stereotype is hard to know now. But
something of his environment comes through in photographs of the
camp's theatrical performances, concerts, tennis games, and boxing
matches. The men engage in snowball fights, dwarfed by a towering snow-
man labelled as "Made in Germany, built by Russians." In many of the
photos, the prisoners wear wooden shoes, presumably to make escaping
more difficult. If one cartoon had it right, the men believed they would
be there a long time: titled "Exercise—Rennbahn, Münster—1946,"
the drawing depicts prisoners as *grizzled veterans* gripping canes and
hobbling around the exercise yard, still in their wooden shoes, but with
long scraggly beards and hunched, aged bodies.[39] Cobwebs cling to the
signs—"Dropping out is *streng verboten*"—and the buildings in the background are warped and sagging, with broken windows.

Tom's record shows that he worked for the Red Cross while he was
at Münster, but doesn't offer specifics. Others worked on farms, or in a
nearby mine, or for the postal service, bringing wagonloads of letters and

parcels to the camp—and sometimes makeup and costumes needed for the theatre. Some men simply refused to work, and these were the ones who were treated most harshly. William Alldritt's refusal to work, and his multiple escape attempts, saw him transferred to increasingly harsh environments during his years in captivity. In 1918, when he'd reached neutral ground in the Netherlands as part of a prisoner exchange, he was "at long last" able to write to his girlfriend a letter that the enemy would not read. "I scarcely know where to start but I will begin by saying that although I suffered in the early days for want of food I was not really ill-treated." Only when he became "one of the most persistent runaways in the country" did things turn dire. He was "knocked insensible," and punished with forced labour in the salt mines. "[But] enough about myself, and Germany," he wrote. "I want to forget if I can."[40]

Though Tom belonged to the same company, and spent the same amount of time in Germany, his experience differed from Alldritt's. By July 1915, a couple of months after Ypres, the cough that started with the gassing still hadn't gone away, and a doctor at the camp—presumably German—made notes in his file that his phlegm was tinged red. He continued to cough blood—just small amounts at first, but by September, it had worsened. *Blood came gargling from the lungs*, and his chest hurt whenever he exerted himself. In October, his coughing produced "quantities of bright red blood," and he was sent to hospital after suffering a severe hemorrhage. This was the beginning of his battle with tuberculosis, which settled first in his lungs but spread to his spine.

In all, Tom spent time in three prisoner of war camps before being sent to the Netherlands in March 1918, and finally to England in June. He was soon moved to a hospital in Edinburgh, either a lucky coincidence or a fulfillment of his own request to be near to his mother. Probably he was reminded of the death of his father, so sudden and so unfortunately timed, and just the beginning of a chain of sadnesses. Tom's two soldier brothers were dead now, both killed in action in 1917, and a sister was a Red Cross nurse. War had gutted the family, and his mother was likely desperate to see him. The military hospital had taken over the old poorhouse, home and infirmary to the most destitute in the area, and now Tom and other soldiers lay there, tended by military nurses and doctors. After almost a year of treatment—a spinal brace, complete bed rest, and a special diet—medical staff deemed him ready to return to Canada for more of the same.

Was he anxious to get home? Or did he even think of Canada in those terms? When he'd enlisted in August 1914, he'd been living in the small, remote town of Fort Frances, Ontario, near the Manitoba border, and working as a clerk for the Bank of Commerce. More than 1,700 of the bank's men had gone to war, and "the women of our kind came to the rescue," wrote the general manager in 1920. "Right nobly did they buckle to their tasks," freeing up the "banker-soldiers" for active duty. With so many at war, the staff inspector at the bank had the idea of documenting employee war service, and publishing pamphlets that listed who'd died or been wounded or commended, and which branch they'd worked at. The pamphlets included letters too, and these were eventually collected in book form, as *Letters from the Front: Being a Record of the Part Played by Officers of the Bank in the Great War.* Tom Ronaldson's portrait appears, along with a letter written from Germany in 1917. He mentions a co-worker he's lost track of, and enquires about two others, and he thanks the bank for a package they've sent:

> most of the bread you sent me arrived in good order....
> You are certainly to be congratulated on the work you have
> done for the prisoners. You can scarcely realize how much
> it is appreciated. Outside of the material gift, there is the
> grateful knowledge that the people back home remember
> us and that they appreciate the fact that we cannot help
> our predicament.... It will certainly be very strange to us
> when we return to see such changes in the personnel of
> the officers.[41]

This last might be read as an awareness of the fact that many would not return to their former positions, because they'd been either killed or so badly wounded they were no longer fit for the job. Tom's own record states that his former trade should not be resumed and that he would need to work in the "open air."

Air was abundant on the DOH rooftop, though when the trains passed, or when the tannery belched out noxious smells, it was likely

far from fresh. Still, the soldiers seem to have liked their ward, as did
the nurses assigned to it. They had a commanding view of the city, still
sleepy looking northward, but bustling looking south. The Ford Motor
Company building that could be seen south of the tracks apparently
tested its Model Ts on a rooftop track, so the patients and their nurses
could probably see the boxy little cars doing laps, sun glinting on the
shiny black paint. The rooftop was the hospital's "centre of fun and
gaiety," according to the *Globe*, and also a place where romance "budded
and bloomed."[42] It was said that wedding bells tinkled when a nurse got
assigned to the roof.

The *Hamilton-Mills Weekly*, the paper begun by two of Tom's fellow
rooftop patients, is full of cheeky mentions of nurses and other female
visitors to the ward. One issue suggested that, during the Canadian
National Exhibition, the rooftop became "a sort of annex to the
midway," and women came in droves to assess the patients' "colour and
form." The author called for a turnstile and guard at the door to better
control the "crowds of females" wishing to ogle the men who lay helpless
and scantily clad. Another editorial claimed, "The other day a sprightly
young matron came bustling into the DOH and danced merrily down
the line of beds dispensing a smile here and there until she reached her
goal . . . [and] leaning over his bed she planted a sweet lingering kiss on
his responsive lips."[43]

It wasn't all wishful thinking. Romances did flourish on the rooftop,
and several of the spinal patients married their nurses, though these
were probably women who'd never expected to marry when they first
entered the profession. Nurses didn't, as a rule; and if they did, their
nursing career was usually over. It was an achievement that had been
hard won. Women had to be twenty-one before they could begin their
nurses' training, which took three years and an abundance of courage
and stamina. Mabel Lucas, who worked on the roof ward at Christie
Street, first applied to the school at Toronto Western Hospital in 1908.
She weighed ninety-four pounds and was told to come back and apply
again when she weighed one hundred. Finally accepted, she lived in
a tent on the hospital grounds, and spent her probationary period
making beds and emptying bedpans and learning about anatomy, surgery, and pathology. There were lectures on diet, and training sessions

from masseuses, and there was ample opportunity to reach a new level of comfort with the human body, for some patients were horribly filthy, or riddled with disease. Emotional fortitude was built into the curriculum: you had to learn to let people go. Mabel's first such ache was for a frail old lady no one ever visited. "I used to look after her and sort of give her a little extra attention whenever I could....I knew she was very ill and they said there was no chance for her." But when the woman died, Mabel was called on to assist as the old woman's body was tended to. She stood "crying and crying" as the staff washed the woman, packed her rectum, put bandages under her chin, closed her eyes, and laid pennies on her eyelids. "It was the first death I had ever seen. [The senior nurse] said to me, 'I wonder how much use you're going to be around here if that's the way you act.'"[44] She couldn't have imagined, then, what she'd be able to endure later: tent life, again, but in Salonika, with scorpions and spiders; the rotting-meat smell of gangrene; buckets spilling over with severed arms and legs; *the groans and screams of mutilated life*; letters that needed careful writing to mothers and fathers. Once, during a bombing raid, rather than finding shelter, she stayed in place, guarding her unconscious patient. "He was dying," she said, "[and] a nurse had to be there."

With her on the rooftop at Christie Street—another "rose"—was Ada Winifred Hammell, known to her family as Win.[45] She'd done her training around the same time as Mabel Lucas had, but at Toronto General Hospital, and she'd also had army nursing experience at "five camps at Niagara," according to her service record, so it's not surprising that Win was among the first one hundred or so nurses readily accepted to serve overseas. Her record puts her at Valcartier Camp near Quebec City in September 1914. Ships were gathering in the harbour by then, and the camp bustled with troops and officers. Each night for a week before leaving, the nurses heard troops and artillery wagons passing their quarters—a continuous line that would branch off in many directions over the next four years, just the way nerves branch off from the spinal cord. Like the soldiers, the women were kept busy receiving medical examinations and the necessary vaccinations, and generally familiarizing themselves with each other and the military world. Only a handful of nurses had served in the Boer War, and now, for the first

time, women from across the country, holding the rank of lieutenant,
were uniting as a force of their own, about to embark on a perilous,
unforgettable time.

Details of the pending departure had not been specified, and rumours
swirled with the dust kicked up by the constant traffic. Several times
the women were ordered to pack their kit bags and get ready to board
ship, and then to unpack them again, with no explanation. But finally,
one evening at the end of September, the real call came. As the nurses
climbed the gangplank with their kit bags, soldiers from the Winnipeg
Rifles—Tom Ronaldson's regiment—cheered them on from above.

Did Tom spot Win that day, red hair peeking out from beneath
her veil, hazel eyes finding him? It seems unlikely there would have
been a spark. Though Tom grew into an exceptionally handsome man,
with dark hair and dark eyes and a commanding presence, he was just
eighteen when he enlisted, and appears a gangly boy in a photograph
taken with the rest of his company. Win, on the other hand, was thirty-
three—tall, accomplished, and seven years into a serious career. But
somehow, somewhere, a relationship developed. Family stories from
Win's side suggest that Tom and Win met overseas, and yet, after
Valcartier and the *Franconia* in 1914, their paths don't seem to have
crossed again until Christie Street in 1919.

On board the *Franconia* with Win was a nurse named Constance
Bruce, known among the other nurses as Connie. Like Tom, Connie
had worked for the Canadian Bank of Commerce, perhaps as an
industrial nurse tending to bank employees.[46] Did she know Tom, and
introduce him to Win? Connie's name appears in the bank's wartime
collection, *Letters from the Front*, but the richest details come from her
own 1918 work, a charming, illustrated book titled *Humour in Tragedy*,
which follows a cluster of nurses from Canada to England, France, and
Salonika.[47] Connie writes in the third person, burying her specific story
in the collective one, and yet personalities shine through in the prose
and the whimsical sketches. The comical and often poignant anecdotes
she recounts about "a Sister" are surely her own experiences, and those
of the nurses closest to her. The book is dedicated "To Winifred," and
though it seems a crazy leap, at first, to hope that Win and Connie were
friends, the evidence does add up: they were both Toronto General

nurses; they were on the same years-long journey through the war, even taking leave and falling ill at the same times; they were close in age; there was only one other woman named Winifred among the first hundred nurses to go abroad, and she was considerably older than Connie. Digging even deeper, the diary of Helen Fowlds, another nurse who served with Win and Connie, and who came with Win to Christie Street, makes several mentions of "Bruce and Hammell" together. "Hammell and Bruce conversed freely as usual," she jotted. The two were "rather inoffensive girls," she wrote to her mother, "but I like them."[48]

Humour in Tragedy opens in *the lull of midnight*, in those very first hours Win and Connie were at sea:

> Silently [the *Franconia*] cut her way through the waters,
> like a phantom, frightened of the night, and of the mystery
> around her. Here and there, framed by the port-holes,
> eager faces looked out, faces of men who understood the
> significance of the widening stretch of water, both to the
> keepers of the firesides and to themselves. Above, the decks
> were deserted, except for a little group of Nursing Sisters,
> who had remained up to see the last of their country, and
> a few lonely-looking figures, silhouetted against the rising
> moon.

In London, the nurses toured the ancient and awesome Westminster Abbey, and "two Sisters, who were very tired," disgraced the others by falling asleep at a service in St. Paul's Cathedral. They were tourists for now, but soon enough they arrived in France and felt the full weight of their responsibilities. Connie wrote:

> In a bed beside a window was a boy, riddled with bullet
> wounds, who always asked for a description of the sunrise,
> that he might picture to himself what he would never again
> enjoy. "Is there lots of pink in it this morning?" he would
> ask, with a yearning expression in his sunken eyes. One
> night, when a storm was raging and the wind was howling
> around, it seemed that his spirit grew weary of this world,

for it drifted out with the tide; and in the morning, as the
Sister stood beside his empty bed, looking out on a glass
sea, she wondered how it seemed to him, now that the storm
of his life was over.

Connie and Win were not in France for long. By the summer of 1915,
they and their band of nurses were travelling to the Mediterranean,
"bound for the unknown East," as Helen Fowlds put it, where the disas-
trous Gallipoli campaign was producing wounded from Australia, New
Zealand, and Newfoundland forces. For Canadians, the war's biggest
stories had featured the Western Front, so this must have seemed an
excursion of wild proportions. Until their arrival the nurses were tourists again, and Helen Fowlds jotted geographical trivia in her diary and
snapped a photo labelled "Gib" for Gibraltar. They passed the craggy
coast of Spain, and the white buildings of Valetta, Malta, which shone in
the light of early morning "like the ghost of a dead city." "Very beautiful
it looked," wrote Connie, "with its lacy spires gleaming in the early morning sun, like a miniature model of a city, carved in white stone, floating
upon the surface of the blue Mediterranean." But then, "everything was
strange in this new world of war."

Over the next couple of years, Win's work in this part of the world
would take her and her fellow nurses into new and fascinating experiences. In Egypt, they rode camels and climbed pyramids. They wandered
through bazaars where vendors hawked perfume and lace, or ground
fragrant plant matter into mounds of vibrant spices. Connie recorded
seeing a tiny child lead two enormous buffaloes through the narrow
streets, and the palm trees fanning themselves in the warm breeze.
Snakes hissed in the arms of snake charmers, and people carried tee-
tering loads on their heads: bundles of hay, trays of bread, crates of
clucking hens. At regular intervals, Muslims were called to pray in the
old mosques nestled throughout the bazaars, a peaceful sound rising
"above the squalor of the earth."

All of this was still ahead of them, and unimaginable, when they
first arrived on the Greek island of Lemnos. With its stones and dust
and flies, it resembled, for Connie, "the actual end of the world." But

being so unlike home, the landscape was compelling, and the nurses had barely settled for dinner that first evening when they noticed two among them had wandered off. "Looking out they discovered, to their horror, two of the most self-respecting and intelligent Sisters"—Connie and Win?—"posing on the sky-line, 'On the way to see something of the Island.' A Sister, who was speedily despatched, caught them just as they came within sight of a column of troops and, it was whispered later, a bathing parade, and they were borne back in triumph from the perilous unknown." The accompanying sketch shows the pair trudging atop a mass of bare earth, their veils stretched out comically behind them.

"Nothing but a sandy, rocky waste" was Helen Fowlds' first impression of Lemnos, matching Connie's. But later that same night, "little specks of light came out through the dusk," Connie wrote:

> As the night wore on, the moon rose, so dazzling and powerful that it was impossible to sleep. Many stole out of their tents and stood spellbound, for the place appeared to be enchanted, and, looking up, the moon and the stars all seemed to have drawn near to the earth. A flock of Indian sheep wandered slowly toward the camp, their bells tinkling through the stillness, and, as they passed, they stared at the strange creatures, who had come to desecrate their pastures. In the morning, through the open flap of the tent, the ground could be seen sloping down to a sheet of water, and beyond, rough land rose, undulating, to the distant mountains, standing defiant and austere.... Here and there, over bleak stretches of brown, Greek villages were scattered, their small white houses snuggled away on clusters of green, giving the impression of a panoramic scene on a stage curtain.

The next day, a convoy of patients arrived, and the nurses scrambled to treat them with few provisions and a shortage of water. These would be ongoing problems at Lemnos, where, for the first while, fresh water had to be brought from Alexandria or distilled aboard the ship. The heat brought a new, oppressive challenge, as did the insects. "Flies swarmed everywhere," wrote Connie, "until, at times, the ground seemed to rise and fall like a grey blanket." And there were lice. Helen Fowlds wrote that "Hammell has started a beauty campaign á la kerosene," and took a photograph to mark the occasion. The women in the image aren't named, but the one standing tall and striking, holding a brush to her hair, is a match for other photos of Win. Her companions, looking wild and dishevelled, pose beside her, as one combs the pests from the other's tresses.

One of Connie's sketches depicts a nurse stretched out in bed, "hoping for five minutes' repose," only to hear the buzz of a mosquito searching out a hole to find its way through the netting. Another shows a nurse lying corpse-like, enduring "a malarial day-dream," an illness both Win and Connie contracted, according to their service records. Nurses nursed each other, in these times, occasionally without success. Owing to the sanitation challenges, two of the nurses on Lemnos died of dysentery not long after the group had arrived there, and though Connie doesn't refer to it specifically in *Humour in Tragedy*, there are sketches showing "Sisters weeping for an unknown reason," or "Sister on verge of tears" or "Weak-minded Sister fainting." But there is also "Sisters relieving tension," in which two women dance and kick their legs in the air, veils flying. In the midst of *the pity of war*, if you couldn't find humour in tragedy, you'd be lost. Or, as Helen Fowlds put it, "There is plenty of sorrow and sadness over here—but one can't worry much or one would go insane."

When the first nurse died on Lemnos—fifty-year-old Mary Frances Munro—CAMC officers made a rough casket, covered it with black fabric, and chalked a white cross on the top. "It was rude and bare in the extreme," Helen wrote, "but the best obtainable.... The officers brought the body in and though we all knew it wasn't wise to let our feelings get the better of us, the sight of her cap and belt on top of the flag was the crowning touch of pathos." The service, by a less than gifted padre, was "weak and unconvincing," in Helen's view, but maybe it was better that way, because the nurses were already despairing. "It had been arranged previously that no Sisters would go to the grave and it was perhaps wise but it seemed too bad to see her go away without a

Nurses on Lemnos combing lice from their hair
(Trent University Archives, Helen Marryat fonds, 69-001-4)

single woman near her." After a while, from a distance, they heard the guns firing a salute, and the sound of a bugle "wailing across the valley." Matron Jessie Jaggard had arranged the funeral, though "nearly crazy, and half sick herself"—but within weeks, she also died of dysentery. These two were the first Canadian nursing sisters to die during the war, and Helen Fowlds acknowledged the fear their deaths must have stirred for families of nurses back home. "I am awfully worried about the anxiety you must be feeling about us," she wrote to her mother. "If you could see me now you would be quite contented for I am feeling absolutely fit.... Our only nightmare is that we'll be recalled. Mrs. J. is some relation of [Prime Minister] Borden's and we are afraid that there will be a demand for us to go home."

Despite Helen's reassurances, it must have been difficult for the nurses to manage their grief for their colleagues and their fear for themselves. But as with the soldiers, it was likely these extreme experiences that brought them close to each other, and made them know themselves differently. Of war in general, a Canadian stretcher bearer wrote home to his wife, "This is a good place to find out about yourself."[49]

Helen writes that on the night of Miss Munro's funeral, the nurses gathered and sought comfort in each other's company. They read aloud Rudyard Kipling's forlorn poem, "Dirge of Dead Sisters," honouring British nurses who'd died in the Boer War:

> Who recalls the twilight and the rangéd tents in order
> (Violet peaks uplifted through the crystal evening air?)
> And the clink of iron teacups and the piteous, noble laughter,
> And the faces of the Sisters with the dust upon their hair?

Just when they were all on the verge of despair from the maudlin ode, one of the women—Myra Goodeve, who'd become matron at Christie Street in its early years—asked the others, "Do I have a piteous noble laugh?" and suggested they all try to cultivate one. "Our Colonial giggles just won't do at all.... no one will ever write poetry to us if we don't acquire more of a Florence Nightingale manner." Helen's writings suggest that Myra was always saving the day with humour, and in spite of grim circumstances, the women often laughed until tears came. These friends were "my mainstays in life," writes Helen, and the same bond is evident in Connie's sketches and stories, where the sisters are depicted in all shapes and sizes, all ages and temperaments, and yet as a single, robust force who "stuck it out together." Even the physical challenges of Lemnos were remembered fondly when Connie penned a farewell to the island in Helen's autograph book, the same rhyme that appears in *Humour in Tragedy*. It opens:

> Ragged little Isle of Lemnos,
> In the blue Aegean Sea,
> We have cursed you, but we like you
> Just the same.
> And when the mists of time obscure you,
> And we're scattered far and wide,
> I am sure that we shall long to
> Hear your name.

Service records show that Win and Connie contracted malaria at the same time, early in 1917. They recuperated together in England, and afterward served in the same hospitals there. Connie must have been writing her book by then, for it was published in London in 1918, "with 64 very original pen and ink sketches," but by 1919, she and Win had parted ways. Connie would marry and live in India for years, and Win—with Helen Fowlds, Myra Goodeve, Mabel Lucas, and May Bastedo—would enter the Christie Street Hospital, just weeks before Tom Ronaldson and the Prince of Wales arrived.

By now Tom had just turned twenty-three, and Win was thirty-eight. But love was a powerful ingredient in the heady atmosphere of the Christie Street rooftop, amid Chappie's pigeons and the music of Frenchy's fiddle. The *Hamilton-Mills Weekly* wrote of "Little Frenchy, lying here, swilling pop and ginger beer, thinking of his future life, picking out a comely wife."[50] Mills himself, who penned the poem, married his DOH masseuse; and Chappie married his nurse—though for the majority of his remaining years, he continued to live at the hospital, and became one of its most beloved patients. Chappie had actually never seen battle: he injured his back while still in training in Toronto in 1916, and upon closer inspection of his case, doctors discovered tuberculosis. So he remained on the Canadian home front, convalescing in military hospitals, and moving to Christie as soon as it opened in February 1919. He'd been among other soldiers for years by that point, and seems to have been embraced as an emblem of cheerfulness. It was Chappie who coined the term "the marrying ward," and who came up with the idea of "tuck boxes" that hung at the heads of patients' cots, so they could reach books and newspapers, or anything that helped them pass hours of recumbency.[51] Fish Hamilton's sketch book might have been kept there, and Robert Mills's notebook, in which he penned ideas for the next issue of the *Hamilton-Mills Weekly*. Frenchy's tuck box would have been full of beads, for Mills made several mentions of Frenchy's "criminal squeezing" of the bead bag market, and Fish drew a sketch of him dangling a pretty creation as he lay in his cot on the DOH roof. There was even a mock advertisement:

Bead Bags!!
$5 and up, mostly up.
I make 'em.
Why let others cheat you — come to me
FRENCHY
Roof Ward[52]

Stringing tiny beads into a pretty purse was also, of course, a form
of treatment, for occupational therapy was beginning to be recognized
as a crucial tool in healing from any number of physical or mental
wounds. For the men on the rooftop, making crafts provided a helpful
distraction. Lying around with little to do, patients might easily "suffer
from introspection," as one early OT specialist at Christie put it.[53] Fish
Hamilton's cartoon, showing himself and Mills in their cots with long
beards in 1970, suggests the men did agonize over the fact that they'd
never fully recover, and experts understood how that dip in confidence
could affect rehabilitation. Occupational therapy, whether beadwork or
embroidery, busied the mind and offered physical evidence of an accomplishment. "When [the patient] gradually recovers self confidence and
realizes that there is still something left for him to do in the world, he is
on the road to recovery and attaining a useful place in society....Many
a soldier who has entered Christie St. hospital a broken man has walked
out restored in mind."[54]

Maybe the music Frenchy played filled a similar need. Mills mocked
it, and said it made dogs howl "in mournful accompaniment."[55] But
how did it really sound, walking along Christie Street in the moonlight
a hundred years ago, with the fiddle's melodies *coming out into the dark-*
ness, drifting from the hospital's rooftop? It must have seemed *there was*
a healing magic in the night. The breeze blew cleaner than it did by day, and
sorrow sank insensibly away.

Most of the stories that remain about the roof ward skim over its tragedies and present the place as a postwar haven, open to the elements and imbued with love and humour. The meeting place of Win and Tom, of Mills and Kathleen Jones, of Chappie and Margaret Sullivan. But there were other realities. Photographs show how thin some of the men were, with prominent cheekbones and sunken eyes. Fish Hamilton, who stood five foot nine, weighed just 107 pounds at one point, according to his record. Beloved Chappie died in 1939, still a patient at Christie, which would soon begin to fill up with soldiers from another war. Others were gone much sooner. The bright and jokey *Hamilton-Mills Weekly* announced in its first issue in August 1920 that a message had been intercepted from Mars, stating that a serum had been discovered, and would cure spinal tuberculosis. "Wonderful! Shipment expected via Humming Bird Express direct to DOH!"[56] But the joke quickly lost its humour. TB patient George Hollett died in September, between the publication dates of the first and second issues of the paper, and just a few days after Jack Hoar's suicide.[57] George was a fisherman from Newfoundland whose record includes a note he wrote to the Newfoundland War Contingent Association, from a hospital in England, where he'd been recovering from a leg wound and was then diagnosed with tuberculosis.

> I should be grateful if you would inform me if there is any
> likelyhood of my early return to Newfoundland and if you
> would be kind enough to hasten my return if possible.
> Some weeks ago the Medical Officer here told me I was fit
> to travel and being fit still I am naturally anxious to return
> to my own country. I have been in hospital for ten months
> and I feel sure my recovery would be hastened if I could
> get home.

The letter seems to have worked, for after sorting out the bureaucratic tangle of his attachment to the British Army rather than the Canadian Expeditionary Force, he was soon on board a ship with returning

Canadian troops. But he never made it home to Newfoundland. When he arrived in Halifax, his condition began to deteriorate, and he was sent on to the Dominion Orthopaedic Hospital.

Army officials wrote to George's brother, Cyril, and urged him to get to Toronto quickly because George was certainly *soon to die*. Cyril wrote back, "Can you tell me what [it] will cost me to go [to] Toronto to see my brother." He'd never travelled, he had no money, and the call came at a critical time in the cod industry. After the rules were bent to allow the Newfoundland government to cover the costs of his trip, Cyril set out armed with letters to smooth his journey—"This will introduce [Cyril Hollett] of Burin, who is proceeding to Toronto to visit his brother who is seriously ill there"—and though Cyril arrived before George died, he could only stay a day or two for this final goodbye. The brother he saw at Christie Street probably barely resembled the brother who'd left for war years earlier; pale and emaciated now, with no hope of recovery. Some time after George's death, his belongings were sent home to Burin, along with a note that read, "It is my regrettable duty to have to forward to you [this] parcel of effects which belonged to your late brother....Assuring you of my deepest sympathy in your recent bereavement and in the added sorrow which the receipt of these effects must entail."

George Hollett's story is a reminder that many of the men at the DOH had no family nearby. Tom Ronaldson was another such example, with his mother back in Edinburgh and two brothers dead in France. But unlike George Hollett, Tom thrived at Christie Street. The disease had almost killed him, but by October 1920, though traces of active tuberculosis lingered in his right lung, he was considered healed. He still wore a spinal brace, and an x-ray showed erosion of the vertebrae, but he had no pain and no muscle spasms, and was easily up and about each day for a period of four hours. He had gained weight consistently, and though he still required treatment, he was considered one of the rooftop's success stories. If Win's presence had anything to do with that, not even the *Hamilton-Mills Weekly* lets on—though Win does make it into those irreverent pages.

> One day recently our worthy sister Hammell drew that
> greatest of dissipations, a half-day "off" — otherwise known
> as a "PM" or long hours. She tripped lightly off duty won-
> dering how she would dissipate "the half day's dissipation."
> She might spend the afternoon shopping among the beauti-
> ful creations so dear to a woman's heart... or she might even
> indulge in the wonderful luxury of a heart to heart gabfest
> with other congenial feminines... But the fact of the matter
> is—and herein lies the mystery, knowing Miss Hammell as
> we do—how on earth can one account for her doing her
> hair in papers, taking her favourite book & going to bed.
> *We are investigating.*[58]

Fish Hamilton drew her snuggled under the covers with her book
and curlers while the sun blazed outside her window. Cartoons like this
hint at the warm relationship between nurses and patients. In another,
nurses are accused of stealing the patients' chocolate. The men were
turning pale and thin, while the nurses felt ill, and had telltale smears
of chocolate on their teeth. The nurses must have laughed at these
depictions. The bond between caregiver and patient was strong, forged
over a period of years. It's often said that once veterans got home, they
rarely spoke to their loved ones about the shocking truths of war, but
nurses' letters and diaries suggest they did confide in these women who
took care of them. Sophie Hoerner, nursing in France, wrote that "the
stories they tell of what they see in the trenches are harrowing. They are
not boastful, any of them, but seem so glad to find someone that is interested in them. They say that they like the Canadian sisters and that it is
Heaven here."[59] Nurses saw the men in their most vulnerable moments.
One soldier revealed to Connie Bruce how he'd been standing next to
a friend when the friend was killed. "I could see his boots and part of
his leg." A stretcher bearer with shell shock told Clare Gass of a shell
bursting as he and a friend were transporting wounded. When he woke,
he saw that the friend's head had been severed from his body. Clare
recorded the exchange in her diary, her handwriting getting smaller
and smaller as the awful story unravels. "I sat beside him for a long time
tonight & he wispered the long sad tale to me while the others slept

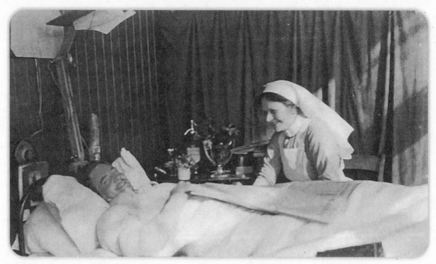

Tom Ronaldson with a nurse who is likely Winifred Hammell
on Christie Street's roof ward (Courtesy Jean Zazelenchuk)

around us. Then when we had both wept a little over it he became quiet
again & I gave him a sleeping draught & he had a dreamless sleep till
daylight."[60]

Were Win and Tom, so far apart in age, drawn to each other because
of a shared war experience? Or was it a practical choice? Or both? They
married in 1921 in Win's hometown of Beeton, Ontario. The marriage
certificate records both bride and groom's address as Christie Street
Hospital, but eventually Tom was discharged, and the two left the roosting box and lived for a while on a farm, where Tom kept bees, one of
several occupations recommended for men who couldn't yet return to
office jobs. For years, Tom was still recovering, and his own family members suggest Win was more friend and nurse than wife. And yet they
remained married, through ordinary days and then through another
war, for more than twenty-five years.

Was it difficult to go from prisoner of war to patient to man of the
house? It's hard to find honest accounts of these transitions. But there
are playful ones. A prisoner of war writing in the Münster camp's paper
foresaw "the perils of peace," and imagined the steps he would take "to
render the transition to new conditions less hard and painful. ... But,
well-prepared as I may be, troubles are sure to arise. I may try to avoid

these in due time by a system of trenches and wire entanglements in the garden, or by the improvisation of a comfortable dug-out in the region of the coal-cellar, to which I shall be able to retreat with drumming-up tin, pipe, and music, from the troubles of the world, there to reflect on the dangers and difficulties of a free life, and the means of overcoming them."[61]

Unusually for that era, Tom and Win's marriage didn't last. They divorced in 1947, yet another event in their lives — like war and imprisonment — that must have seemed improbable before it actually happened. Tom remarried to a much younger woman and had a family, and Win carried on living in Toronto, her name appearing now and again in newspaper articles to do with nursing functions and ladies' luncheons, so she must have kept in contact with her old colleagues. Her pension record includes vague mentions of health concerns that were not deemed pensionable by doctors, or taken particularly seriously. "Patient believes that she is becoming quite deaf....She is a nervous individual whose family life has been quite upsetting. Her hearing is poor when she is upset." A specialist determined that it was unlikely she was actually experiencing the level of hearing loss she complained about, and that "psychological disturbances" were probably to blame. "She herself believes that if her personal life could be put on a more solid basis, her hearing would be alright."[62]

The notes were made two years after Win's divorce from Tom, but linking the details to heartbreak is guesswork at best. Still, over the years she would have known about Tom's life and his three growing children, for Win's cousin married Tom's sister, linking the two families further. Whether that was painful for Win, no one can say. Tom's daughter Jean remembers, as a child, seeing a photo of Win and asking, "Who's that?" Her aunt answered, "That's Winifred." But then she must have realized that Jean knew nothing of her father's first wife, for she shuffled the picture away and changed the subject.

Winifred Hammell lived to be ninety-one, but dementia set in during her final years. The Sunnybrook veterans' hospital, which replaced Christie Street in later years, became home for an old nurse who could no longer care for herself, let alone others. The nurses checked on her regularly, and a devoted sister visited once a week, wearing proper hat and gloves for the outing. In the early years of Win's stay, Tom, too, was admitted to Sunnybrook, but no one knows, now, if they saw each other there, or even if Win would have recognized handsome Tom as a seventy-one-year-old man dying of cancer. Though he'd remained a strapping and striking man in his later years, doctors noted that he looked nervous and unhappy by the end, and had "weakness, anorexia and cough" as the cancer ate away at his lungs.[63] He rallied briefly, fell ill again, and died at Sunnybrook on New Year's Eve, 1966.

Win lived on. Which parts of her old life came back to her as the rest tangled or fell away? Perhaps she sometimes believed she was back on the Lemnos island beach with Connie and the rest of the nurses, combing kerosene through her long red hair and avoiding scorpions. Or she was travelling by train through the English countryside, *along the valleys, past gardens, crofts, and homesteads*. Or she was on the rooftop at Christie Street, a rose in a bluebird uniform, measuring out doses of sunshine as Frenchy played his fiddle. Or the war was still ahead of her, and she and her fellow passengers, soldiers and nurses alike, were on board the *Franconia*, leaning into a salty spray. Stars sparkling in the black sky above and phosphorescence sparkling in the black sea below. All of them moving toward a great unknown.

Faces

When A.Y. Jackson returned to Canada after the war, his sketchbook rippled with drawings and notes he'd made in the field to jog his memory—"sudden bursts of flame...Bright green lights...shining through gas clouds."[1] His work as an official war artist continued past armistice, and he spent the chilly days of early 1919 on the east coast, documenting the troops arriving home. In *The Entrance to Halifax Harbour*, there is no sign of the destruction caused by the Halifax Explosion more than a year earlier, but in the distance, war ships boldly done up with "dazzle painting" float on the blue water. The idea behind dazzle camouflage was not to attempt to hide the lumbering war vessels as they moved across the ocean, but to confuse the enemy with such an array of patterns that U-boat captains had trouble determining a ship's placement and speed in order to make a successful torpedo attack. As both painter and soldier, Jackson must have been intrigued by

the ships, decorated with wild geometric shapes. They make an ominous backdrop for his otherwise tranquil scene: colourful Maritime houses sitting on *land freckled with snow,* brown patches of spring grass poking through. For many, this was how the war would be from here on in, ever-present in the background, a point of reference against which all else was measured. In the early 1930s, Jackson was still referencing his army ID when he wrote words of encouragement to his dear friend, the artist Anne Savage: "If you get in any more difficulties just send for 453716 60th B[attalion] and to him anything you do will be right."[2] He would always, in some small way, be a soldier now, and if it was true for an artist, perhaps it was also true for a clerk and a farmer and a teacher and a bricklayer.

Anne Savage and A.Y. Jackson kept up a fifty-year correspondence, and it seems to have been art but also war that bonded them, *the past hovering.* "I was just thinking back to another June 3rd," he wrote to her on that day in 1932, "crawling along a trench in Sanctuary Wood, and an aeroplane circling overhead like a big hawk, signalling to the artillery who were trying to blow us up. It was a day of glorious sunshine and only man was vile, in general, individually they were magnificent. I thought a cup of cocoa in a dressing station was an undreamed of luxury and sixteen years have rolled on and I am writing to a girl I knew nothing of then."

Anne, for her part, was twenty years old when A.Y. Jackson was wounded in 1916. She was studying art in Montreal, and worrying about her twin, Donaldson, who was a lieutenant with the Royal Engineers. Two older half-brothers were also at the front, but it was Donaldson who was struck that November, swallowed by the Battle of the Somme. A friend at art school, who'd known Anne as "full of life, with high colour and bright eyes and an infectious sense of humour,"[3] later remembered how she had changed her red smock to a black one when Donaldson died, the kind of quiet gesture Van Buren Whetsel made with his simple black tie.

According to Anne, Donaldson was so bright and full of potential that after his death her own ambitions deepened. "I was left with this feeling of trying to do something to make up for that loss."[4] In 1919, when Jackson was working sketches into paintings in his Toronto studio,

Anne found her own niche in war work, drawing the wounded faces of patients who'd come to Ste. Anne's Military Hospital near Montreal. The work was described to a newspaper reporter by another woman around the same time in Missouri. "My duty is to make an exact drawing of each soldier's wound before he is operated upon, to attend each operation, make careful drawings of each step taken by the surgeons, and finally after the man has convalesced to make a drawing of his face as it then looks."[5] A soldier whose ear had been shot away lifted his bandage to show the new one surgeons had created, and the reporter noted that the drawings on the artist's desk conveyed exactly how the surgery had been done.

The work must have been distressing, but also fulfilling in that it used Anne's skills in new and challenging ways; she was helping men who'd experienced Donaldson's military world — her brother's brothers, in a sense — and she was earning her own money. The Savages were wealthy and well-connected in Canadian society, but Anne's father's business had failed during the war, which had also stolen the promise Donaldson had embodied. At Ste. Anne's, she worked with another young artist named Dorothy Coles, who excelled in portraiture. The facial unit — about a hundred men, the artists, the two lead surgeons, and the rest of their support staff, who formed the only specialized team for such work in Canada — moved with their equipment to the DOH in December 1919, just in time for Julia Marlowe's show on the hospital's new stage, and on the eve of Jack Hoar's departure for Chicago.

What was it like for this entourage to join the more diverse group of wounded at Christie Street? Most of the men had gone through their early stages of treatment in England, where the Queen's Hospital, southeast of London, had been established to treat facial wounds. The hospital had British, Australian, New Zealand, Canadian, and eventually American sections, but the staff shared their experiences "in friendly rivalry and healthy competition,"[6] learning from each other's mistakes and successes, and sometimes referring their patients to another section that could get better results for a particular type of injury. The brilliant New Zealand doctor Harold Gillies had pushed for the facility's creation after treating facial wounds in France, and learning bold medical procedures that moved bone and cartilage and skin from one part of the body to another. "A strange new art," Gillies called plastic surgery.[7] He was also acknowledging the supporting work that made such wonders possible—traditional art practices put to new purpose. Expert doctors were figuring out how to rebuild faces and restore their functions, but artists who'd studied the human form understood just how the faces should look. As Gillies put it, "Surgery calls Art to its aid."

Artists like Anne and Dorothy made diagrams and charts of each stage of the operations, and sculptors made plaster and wax casts of the men's faces and their individual features. Pastel drawings brought the features to colourful life, and showed the blue collars and red ties of the men's flannelette hospital uniforms. Paintings, films, and photographs captured not only the patients but the hospitals and the operating rooms where the surgeries went on, and the workshops where bandaged men sat making toys as part of their rehabilitation. When the doctors had done all they could, or when there were long gaps between the multiple operations a man required, artists stepped in again, and fashioned facial prostheses: a nose attached to a face with a pair of glasses, a chin held in place with ribbons that fastened behind the ears.

Facial wounds were a shocking consequence of trench warfare. Peeking up out of the trench for even a fraction of a second could cost a man his life, or the face with which he had always greeted the world. Though a move to steel helmets in 1916 reduced deaths and head injuries, the face itself remained vulnerable, and received what many believed were the most grievous wounds of all because they rendered a man "an object of horror to himself as well as to others."[8]

The Queen's Hospital was situated on a beautiful, sprawling estate, where men could roam outdoors without fear of encountering anyone unfamiliar with their wounds. Patients were also free to wander off the property. Along the road to the nearby village of Sidcup, benches were painted blue to alert locals that a Queen's patient might be sitting there. The warning supported the man who didn't want to be seen, as well as the civilian who ran the risk of being shocked by his image. Either way the implication was the same: a ruined face profoundly changed a man's place in society. The service record for one of the men treated at the Queen's and then at Christie Street clearly states that he couldn't resume his pre-war occupation as a shopkeeper "on account of disfigurement."[9]

Even if a disfigured man was otherwise well, it was assumed that his changed appearance created a huge gulf between him and the rest of the world.

Inside the Queen's, there were no mirrors on the walls, and staff was admonished to look straight into a man's face without flinching. For some it was a difficult skill to learn. Ward Muir, a writer who worked as an orderly during the war, confessed to feeling real discomfort looking at disfigured men. "I had not known before how usual and necessary a thing it is, in human intercourse, to gaze straight at anybody to whom one is speaking, and to gaze with no embarrassment."[10] It surprised him to realize that the raw wounds still requiring treatment and bandaging were far less disturbing to him than the healed wounds, when the patient was "going about with his wrecked face uncovered....I feared, when talking to him, to meet his eye."

Muir's friend, the artist Francis Derwent Wood, ran what was nicknamed the Tin Noses Shop, making masks for men whose features could not be sufficiently restored by surgery. Too old for soldiering, he'd been working as an orderly in a London hospital when he began to notice an increase in facial wounds, and approached his superiors about making masks. A studio was soon up and running. "My work," he wrote in 1917, "begins where the work of the surgeon is completed. When the surgeon has done all he can to restore functions, to heal wounds, to support fleshy tissues by bone-grafting, to cover areas by skin-grafting, I endeavour by means of the skill I happen to possess as a sculptor to make a man's face as near as possible to what it looked like before he was wounded....As [the features] were in life so I try to reproduce them, beautiful or ugly; the one desideratum is to make them natural."[11]

His first step was to make a cast of a man's face with plaster of Paris. To ensure that the contours were perfect, wound cavities were filled with cotton wool and then covered with goldbeater's skin, the tough membrane of an animal's intestine. Depending on the area of the wound, cotton wool also filled the nostrils or the mouth, and a quill was inserted for breathing. Once the mould had been created, it was coated with talc, and filled with clay or plasticine to make a positive model of the face with all its features perfected. And then the man sat again, and another negative cast was made with the features as they were, so that

"the manipulator" could build up the deficient areas to match the perfect version.[12] Using photographs of the man before he was wounded,
the sculptor added detail to the face so that "a plaster likeness emerges
of the man not as he is but as he was," and from this portrait, a paper-
thin copper mask was forged.[13]

With their delicate eyelashes and flawless complexions, the masks
themselves were objects of strange beauty—pristine, fragmentary portraits that bring to mind masquerade balls and fancy dress. The hope
was that they would banish "timidity and self-consciousness," and that
the men would find "they are no longer objects of repulsion to every
onlooker."[14] But whether fastened by spirit gum, ribbons, or glasses, the
attachments sometimes failed to stay in place, or the enamel paint, carefully matched to a man's skin tone, chipped or faded. Worse, of course,
was the mask's inability to convey an array of emotions. In this sense, a
mask's perfection was also its greatest flaw: however expertly sculpted,
painted, embellished, and adhered, it remained lifeless. "The illusion
should be complete at a couple of yards' distance," but closer in, when
the face couldn't change to reflect the moods of the person behind the
mask, that illusion was broken. So while a mask allowed a man to go
out in public, at the same time, it concealed him. Experts maintained
that, "by means of these masks, horribly disfigured men have been able
to accept and hold positions as chauffeurs, elevator attendants, clerks,
and, in fact, any position involving appearance among their fellows,
who are quite unconscious of the grisly gap present beneath this fair
exterior.... Self-respect returns, depression departs, and physical health
follows the upward trend of their spirits."[15] But did a mask restore a
man's identity, or obscure the person he'd become? How did it feel to
believe you couldn't get a job *involving appearance among your fellows* if
your mask was not in place? How could anyone get used to features that
were always hidden?

Joseph Pickard, a British soldier wounded in 1918, lost his nose and
underwent multiple operations to restore both appearance and function. The face had to heal between each painstaking procedure, which
meant that years passed before he began to look "normal." Interviewed
in his late eighties, he remembered his twenty-year-old self, going out
for a walk before his nose had been rebuilt. A group of children saw him

and stared, and ran ahead beyond a hill. By the time Joseph got over the hill, "All the kids in the blinkin' neighbourhood had gathered, talkin', lookin', gawpin' at me.... I could've taken the crutch and hit the whole blinkin' lot of them. I knew what they were lookin' at. So I turned round and went back to the hospital. Got no confidence. I turned straight on and went back. And I was sittin' one day and I thought, well, that's no good. I can stop like this for the rest of me life. I says, you've got to face it some time. So I went out again. After that I just walked out any time. Any time I was goin' anywhere I just walked out." People still stared, but "if it got bad," he just stared back.[16]

As at Christie Street, the hospital was a safe zone, and a place to *calm the restless brain*. Pickard praised the staff at the Queen's, and said, "You could talk to them, the doctors.... They'd do anything for you, and the nurses, the sisters, was the same." The *human tenderness* seems to have gone both ways. Returning to Toronto after the war, Canadian nurse Edith Jolliffe told the *Star* that the men at the Queen's Hospital were "the brightest patients I ever came in touch with." Some of them were so heavily bandaged they were hard to distinguish at first. "We had to remember them by their walk or some little peculiarity." After she'd seen them again and again, their individualities shone through. And tending to the men through their treatment was gratifying. "We merely looked at their normal features and forgot about their ghastly wounds."[17]

More than five hundred patients passed through the Canadian unit alone in Jolliffe's months at the Queen's Hospital, and although she'd assisted in surgeries for years before the war began, she'd never seen anything like the operations performed on these men. "For instance, in the case of building up a jaw bone, a portion of bone from the crest of the hip joint was removed. This was wired in place [in the face] with the loose fragments, and after it knitted a piece of flesh was cut from the chest, neck or shoulder, and was stitched on over the bones. The flesh was still attached to the place where it was removed from, and by means of a tube the circulation kept up which kept the flesh in the course of being grafted in a healthy state until it healed, and the flesh was then severed from the base it was taken from. Ears, noses, eye sockets, cheeks and other portions of the face were built up in the same manner, flesh, bone or cartilage being removed from whatever part of the body it was

Anne Savage, left, and Dorothy Coles, 1921, pictured
in facial patient Stewart Colquhoun's photo album
(Bunker Military Museum, Cobalt, Ontario)

considered would work in best." Such procedures, in which the patient's
own body contributed to his repair, were slow and painful. After each
operation, the areas had to heal before another step in the man's treatment could proceed. "The boys suffer more than anyone has any idea."

These were the types of surgeries that Anne Savage and Dorothy
Coles charted in Montreal and later at Christie Street. They were young,
creative women, participating in ground-breaking medical work, but
there's little left, now, that reveals much about this unusual chapter in
their lives. The Montreal *Gazette* briefly mentions Miss Dorothy Coles
and Miss Annie Savage travelling as a twosome from one hospital to
another to accompany the surgeons, and the Social & Personal column

Sculptor Frederick Coates with plaster facial models
(University of Toronto Archives, Frederick Coates fonds, 2014-53-1MS)

tells us they went home for Christmas to visit their families. The *Globe* lists "Dorothy Coles, a Montreal artist," among the guests at a performance put on by soldier-actors that same December, with one of the facial surgeons also in the crowd. "A very interesting exhibit of pictures by Mr. J.E.H. MacDonald was on the walls," the article notes, and it's easy to imagine Dorothy's gaze wandering away from the stage and over to the striking, wild landscapes bursting with colour.[18] The year 1919 was also when Anne Savage first saw Tom Thomson's oils of ragged oaks and crimson sunsets, and knew she wanted to be part of this revolutionary time in Canadian art. But of the women's jobs with the facial unit, and the impact it had on them, few details surface.

They worked closely with the sculptor Frederick Coates, who made plaster casts for the Canadian surgeons, and whose impressive talents led him to be called "the facial architect."[19]

Anne Savage, Frederick Coates, and Dorothy Coles in
the workshop of the Dominion Orthopaedic Hospital
(University of Toronto Archives, Frederick Coates fonds, 2015-49-3MS)

A photograph shows Coates at work at the DOH in 1920, intent on
the details of some intricate facial prosthesis and surrounded by the
tools required to build his creations. Photographs and hand-done portraits of patients cover the large wall behind him, and in the foreground
Savage and Coles sit studiously working on yet more renditions. Despite
the nature of their work as artists, the women are clothed as nurses'
aides, in uniform dresses and aprons, with white veils covering their
hair. Sunlight pours through the wall of windows at the edge of the
frame, and casts a glow over their workspace, a pleasant mess of enamel
bowls and paints, bottles of inks and oils, scraps of paper, and bits of
cloth for rubbing out errors or for smudging and smoothing a man's
complexion to just the right tone. Who were these women whose wartime contribution has nearly disappeared from the Great War story?

Anne—christened Annie—dropped the "i" from her name, "a minuscule change," writes her niece, but one that gave her "a real sense of
emancipation and daring." She became part of the postwar painting
renaissance that included the Group of Seven, and went on to a long

and respectable career as an artist and art teacher, though she never enjoyed the successes her male counterparts did. After her death in the 1970s, her niece wrote a biography about her, drawing on the cache of letters from A.Y. Jackson and on the memories of family and friends. "She would fly out of the house, her hair tied up in a scarf, and get out in the canoe in the pouring rain to finish a picture she had started on the lake, no matter who tried to stop her. It was not a hobby; it was a compulsion."[20] But of Anne's time as a medical illustrator just after the war, there is only the suggestion that it was "grim work."

She probably knew Dorothy before their hospital jobs, since the two were of similar age and background, and showed in exhibits together. A newspaper account reveals that in 1916, the year Anne's brother died, Dorothy and her sister rode their bicycles from Montreal to Ottawa and back, and encountered roads full of deep ruts and holes filled in with loose stones. Rain made the trip more challenging, and they were caught in a downpour so extreme that they skidded from side to side and couldn't see where they were going. "There was nothing to do but get off and walk to the nearest shelter," Dorothy's sister recalled. There, in a little woodshed, they waited out the storm, "with a pig and several hens for company."[21]

The story suggests that Dorothy was not a conventional girl. Like Anne, she didn't marry, and though war had brutally altered the demographics, it was still usual for that generation to do so. Letters between Anne and A.Y. Jackson imply that they considered marrying — "You are the dearest and sweetest soul I know and if you will be my wife I will try so much to make you happy," he wrote; and she once told him, "My heart stands still when I imagine existence without you."[22] But a union never took place, probably because Anne valued her independence and put her career first. Was the same true for Dorothy? She lived to be ninety-two years old, and donated her remains to the Faculty of Medicine at McGill University, an interesting decision given her hospital work after the war. She also made gifts to the university's medical archive: sketches of operations she'd attended at Ste. Anne's and Christie Street.

There are about fifty drawings included in the collection, each image labelled with the patient's name and a carefully printed description of the work done: palate closure, chin restoration, or a multiple-feature

reconstruction, as in the case of Stewart Colquhoun.[23] Dorothy's drawing shows the stages of just one of Stewart's twenty-nine surgeries, so it's
possible she sat through other procedures too. She must have come to
know the men's faces well, for each drawing shows a distinct individual
as the well as the steps of restoration.

Dorothy Coles's drawings of Stewart Colquhoun's surgery
(Osler Library, McGill University, Dorothy R. Coles fonds, 703454420)

Stewart arrived at the DOH with Dorothy, Anne, and the rest of the
facial unit just as the second winter of peace time began. The snow fell,
as it always had this time of year, interspersed with autumn's last cold
rains. Late afternoons, the sun went down and the rooms of the old
cash register factory turned chilly, but most of the hospital's people had
known greater discomfort in recent times. Inside, tucked under clean
blankets, the harshness of winter seemed a small matter to a man who
had slept in his uniform in the trenches, and fat rats had scampered
over him, and the constant dampness had eaten away at his feet, and
he was often achy, exhausted, and feverish. Here, he could *slumber by the
fireside.* Day by day, *the rankling scars grew old,* even if they snaked across
cheeks or around noses.

Four years had passed since a twenty-year-old Stewart Colquhoun
had enlisted with the Grenadier Guards in the company of his cousin
Allan. Each recorded his occupation as farmer. The two had travelled to
Montreal from their hometown of Lakeview, Quebec, in the Laurentian
Mountains, very near the area where Anne Savage spent her summers,
painting the woods and streams. Stewart was a wiry man, with wavy red
hair and blue eyes to match his Celtic ancestry. A photograph taken
in uniform early in his army career shows a pleasant face with a gentle
smile, and features that match the ones Dorothy Coles would later

capture. Family lore says he had a grade-five education, which wasn't uncommon for the working class at that time, but he was an avid reader, and curious about the world. By May 1917, his worldview was expanding, and he and Allan and their fellow soldiers boarded the *Justicia* for England. By August they'd arrived at the front. It may have been some comfort for the cousins to have come this far together, but Stewart's war experience, like that of so many men, was fleeting and intense. Caught up in weeks of fighting at Passchendaele, where *flesh and blood and brains* stained the landscape, he was wounded as the battle drew to a close, and it was likely Allan who informed the family back home of the gravity of his condition. Shrapnel had pierced Stewart's elbow, shoulder, chest, thigh, abdomen, and back, and blown apart the centre of his face. The first notes were made the day of his injuries, in cramped writing on a field medical card. Each wound was numbered and detailed, the last being "Face badly destroyed." His upper lip was lacerated; his upper jaw was loose; his left eye was damaged; his nose and right eye were gone. He was given morphine, and "foreign bodies" were removed from the wounds. The soft tissue around his eye socket and nose was sutured into place, and he was bandaged and sent on, listed as dangerously ill for almost two months and landing at the Queen's Hospital the following March.

How did it feel to endure such wounds? Joseph Pickard, the British soldier who recalled the stares of children, remembered the day he was "blown up." He'd been leaving a village with the rest of his company, and saw a great black cloud rise up, and when he came to he'd been blown into the woods and was lying among a pile of dead bodies. He fumbled for his first aid kit—nothing more than a length of gauze, an ampoule of iodine, and a big safety pin. He knew something had happened to his face, but it was the wound in his leg that he could see, and so tried to bandage. Then he crawled on his hands and knees and shouted for help, and some stretcher bearers appeared and took him to a Red Cross van. Someone leaned in and told him, "You'll be all right now, chum." He believed the shock was probably what saved him: "it takes a lot of the feeling away." Later, at his own request, a nurse helped him cut his bandages away and gave him a mirror to see his face without his nose. "She said, 'What do you think about it?' And I said, 'Well, what can I? It's off. It's gone.' ... I think in a case like that you want to live and to hell with what you look like."

Joseph Pickard and Stewart Colquhoun followed similar paths that led to the Queen's Hospital, where their time as patients overlapped, though Stewart was under the care of a Canadian doctor who would continue to treat him for years to come. Ernest Fulton Risdon, the Toronto surgeon who made many of the notes in Stewart's file, married in England in 1919, not long before the facial unit returned home. A wedding portrait shows the bride and groom surrounded by patients in their hospital blues, with the bride's stately family mansion as the backdrop. The picture is not a typical wedding shot, and suggests a strong bond between Risdon and the men he cared for. It's also an example of how war had permeated everyday life. Carl Waldron, Risdon's surgical colleague at the Queen's and later back at Christie, witnessed the marriage, and both pose with other officers in full uniform. The bride, Sylvia, who had German family ties, had worked for British Intelligence doing translations, but she also volunteered at a convalescent hospital affiliated with the Queen's, and it was probably this duty that led her to meet Fulton Risdon. She may have even known some of her husband's patients.

Some of the men in the wedding photo can be matched up with other images. The revered surgeon Harold Gillies is there, bald and moustachioed, standing just behind Risdon. The Nova Scotia sapper Frank Langley stands in the back row, with a bandage where his chin should be, showing an injury that corresponds with Dorothy Coles's drawings and with the photos in Frank's own record. Though several of the guests wear facial dressings, no one quite fits Stewart's description —and yet he must have been there, for his own photo album, brimming with hundreds of pictures from his time at the Queen's, Ste. Anne's, and Christie Street, also contains a photo from the day: about forty patients, posing casually in the comfy, flannelette uniforms issued to men when they were convalescing.

Stewart's record shows he'd undergone an operation just a week before the doctor's wedding. Many more would follow, for addressing such serious wounds was a slow, meticulous process, and Risdon was still operating on Stewart more than two years after he'd been injured, when they arrived at Christie Street in December 1919. Using Harold Gillies's tubed pedicle method, the same procedure nurse Edith Jolliffe had described to the *Star*, Risdon attempted to rebuild Stewart's face. Dorothy Coles's drawing shows how a flap of skin from his cheek was raised to cover the hole where his nose had been, and a flap from his chest in turn covered the undermined cheek. In each case, the skin remained attached at its original source, and was stitched into a tube that travelled over to the wound, where it was patched in place. The procedure meant that the tissue stayed connected and alive, and had a better chance of regenerating in its new location. Once it had taken root, the tube could be cut away.

Stewart was due for yet another procedure in the new year, but he had a persistent cough that continued to grow worse as the weeks went on. By late January, he was complaining of "pains all over" and his temperature was soaring. Suspecting influenza, the doctors isolated him at St. Andrew's Hospital, since Christie's own isolation units were full. The hospital was winding down, and all of its patients would soon move to Christie Street, so there was likely ample room there for contagious cases. Notes in his record track his condition: the pain behind his eyes and across the small of his back; the chills, the nausea, the vomiting. To experience these symptoms while still recovering from such horrendous wounds must have meant enormous discomfort, not to mention fear: successive waves of "Spanish flu" had wiped out millions of lives since its original surge in 1918. But once more, Stewart Colquhoun survived. Early in February he was well again and moved back into the DOH, just days before three orthopaedic patients died of the same complaint. Attempts at isolation had failed, and it was impossible to keep the virus from spreading in a crowded environment, where men slept and dined and lived out their days side by side, and where staff had to get close to care for them properly.

A photograph of Stewart with a nurse at Christie Street shows just how close the beds were to each other. And a wider shot of the facial ward in the *Illustrated Souvenir* likewise conveys how little privacy there was, and how well the men must have come to know each other, living in such close quarters. The picture shows about twenty-five men lounging, some bandaged and bedridden, but most dressed and standing in

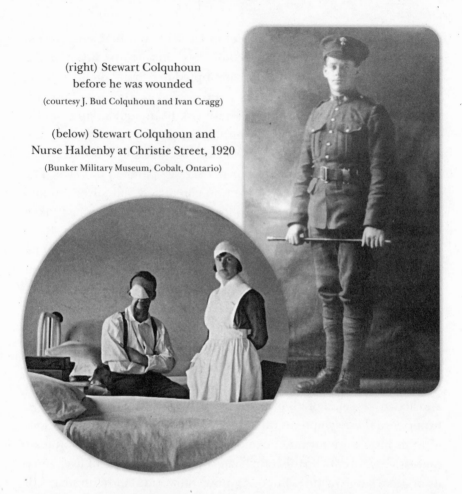

(right) Stewart Colquhoun
before he was wounded
(courtesy J. Bud Colquhoun and Ivan Cragg)

(below) Stewart Colquhoun and
Nurse Haldenby at Christie Street, 1920
(Bunker Military Museum, Cobalt, Ontario)

groups, or perched on the edge of a mattress. Frank Langley is there, bandaged but smiling at the camera. Stewart is there, too, at the back of the room, barely visible but still distinct with his mask and wavy hair. The others are men he went on outings with, to High Park and the Toronto Islands. Many had received gunshot wounds to the face, but there were surprising reasons for their injuries too: one had been kicked in the jaw by a horse, and another had had his lip bitten off when he was attacked by a fellow soldier. A third had suffered burns in an explosion he'd caused himself—his injuries were so grave that his superiors decided they were punishment enough, and wouldn't lay charges. For the most part, though, the men missing chins, ears, eyes, and noses had been wounded in battle, and just like the amputees, the sun worshippers on the roof ward, and the nurses, the facial patients featured in the pages of the *Hamilton-Mills Weekly*, where Robert Mills joked about miraculous transformations under the surgeons' knives. "Wonderful!! . . . Astonishing!!" read the headline. "The case was one of practically complete disability and doctors were at a loss as to what to do to help the man get back into civilian life as a self supporting and producing member of society. But [the surgeon] was equal to the occasion. He procured a well-developed monkey from the Riverdale Zoo, removed the large jaw muscles and grafted them on to the jaws of the patient. The operation was successful and the man has already had several offers from large walnut factories to accept a position as CHIEF NUT CRACKER."[24]

It was common for soldiers to joke about disturbing topics, and perhaps, reading through the *Hamilton-Mills Weekly*, Stewart saw the humour in the piece. But the dark reality was that money would always be in short supply. With his numerous wounds, he was entitled to free medical care, rehabilitation, and a full pension — progressive ideas at the time — but right after the war, that amounted to just $600 annually for a man with no dependants. By September 1919, with the implementation of the Pension Act, full disability had inched up to $720, still far from satisfactory in the minds of many veterans whose lives had been so profoundly altered.

Pensions were only available to those who'd suffered a disability as a direct and provable result of war service, and these were classified by severity at rates between 5 and 100 per cent. Losing an eye, like Stewart had, was considered a 40 per cent disability, and suffering facial disfigurement brought him 60 per cent more. His fused elbow was worth another 40 per cent, and other lesser wounds put him well over the maximum amount he could receive, but in this he was a rarity, for while Canada's pension rates were considered generous by international standards, many didn't qualify at all, and most of those who were eligible qualified for only the smallest amounts, as well as for the thirty-five dollar clothing allowance that every soldier got when he was discharged, and for the war service gratuity, less than a couple of dollars a day times the number of days served. Pensions could be adjusted over the years, depending on how a wound or illness developed or faded away, but often the adjustments were not in the applicant's favour — as with Jack Hoar,

who killed himself when his "helplessness allowance" ended, and John
Spaniel, whose old gunshot wound was deemed never to have existed.
Frustrated by the snarl of bureaucracy regarding what they were or
weren't owed, veterans and their families often turned to newspapers
and wrote in with questions as to why venereal disease wasn't considered
a pensionable disability, or whether a man who'd only served in Canada
could receive assistance, or whether the mother of a deceased nurse was
entitled to her daughter's pension.

Women's questions were always tricky. It seems a huge, enlightened
step that nursing sisters were now eligible for pensions at all, and that,
at least in this sense, they were regarded as veterans by the Canadian
government. If a nurse died and her family could prove dependency,
they would receive a full pension. But most nurses applying to the pension board had fallen ill rather than been grievously wounded, so the
amounts received were tiny—six dollars a month, for instance, for one
who suffered from nervous debility. Even these minuscule amounts only
came when the nurse could prove a direct link between the illness and
her war service. Still, it was significant, in this era, that a woman could
receive a pension in her own name and not just as an extension of her
husband.

The latter were the more usual recipients. Married veterans like
Charles Harrowsmith, Walter Dunn, and Arwood Fortner got a little
more than a single man did, and more still if they had children. When
a man died, his widow was entitled to a pension, but only if she'd married him *before* he was wounded—this rule was intended to dissuade
so-called deathbed marriages, or a woman marrying a man just to get
his pension in the years to come. So when Jack Hoar committed suicide, with his letter from the Canadian government beside him on the
kitchen floor, his wife Kitty was entitled to nothing. It seems a ludi-
crously punitive rule, considering how small the pensions were, and
must have also made the idea of marrying a man with a disability even
less attractive, knowing the greater hardship that would come if and
when he died. Yet as with prosthetic designs, medical and mental health
treatments, and other types of government assistance, pension details
shifted over time, as veterans and their allies advocated for changes that
also affected the wider society.

Maybe Stewart Colquhoun thought, in those days, that he would never marry, but just as it did Tom Ronaldson and others on the roof ward, love found Stewart at Christie Street. Throughout the 1920s, young women often visited the hospitals on weekends, turning dull drudgery sweet and bringing cigarettes for the men or taking them out for tea, or just sitting and keeping them company. Newspapers carried notices to encourage volunteer visitors, who came on Saturday and Sunday afternoons to the reception hall, which was brightened with flowers. The visitors were instructed to bring not just friendship, but practical information. She—for these were usually female roles—"should take pains to inform herself with regard to soldiers' pensions, patriotic societies, and the like." And she had to understand that she wasn't engaging in a self-gratifying act of charity: "the visiting...is for the good of the men, not the good of the visitor."[25]

According to his son Bud, it was in this way that Stewart met Florence Leggett, a woman born and raised in Toronto who worked as a stenographer. She began to visit regularly, and eventually, Stewart proposed. That night, with all his wardmates nearby, he wrote her answer in his diary: she said, "Well, I guess so."

What caused Florence's hesitation? Was it that she was "a city girl in love with a soldier boy," as Bud puts it, and that upon Stewart's release from the hospital he'd take her north, to rural Ontario, where his family had gone? Was it that Stewart would have little opportunity to make a decent income? Was it that his wounds—leg, arm, chest, back, abdomen, eye, nose—would cause ongoing trouble and discomfort? Despite operations that continued into the 1930s, his nose was never successfully rebuilt. Under the mask there was just a large, deep depression covered by grafted skin. Rubber tubes held the nostrils open and required cleaning each day, since his nasal passages ran. His remaining eye teared regularly, and with his elbow fused at a 100-degree angle, he couldn't reach his face with that hand. "This is a greater disability than usual," one doctor noted, "since his facial condition requires constant attention involving the use of his hands....He complains of disfigurement and liability to cold. Unable to stand any exposure."

However tentative, Florence answered yes to Stewart's proposal, and they were married in Toronto, the ceremony officiated by the Christie

Street chaplain, Sidney Lambert, himself an amputee who'd married a nurse. So the war was still with them at the wedding, as it had been at Sylvia and Fulton Risdon's wedding, and at so many other unions that took place in those days. It's easy to romanticize these couples, with their stories of war and bravery and survival and love, but the truth is more complex. Florence never completely settled into rural life. And Stewart was sensitive and sometimes moody. If something set him off he would "go into himself" and hide away for a while. "If it would've been nowadays," says Bud, "they probably wouldn't have stayed together."

Stewart always wore what he called his bandage — not the elaborately painted copper masks made by artists, but a simple cotton style first supplied by the hospital in England and later knitted by his sister. It came up over his missing eye and down over his crudely rebuilt nose, and tied behind his head where it left a permanent groove, the way that glasses deepen the bridge of a nose after years of wearing them. Bud doesn't think Florence ever saw Stewart without the bandage, through nearly forty years of marriage. But Bud did. When Stewart washed and shaved, young Bud helped him re-tie the mask, and hooked in the single framed lens that improved the vision in his remaining eye. For a while, he wore a glass eye too — a mesmerizing artifact that Bud says was "wonderfully cleverly made" — but because Stewart wore the mask over that eye anyway, there was really no point in putting it in. The mask must have felt, after a time, like part of him. It's there in the hundreds of photographs that remain in Stewart's worn old album: Stewart at the hospital in England, posing with a woolly sheep; and then on the *Araguaya* on his way back to Canada; Stewart on the skating rink at Christie Street, grasping a hockey stick and grinning widely; and in a formal portrait with a boutonniere pinned to his lapel. Many of the photos show Stewart at his family's lumber mill, wearing snowshoes, rolling logs, or driving a team of horses, the mask always in place.

"My father was a pretty scary-looking creature without his bandage," Bud confided. But not to Bud, one of the few who saw Stewart's face as it was, and easily grew accustomed to it. A tenderness accompanies each story Bud shares. Stewart was "all blown up out of hell" in Europe but found solace on his patch of land in Krugerdorf in northern Ontario, where he loved to walk in the garden and watch the plants open and

(left) Stewart Colquhoun at
the family lumber mill, 1920s
(Bunker Military Museum, Cobalt, Ontario)

(right) Stewart Colquhoun
skating on the Christie Street
Hospital rink, 1923 (Bunker
Military Museum, Cobalt, Ontario)

grow sweet and blossom. He dug a pond that ducks frequented, and though Florence never cared for it, to Stewart, it was a small bit of paradise. "He got so much joy from that place," says Bud. "I can't explain how much that meant to him."

As a child, Bud sometimes accompanied Stewart on the long trip south to Toronto for appointments at the Christie Street Hospital. He remembers a blind man who worked at the entrance, where you could purchase items for patients you were visiting. When you placed the coins in the man's hand, he studied them with his fingers to determine the denomination. The offerings Stewart purchased were for his friend Percy Rimmell, who'd been gassed at Ypres and paralyzed in a workplace accident after the war. Percy was admitted to Christie Street a year or so after Stewart arrived, and more than twenty-five years later, he was still there. Comparing his life to Percy's, and considering his children, his wife, his ducks, and his land, Stewart must have felt that he'd done okay. Certainly his album, with pictures of Christie Street friends, medical staff, and artists stretching on into the years, suggests a contented life.

A few years before he died in the 1960s, Stewart filled out a form related to his pension claim. Next to the heading "Man's complaints," he wrote, "I actually haven't any complaints," and went on to explain that his doctor had suggested he add a chronic chest condition to his list of health problems. "I have shrapnel on both sides of my chest," he stated matter-of-factly.[26] The shrapnel had sat there, as well as in his pelvis, for forty-six years, beneath skin that was scarred and pitted from excavation, for facial surgeries. What was it like to carry artifacts of war in your body, next to your heart and lungs? To take the war everywhere you went with your omnipresent bandage and the ruins of your face beneath? More than a century after Passchendaele, ninety-year-old Bud wears Stewart's regimental badge pinned to his ball cap and states plainly, "[He] was the most courageous man one could ever know."

Lungs

Shortly before Stewart Colquhoun got sick in January 1920, the death of a young Toronto boy prompted a front-page story in the *Star*, asking, "Is flu back again?" Over the course of the month, both the *Star* and the *Globe* reported on outbreaks south of the border with such increasing alarm that it soon seemed inevitable the virus would return, swirling over the city like frenzied snowflakes and falling wherever it chose. In Chicago, where Jack Hoar had relocated, California-bound trains were "crowded to the limit" with people fleeing to escape flu. And in Detroit, the coroner announced the county morgue was "filled to its capacity with bodies.... If bodies continue coming in as they have in the last two days extra arrangements for their care will have to be made." Ads appeared for cure-alls like Hamlin's Wizard Oil: snuff it up the nose at the first sign of a cough or sore throat and you could stop the symptoms from turning into "dangerous influenza."

By the end of January, one headline warned there were "more than 500 cases of 'flu' at the border," characterizing the illness as a band of murderers poised to invade.[1] Within Toronto, the city's medical officer of health, Dr. Charles Hastings, announced that one hundred cases had been officially reported so far, but he believed some doctors had failed to submit their numbers, and that it was therefore a low estimate.

In February, when Stewart returned to Christie Street from the isolation ward at St. Andrew's, several other events were unfolding as the flu raged on. With so many patients and staff, the DOH was like its own village, populated with *human joys and cares* and humdrum moments, but also drama. That month alone, an arm patient had been charged with stealing from a facial patient, and been carted off to the jail farm in Richmond Hill; Tom Ronaldson of the rooftop gang had been awarded the Military Medal, but the ceremony had been put off due to the flu outbreak; a member of the kitchen staff had died in a suspicious fire in the fall, and the trial of her husband, accused of murder, was now underway. But it was influenza that took centre stage.

And no wonder, really. The hospital was meant to breathe life into its patients, and heal them from all wounds, but now they were falling sick inside its wards. With no effective vaccine for the flu, there were no safe havens, and the pandemic that had followed the first outbreak in 1918 was still a fresh and terrifying memory. Then, it seemed the whole world had burned with fever. One young soldier in England had written home to his mother in Kelowna to say that "everyone seems to have it" and that "lots of them drop in [their] tracks when marching." Another, stationed with a field ambulance near Arras, had written to his wife of "running day and night, hauling Spanish flu patients.... Our ambulance base covered more miles in the last two weeks than they have since we have been in France."[2] Such letters travelled in all directions: in October 1918, a Toronto woman wrote to her soldier-son of the deaths of family friends and told him the situation had grown so serious that theatres and picture shows had closed and churches were limited to a single service. That same month saw the official opening of the Bloor Street Viaduct after years of construction. The flu was a "decided factor" in the ceremonies, the *Star* reported, for the project's construction engineer was too ill to attend, and speeches were cut short in the name of safety.

"If we keep you any longer," said the mayor, "we will be violating Dr. Hastings' regulations as to gatherings of people." Hastings was probably already annoyed: another little note in the paper that day claimed that, because several of the city's automobiles had taken an entourage to the bridge, "the department of Public Health was forced to call on private owners for cars to carry doctors and nurses for Spanish influenza emergency cases."[3]

From its first surges, this new and deadly strain of influenza had many names. Though the sickness didn't originate in Spain, "Spanish flu" seemed an appropriate term given the high number of cases there—but this was only because Spain reported its cases freely, and countries still at war downplayed the sweep of the illness. Soon, though, "the Purple Death" became impossible to ignore. One doctor, watching the sickness spread through an army camp, wrote to a colleague that "these men start with what appears to be an ordinary attack of LaGrippe or Influenza, and when brought to the hospital, they very rapidly develop the most vicious type of pneumonia that has ever been seen.... A few hours later you can begin to see cyanosis extending from their ears and spreading all over the face.... It is only a matter of a few hours then until death comes. It is horrible."[4]

Some estimates suggest a minimum of fifty million people worldwide died from influenza during three waves in 1918 and 1919; there were at least fifty thousand deaths in Canada alone, where the disease seemed to arrive at the eastern shores and then rush west across the country. With inequitable access to health care, Indigenous communities were struck hard. "Big Chief" John Spaniel's niece later recalled that at Biscotasing in northern Ontario, where Louis Espagnol had signed the James Bay Treaty, flu "wiped out practically all the Indians."[5] As always, all across the country, the hard done by were the hardest hit, and wherever there were communities oppressed by poverty, overcrowding, poor ventilation, and lack of access to running water, the virus flourished.

In the general population, the most vulnerable were the very young and the very old, but also those who were typically the strongest, between twenty and forty years old, and the group most intrinsically tied to the war. The spread of the sickness intensified over land and sea because of soldiers and sailors on the move in great numbers, or living in barracks, prisoner of war camps, or onboard ships. Even on the home fronts, people regularly gathered in large groups because of the war: in processions and demonstrations, or in factories that made the more obvious weapons of combat. Hospitals were already overrun before the outbreak, treating wounded soldiers; in towns and cities far from the war zones, local doctors and nurses were missing because they'd gone to assist their armies. Everything was perfectly in place to grow a pandemic.

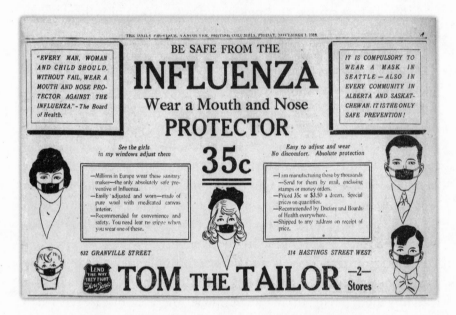

Tom the Tailor ad, November 1, 1918, *Daily Province*,
(now the *Vancouver Province*, a division of Postmedia Network Inc.)

In Ontario, the provincial board of health tried to keep residents calm, and released a statement that "the public should not be unduly alarmed about Spanish Influenza." It advised that people "eat moderately, take plenty of outdoor exercise, sleep with the windows open, drink lots of good water, and do not get excited about newspaper reports."[6] This last request was surely difficult to follow as more and more deaths occurred. Early in October 1918, the *Border Cities Star* reported the dire warnings of G.R. Cruickshank, Windsor's medical officer of health: "Anyone who goes into a crowded streetcar and coughs," he announced, "is worse than the German Kaiser."[7] Medical officials could try to isolate the most severe cases, but they couldn't gather up all the people who came down with milder forms of influenza, so it was up to the individual to ensure he wasn't travelling around making others sick, perhaps fatally. People were urged (and in some places required) to wear masks to protect themselves and each other. "Tom the Tailor" in Vancouver ran a large ad in the *Daily Province*, quoting health experts who said, "Every man, woman and child should, without fail, wear a mouth and nose protector against the influenza."[8] Tom's masks, manufactured by the thousands, were made of wool with a medicated canvas interior and sold for 35 cents, or $3.50 for a dozen. Women posed in the shop's window and showed how they could be adjusted for optimal fit. But there was plenty of debate as to whether masks were necessary. Many people found them uncomfortable or simply didn't like being told to wear them, and others took offence that they put the rest of the population at risk for their own sense of personal freedom. A poem published in a Utah paper captured the mood:

If you think you have the Flu—wear a mask; though some fuss it puts you to—wear a mask; YOU may not believe it's right—cuss about it day and night—keep your faith and conscience bright— wear a mask! If you think that you're quite well—wear a mask; wiser heads than yours can't tell—wear a mask; snare that "bug" before he bites, interrupt his fatal flights, thus you're spared some awful nights—wear a mask! If you think you know it all—wear a mask; if you think your thinks are small—wear a mask; You would fight for Uncle Sam? Then for him give Flu a lam. If you're worth a tinker's damn—wear a mask! Though you swear and sweat and rave—wear a mask; some dear neighbor you may save by that task; doctors say—and they should know—that masks will make this fluzzy go, then do your part or shame will show through your mask! This ONE lesson you should learn—WEAR A MASK; though your mouth and nostrils burn—wear a mask; it's a shame when you or I let this SIMPLE thing go by, then weep and wail when loved ones die—wear a mask![9]

There were "flu veils" too, promoted as an alternative to "weird-looking masks."[10] The veils did double duty as both fashion accessory and virus barrier, and were described in the women's pages as "delightful" and "quite bewitching." The veil extended from a hat, with multiple layers over the lower half, where a "medicated pocket" was stitched into the fabric.

Many of the women who turned up for "Sisters of Service" lectures were wearing flu veils. With so many trained nurses unavailable, the province of Ontario urged young, educated women to volunteer as caregivers for people who fell sick in their communities, and offered daily classes at Queen's Park. The city's medical officer of health, Dr. Hastings, likened the approach to an army raised to fight flu: the women would do their share as nurses, but "we must conscript every human being in Toronto to play his or her part. The enemy is comparatively unfamiliar, and most ubiquitous in character. To be on the watch is the great thing. Precautions should be taken on the first appearance of the disease. It is hard to control the spread of it, but the mortality may be materially lessened by staying indoors as soon as the first symptoms appear."[11]

Eighty-one women registered the morning of the first class, and by afternoon, the room at Queen's Park was so packed with potential volunteers that some stood listening from the hallway. The lectures—a series of three that kept cycling—were delivered by Dr. Margaret Norris Patterson, and printed in the *Globe* as well, so that people who couldn't attend could gain the knowledge shared. In opening her talk, Patterson acknowledged that it was "an absolute impossibility" to transform women into nurses over the course of three lectures, and that the aim, instead, was to impart "certain essentials of the sick room" to deal with the current emergency.[12]

The first lecture focused on "general preparation for nursing at home," such as how to choose the best place in a house for a patient to reside: ideally a well-ventilated room isolated from others in the house, and with a south-facing window. "Patients who are very ill are usually restless in the early part of the night and pass into their soundest sleep in the early hours of the morning. If you have a room that faces east you have to run the risk of the patient awakening or draw the blinds and lose the effect of the sun's rays, whereas, if you have the room with a south or southwest exposure in the afternoon, when the patient feels tired or depressed, let your blind go to the top and flood the room with sunshine, and the effect is almost magical. No disease can stand the direct rays of the sun for any length of time." She advised keeping the room clean and sparse, but also warned against too much bustling while the patient lay resting. "If there is somebody working in the room, it takes some of his nervous energy; and the more things there are in a room the more work there is to be done, the more danger there is of germs being spread about in the air. Keep your room just as clean and neat and free from unnecessary things as possible." Any implements involved in the person's care—from dainty dishes to bedpans—had to be kept in the sick room and scrupulously cleaned after each use. Handkerchiefs were a "prolific source of infection," and no match for good-quality crepe toilet paper: "two or three times a day that can be burned up. It is cleaner, better, and costs less than the soap required to wash handkerchiefs." The lecture went on to explain how to properly clean a room and its contents after the patient had recovered or died, and then finally what to wear and how to keep oneself in the best condition possible for caregiving.

The second lecture focused on "the bed patient," and how to keep a chart that recorded "the date, the hour, the temperature, the pulse, respiration, urine, stool, treatment, medicine, nourishment, and lastly, remarks....You must observe intelligently and systematically and learn to record your operations briefly but clearly....It is very important, indeed, that there should be a very full record made of everything that is observed in connection with the patient." The rest of the lecture detailed each of the categories, ending with the importance of turning the patient and regularly changing her position. "It is considered a disgrace to a nurse for her patient to develop a bed sore." The third lecture looked more closely at the illness itself, and the various ways of treating different symptoms: when to give hot milk, broth, or grape juice; how to make a mustard plaster and a linseed poultice and when to use them; how to monitor not just bluish skin and red spots but facial expression for clues as to how a patient is feeling. "If [a] bluish appearance continues and, in addition, you get a drawn expression around the lips and nose, it is a serious sign, and a sign that would always warrant you in sending for your doctor."

The men at Christie Street always had doctors and nurses nearby, and by February 1920, many of the patients and staff had already been touched by influenza in one of its previous waves. Van Buren Whetsel had fallen ill in March 1918, when no one understood how lethal the virus would become or how long the pandemic would last. He was still training in England when his throat and head began to ache and his temperature rose. Arwood Fortner's brother Edwin came down with the flu in its second wave that autumn, only to recover and die from wounds sustained in battle the following month. Around the same time, young women were arriving in Toronto to study to be ward aides in the new occupational therapy program, but the spread of the illness became so severe that classes were cancelled, and the women were urged to volunteer to help care for the sick instead. Often enough, the caregivers also got sick: the eventual matron at Christie Street, Myra Goodeve, contracted the flu, but after a bout of huskiness, sore throat, and fever, her symptoms quickly subsided and she was back at work. Her friend Helen Fowlds was less fortunate, and wrote in her diary that flu had meant five weeks' convalescence at a hospital in England, which was "worse than jail" and a bleak period that coincided with news of her brother's death. In a letter to her mother, she stressed, "I pray to God that you will escape the influenza—but it's all over the world, and there's no getting away from it apparently."[13]

Flu meant that even when the war ended, loved ones worried for each other over vast distances. When Mabel Lucas endured her seasick journey back to Canada through ice and sleet in January 1919, it was because she'd received compassionate leave to come home early and care for her sister Bessie, who had influenza. Bessie had never been strong. She'd had rheumatic fever as a child, and never skated or climbed trees, or did any of the physical child-play that drew Mabel. When the flu struck, their widowed mother was recovering from a heart attack, and their brother was still in Europe. "The specialist said there was no chance that she would live," Mabel later recalled. "[Bessie] evidently heard the doctor say that she wasn't going to get better. They may not have realized that she was conscious. She said, 'I am not going to die, because my sister is coming home.' She knew they had sent for me." As Mabel travelled back to Canada, a friend she'd trained with years earlier.cared for her sister. "When she found out that they said there was no hope for [Bessie], she said, 'Can I do what I want to do?' The doctor said, 'Anything that you think will help.' She made onion poultices and put them on her back and chest and even on the bottom of her feet. She kept them on for days. When I came home and would give [Bessie] a bath, I could still smell onions. It was right in the pores.... she lived for years afterwards."[14]

Once Bessie had recovered, Mabel resumed her nursing work at the newly opened Christie Street Hospital.

Patient James Campbell seemed little more than drunk when he first grew ill at the DOH.[15] A forty-two-year-old Scotsman, Campbell had been an unmarried labourer when he'd enlisted in Welland, Ontario, in 1915, knocking six years off his age and naming his next of kin as a sister back in Scotland. At Christie Street, he was recovering from a fractured femur received at Amiens around the same time Charles Harrowsmith was wounded, and though he'd had some troubles with a persistent infection in his wound, he now seemed to be doing well. The wound had finally closed, and a note in his record said he'd soon start wood-working classes in the vocational department. But on January 26, the day before face patient Stewart Colquhoun was sent to the St. Andrew's isolation ward, James Campbell was "in bed, apparently intoxicated and nauseated." The next day, he was still drunk, and harbouring a bottle of whiskey, which was quickly confiscated. On the third day, with no booze obscuring his symptoms, he was flushed and nauseous and had a slight cough. That night, his temperature climbed.

And yet his diagnosis was not straightforward. The notes describe tremors, and speculate that an old pulmonary condition "must account for fingernails," which were presumably turning blue. His thigh wound was red and swollen, and there was a "boggy area" all around his scar. The accompanying rise in temperature suggested cellulitis had returned, so hot fomentations were applied to draw out the infection, and the next day a small incision released a great amount of pus. His temperature lowered for a while, but his breathing popped and crackled in both sides of his chest. He sweated profusely and his abdomen ballooned. By February 4—more than a week after his first symptoms—his condition was grave. Turpentine enemas reduced the distension, but it came back two days later, the day Stewart Colquhoun returned from St. Andrew's, recovered from flu. James Campbell was not so lucky. "Moist bubbling rales" sounded in both lungs, and the following day, his condition turned critical. He showed no signs of delirium, as some flu patients did, but his expression was anxious, and he complained of numbness in his right hand. "No radial or ulnar pulse can be felt," the nurse noted, as if that small part of him had already died. With evening, the pulse detected in his left side turned rapid and thready, and soon the death rattle started in his throat, releasing *his very last sound*.

While the official cause of death was listed as "influenzal bronchopneumonia following influenza," the medical details suggest other factors. What's certain, though, is that war was at the root of James Campbell's demise, more than a year after the fighting had ended. The date of his death—February 7, 1920—was added to his file in red ink, and Charles McVicar and nursing sister Bertha Gibbons were interviewed for the coroner's inquest, which was little more than a formality stating his symptoms and the date and time of his death. His record contains a list of all he left behind, the items themselves like *strange ghosts* and *perishing things*:

great coat & puttees	*2 identity discs*
2 pairs drawers (winter)	*brush (hair)*
muffler	*tobacco pouch*
2 pairs braces	*2 shaving brushes*
5 pipes	*book (reading)*
pipe case	*tin tobacco*
three pocket knives	*jar cold cream*
wash cloth & soap	*tin box of x-ray plates*
black match box	*cheque book*
watch & case	*hone*

cap (sleeping)	*2 pairs of boots*
razor strop	*4 handkerchiefs*
2 razors & cases	*2 pairs of woollen gloves*
safety razor	*4½ pairs socks*
bill fold	*khaki tie*
tooth brush	*wallet*
comb	*kit bag*
towel (hand)	*4 letters*
2 khaki shirts	*photographs*

Who was in those photographs? Who were the letters from, and what did they say? Who would miss him now that he was gone?

Coincidences abound among the soldiers who served in the First World War: this many Archies died on such-and-such day, and this many lost *one hand and half a leg*. Searching out the patterns to find meaning within them is in some ways like engaging in the superstitious thinking the men resorted to during their time at the front. "You think of absurd omens and fetishes to ward off the shell you hear coming," one British soldier explained. "A strong inward feeling compels you to sit in a certain position, to touch a particular object, to whistle so many bars of a tune silently between your teeth. If you complete the charm in time you are safe—until the next one. This absurdity [becomes] a dark, overpowering fatalism."[16] Futile or not, the search for patterns in such a brutal wilderness may have been a way of finding order in chaos.

The same day James Campbell enlisted—July 28, 1915—a man about his age, and also a labourer, signed up in Hamilton, Ontario, in the company of his brother. Charles and John Ellis were given service numbers one digit apart, so it's easy to imagine them lined up together, like Stewart Colquhoun and his cousin Allan, one the inspiration for the other. Perhaps they were compelled by news that had come the day before, that Prime Minister Borden had visited Canadians at the front and described it as "the most interesting and inspiring event of my life."

Rising in the wee hours and finishing each day at midnight, Borden had met with officers and ordinary soldiers, as well as wounded men in hospitals; he'd visited an artillery observation point where he'd seen a "magnificent panorama" with Ypres in ruins at its centre. Here and there he'd planted maple seeds on the graves of Canadian soldiers, and returned to England utterly exhausted—though surely not more so than the soldiers themselves.[17]

That July day, the *Globe* also gave front-page coverage to a story about lowered standards for new recruits. The army was losing soldiers quickly now, and still counting on men to volunteer. The chest circumference requirement had initially been 33½ inches, but now it was shrunk to 32½, though just for the youthful who were presumably still growing, "on the theory that the young man will fill out later"—should he survive, of course. For all men, the height requirement was lowered from 5'3" to 5'2", a relief or a disappointment for the small man depending on his feelings toward war. Small men with narrow chests existed in great numbers in the early part of the twentieth century, and often came from poor, working-class backgrounds.

At 5'3½", Charles Ellis was in no danger of being turned away. His brother John was a little taller and a little older, but like Harrowsmith and Tom Ronaldson, these men had come from Britain as adults not long before the war had started, and likely felt a great responsibility to enlist. By November they were still together on board the SS *Lapland*, but eventually John was assigned to the 2nd Tunnelling Company, which placed mines under enemy lines and constructed dugouts and underground chambers, and Charles joined the 4th Canadian Mounted Rifles, which also took James Campbell.

His goodbye from Hamilton must have been hard, for he had a wife named Lillian, a baby daughter, and another baby on the way. The child, a second girl, was born while Charles was still training in England in April 1916, but by early June he'd landed near Ypres, and joined his unit at Sanctuary Wood in the midst of the Battle of Mount Sorrel. It was a black introduction to war.

Southeast of Ypres, in France, the Germans were months into fighting the Battle of Verdun, and like their French opponents were suffering massive losses there. They'd noticed preparations for a large-scale assault building up in the Somme, and wanted to thwart their enemy's ability to get more men and resources to that area while they themselves were so weakened. Early on June 2, under the blue sky of a beautiful morning, the Germans began a heavy artillery bombardment on the high ground held by the Canadian forces. Mines were detonated near the forward trenches, and "sandbags, wire, machine guns, bits of corrugated iron and bits of men were slung forward." In trying to describe the destruction for his official history of the regiment, the writer S.G. Bennett conceded that "the most extravagant imagination cannot picture such a downpour of destruction.... That anyone lived through it is a miracle."[18]

Like Harrowsmith of the 18th Battalion, Charles Ellis arrived with hundreds of other reinforcements just after the Germans' vicious surprise attack, "a day of obliteration," Bennett called it, for the 4th Canadian Mounted Rifles. The dead had not yet been buried, and the living had been reduced to a "handful of weary, grimy, unshaven men," dwindled in number and spirit.[19] The charming woods that had leafed out in the past weeks under the welcome spring sunshine had mutated into sparse, haunting landscapes of charred stumps that had lost their branches. A.Y. Jackson rendered such a scene in oils, all *the colours of the earth* washed to muted browns, and the trees like soldiers, dazed but still standing, and uncertain of the next manoeuvre.

For Ellis, and so many of his future fellow patients at the DOH, next to come was the Somme, and Vimy Ridge, and Passchendaele, and Arras, where a gunshot wound to his ankle put an end to his service. After years of roaming, it must have felt strange to stop. Bennett's official history shows a map of the 4th CMR's movements in the Last Hundred Days, and places the regiment near Vis-en-Artois, between Arras and Cambrai, on the day Charles was wounded. If you didn't know the meaning of the map, you would think it a pretty picture, with little red dashes like footprints traipsing through the countryside, circling back and around in a whimsical tour of the villages of France and Belgium. A decorative script labels the places, which are further defined by simple drawings of churches and windmills and puffy trees. There are no symbols to represent the bodies entombed here, or decaying in tangles of barbed wire, or the trenches gouged into farmers' fields, or the mounds of rubble where homes and buildings had collapsed, but for the people who'd traversed this small portion of the earth throughout the conflict, some of the sights were impossible to forget. On the basilica in Albert, a gilded statue of the Virgin Mary holding her baby high above her head had become legendary among the soldiers. She'd been hit by a shell in 1915, and for three years leaned precariously, at a horizontal angle, holding the child out like an offering or a threat. The church and the town lay in ruins below, and it was said that when the statue finally fell, the war would be over.

Charles Ellis had seen all this and more by September 1918. He had also seen, and even sought *a little safe sleep* in, the less grand ruins of old farms and ordinary houses. Frank Hurley, official war photographer for the Australian forces, captured "pathetic though awesome" images of Cloth Hall and of the Leaning Virgin, as she became known, but wrote in his diary that roaming amongst the "domestic ruins" was especially distressing. "In many cases the roofs and top stories have been blown away and the fronts shorn off, so that the smashed up rooms gape into the street.... Here and there were fragments of toys—what a source of happiness they once were. Bedsteads broken and twisted almost into knots lay about, almost hidden with brick dust. A stove riddled with shrapnel, roofs poised on almost shot away walls, and walls balanced in every impossible fashion, that seemed to defy all laws of equilibrium and gravitation."[20]

Charles Ellis and wife Lillian with their daughters (Courtesy Dawn McNea)

This was the same intimacy A.Y. Jackson depicted in his war paintings: *House of Ypres* shows the fragile remains of a row of dwellings rendered in sombre tones against a bruised sky. *Springtime in Picardy*, with a peach tree in bloom, shows a centuries-old farmhouse blown open to reveal its bright blue interior walls. "Not the struggle of men in action," as fellow artist Arthur Lismer put it, "but rather the sad and wistful aftermath."[21] The exteriors of these homes were different from Canadian houses, but with the interior evidence of intimacy displayed as in a doll house, they were surprisingly similar, and a piercing sight for men who missed their families.

The wound meant that Charles would return home to his wife and daughter, and the new girl he had not yet met, but whom he'd seen in a photograph that shows Lillian in a pretty blouse and broad-brimmed hat, standing outside what is presumably their house in Hamilton, with the two little girls in front of her. She must have sent the photo to Charles, for it's been tinkered with in a darkroom, and made into a new image using a soldier portrait of him with his family depicted like a dream in the picture's upper corner. Photos like these—composite studio portraits—appeared regularly during the war, as if the conflict had forced a new version of the traditional family portrait that under-scored the father's distance from home. They showed men thinking of their families or sweethearts, or they showed a child as the main subject, and the father in uniform in the upper corner. These types of images were also used in post cards with poems that added a more overt sentimentality.

> *You know, dear Daddy, I don't forget,*
> *And I pray for you every day.*
> *And God will bless you I know, but yet,*
> *I'd rather you'd not stay away.*
> *You know, dear Daddy, we're thinking of you,*
> *Always, wherever you be.*
> *And we always know that you're brave and true,*
> *Just the same as Mamma and me.*[22]

The Scottish photographer and potato farmer Frank Findlay advertised such tricks with photography that went even further, promising to
"complete Family Groups when the members cannot all be present....
My method, worked to its present state of perfection through many
years, permits my doing by photography anything that can be achieved
by painting."[23] In 1920, he collected photographs of twenty-six men from
his small community of Auchtermuchty, all of whom had died in the
war, and made a new group portrait that showed the men posed in front
of a view of their town. Though the picture was an imaginative creation
rather than a factual portrait, it told a deeper truth, uniting the dead
and showing the town what it had lost—more moving, perhaps, than a
list of names in stone.

Photographers understood that by manipulating their images, they
could tell a fuller story. Frank Hurley—the man who'd lamented the
ruined homes in Ypres—believed composite photography was essential
to his job as official war photographer, and that the awesome magnitude
of war could only be conveyed by using multiple negatives to bring the
various components together into a single image. Hurley vehemently
believed that these types of pictures were more truthful about war even
though they'd been artificially constructed. One such image showed
soldiers crouching in the foreground while stretchers of wounded men
were carried into the distance, where columns of black smoke rose from
a ravaged landscape. Another showed men climbing out of the trenches
with their rifles ready, and planes soaring in the sky above them, amid
puffs of dark cloud. Another was a simpler yet striking depiction: a
corpse in a pool of muddy water, with a shell bursting behind him, and
clumps of earth tossed up and caught mid-air, like birds flying.

An incredible amount of work went into making such images—
meticulously cutting, pasting, re-photographing—all of which was
much more complex than the merging of two negatives that had created
a new family portrait for Charles and Lillian Ellis and their girls. But in a
similar way, the portrait conveyed something larger: a unity, and also
a division. The soldier *and* his family, rather than the soldier *with* his
family. Charles returned to Canada in April 1919, when the air was
turning *warm with spring,* and A.Y. Jackson was putting finishing touches
on the pink blossoms of *Springtime in Picardy.* He was given a couple of

days leave at home in Hamilton with Lillian and the girls before he entered Brant Military Hospital in Burlington. It was here that an x-ray was taken of his ankle, and the picture, *suspended still and ghostly white*, appears in his service record, with little arrows carefully drawn to point out the fracture.

In October, he was among the one hundred patients moved from Brant to the DOH, in time for a Thanksgiving celebration so splendid it was written up in the *Star*.

> When the appeal went forth for a supplementary contri-
> bution to the treat of ice cream, cake and *charlotte russe*
> supplied by the Red Cross to the soldiers in the military
> hospitals, Toronto expressed her thankfulness this
> Thanksgiving Day in terms of jellies and jams, pies, crisp
> cookies, and delicious home-made cakes; in candies and
> maple sugar; fresh vegetables, luscious grapes, and rosy
> apples. Then, feeling she had cared for the inner man, and
> remembering the long hours of a hospital day, she sent
> games and magazines, books, and smokes. And over all
> her gift she poured a shower of good wishes, hoping the
> combination would bring the soldiers the pleasure and
> happiness she wished them to have.[24]

The same page of the paper carried a small ad, disguised as an article, and headed "The 'flu is here. Are you well enough to resist it?" The ad advised people to "Make sure that the general system is kept in the best possible condition by taking a glass of Abbey's Effervescent Salt every morning. This reliable saline—so pleasant to the taste, and so invigorating in its action—cleanses the body of all impurities and so keeps up the strength and vitality that the system has the power to resist disease."

It was late in the season by the time influenza found Charles Ellis. He came down with symptoms a couple of days after James Campbell fell ill, and the details recorded were almost identical to Stewart Colquhoun's: pain behind his eyes and across his back; nausea and vomiting. He was isolated, but he quickly grew worse. A chart shows his temperature

dropping and soaring like notes on a musical score. By February 5
he was delirious, and by February 6 he was in critical condition, with
wild eyes, pulse "uncountable," and temperature nearing 105 degrees
Fahrenheit. He died on February 7—the same day as James Campbell,
a bizarre coincidence since they'd also enlisted on the same day. His
brother John served as the informant upon his death, perhaps because
Lillian was overwhelmed with a collision of emotions that must have
erupted just after Charles had gotten sick: on February 1, she'd given
birth to twins.

What was it like for doctors and nurses to lose such huge numbers of soldiers to influenza, given all the wounds they'd treated, and the medical
advances that had been made during the war years? Both the soldiers
and the caregivers had *seen men broken* in ways that civilians could never
comprehend. The nurses, especially, risked their lives caring for the ill,
for they were the ones who got closest to the patients and everything
that came out of them. Bertha Gibbons, the nurse who'd frequented
James Campbell's bedside and noted first his drunkenness and then his
raspy breathing, had enlisted in 1915 and served in England and France.
She was a farmer's daughter, tall and strong, but the work was exhaust-
ing, and twice during the war she'd taken leave in convalescent homes
for nurses. La Villa Orphée was one of these: a beautiful old house
in Étretat, overlooking the cliffs of Normandy. It had once been the
summer home of operetta composer Jacques Offenbach, and the brightness and gaiety of his work seem to have seeped into the very structure.
Lacey, wrought-iron cresting ran along the roofline, and pretty finials
poked up from the gables. A façade full of large windows offered stun-
ning views out to the North Sea and caused nurse Elsie Tranter to write
in her diary: "The view from our bedroom window is glorious. Tonight
at sunset there was the softest, prettiest light over everything. It is hard
to tell where the sea ends and the sky begins."[25] The scene was just
what Claude Monet had captured in a sunset painting of the spot years
earlier: a fiery ball of orange slipping down a broody sky toward the

water. The white chalk cliffs, the pinnacles and arches—all were so magnificent that Monet had returned year after year to convey Étretat in his paintings. It was a place steeped in magic for the local people too. Tranter wrote that "fisher folk" believed a secret stairway led deep through the rock, to the ancient home of sea fairies.

Such places must have been soothing to visit in the middle of a war, but disquieting too; to see the effect of thousands of years of wind and water on land, and to have seen, also, the constant ruin of the natural world by warfare. Like Elsie Tranter, Bertha Gibbons must have walked the paths along the top of the cliffs, and taken the slippery route down to the base, clinging to a wooden railing. Looking up at the massive cliffs—"so straight and so solid"—was awe-inspiring. From there she could creep through a pitch-dark tunnel toward Le Chaudron, where the water seethed and roiled at high tide. About halfway in, immersed inside the cliff, "the vibration of the waves beating on rocks sound[ed] like distant cannonading."

Bertha stayed in Étretat for a week in the spring of 1918, revelling, if only briefly, in *birds singing, and clouds flying, and sleep, and freedom*; months later, when the war had just ended, she spent two weeks at another convalescent home for nurses on the southern coast, near Cannes. Both times, her record said she was suffering from debility, a condition frequently noted in nurses' records, with little wonder. Nurses saw the suffering up close, and were often unable to alleviate it. On top of frazzled nerves and depression, they came down with typhoid and dysentery and flu. Well behind the front lines, they were victims of bombing raids, where they had the added pressure to protect not only themselves and their colleagues but the patients they'd been treating. Even at sea, on board floating hospitals the enemy couldn't lawfully attack, their world was perilous.

One night at the end of June in 1918, the hospital ship *Llandovery Castle* was rounding the southern coast of Ireland, returning from Halifax to Liverpool, when it was torpedoed by a German submarine. Though the ship had been brightly lit and identified with huge red crosses, German intelligence suggested it was a disguised troopship loaded with munitions. Once the torpedo struck, the ship cracked open and rapidly began to sink. The passengers—some 250 of them—scrambled to get themselves into lifeboats and away from the immense ship as the ocean swallowed it. But then the submarine bubbled up to the surface and hauled some officers on board, demanding evidence that their suspicions had been correct and *Llandovery Castle* was masquerading as a hospital ship. When the blunder became obvious, they opened fire on the lifeboats, hoping to kill everyone who'd witnessed the event. Only twenty-four people survived, and afterward they lived with night terrors and visions of their shipmates in the water. Many among the dead were members of the Canadian Army Medical Corps. Fourteen were nurses who'd piled into a lifeboat as the ship was sinking. Sergeant Arthur Knight, one of the men in charge of the lifeboat, recalled how it had pounded against the side of the ship over and over again, and how, once they'd broken free and tried to row away, the suction from the enormous vessel sinking had pulled them back. As they drifted toward the ship, one of the nurses asked him, "Sergeant, do you think there is any hope for us?" and he answered "No."[26] The lifeboat tipped and the passengers plunged into the whirlpool. Knight himself sank and surfaced three times before grabbing a piece of wreckage and finding safety in another lifeboat. He never saw the nurses again.

Weeks later, another ship steaming through the same waters came upon corpses that had floated to the surface. Kenneth Cummins, a young midshipman, was on his first voyage when he witnessed the appalling sight. "We were not allowed to stop—we just had to go straight through.... It was something we could never have imagined... particularly the nurses: seeing these bodies of women and nurses, floating in the ocean, having been there some time. Huge aprons and skirts in billows, which looked almost like sails because they'd dried in the hot sun."[27]

The deaths of 234 people on a hospital ship were shocking, but the loss of all fourteen nurses particularly horrified both soldiers and civilians. *Llandovery Castle* was one of five Canadian hospital ships that carried wounded men home during the First World War. A young private named Edward Roberts had been on board the ship on its last trip to Canada, a couple of weeks before the sinking, and would have remembered some of the nurses, doctors, and crew.[28] He was a twenty-five-year-old painter when he enlisted in London, Ontario, in 1915.

Like Charles Ellis, he was just 5' 3½", but with a dark complexion, grey
eyes, and brown hair. He had an anchor tattoo on his right forearm
and a woman's face on his left—perhaps that of his wife, Mary Kate,
with whom he had three daughters. The youngest had been born the
week before he enlisted. Within a few months of joining up, he sailed
for England, and was wounded there before he reached the front; stationed in Bristol, he was flying down a steep hill on a bicycle when he
lost his balance and hurtled to the ground. He suffered a concussion
and needed stitches above his eyebrow, but recovered within a few days.
Before he sailed for France, though, he was again hospitalized for "poisoned feet" and an ingrown toenail, so it seemed, perhaps, as if some
higher power was trying to keep him from seeing action.

But by October 1916, he'd joined the 21st Battalion in France, one
among eighty reinforcements sent to replace the dead and wounded.
The battalion had just come through severe fighting at Courcelette,
and the weather had been cold and rainy. "Men very uncomfortable,"
the war diary noted.[29] The bodies of both German and allied soldiers
lay rotting in the battlefield because of regular shelling, and when the
stench and the sight of them became too much to endure, two chaplains
took on the dangerous work of burying the remains.

In Edward's first week, the battalion proceeded from one billet to
the next, and day after day was quiet, with little to report other than
the fact that the men had bathed, "and received, in the majority of the
cases, fresh underwear, which was appreciated by all." Edward likely
didn't realize yet why such ordinary comforts would mean so much to
the men, but surely the soldier's challenging existence became apparent
soon enough, as the weather grew colder.

The war diary occasionally mentions extreme cold, bitter winds, and
blowing snow through the winter months, but the memories of the soldiers themselves offer a clearer picture. One British soldier felt he'd
"tasted the depths of misery really, what with the cold," and another
remembered, "Our boots froze while we were sleeping—it was painful."
"The coldest winter was 1916–17," another man claimed. "[It] was so cold
that I felt like crying. . . . I'd never felt like it before, not even under shell
fire."[30] When the temperature rose again, the thaw turned the hard
ground back to mud, which clung to the long great coats, and made

them heavier to wear, so the men used their jackknives and hacked away
at the fabric to keep it from dragging in the mud.

By the following April, Edward had come through that harsh winter,
though some days the snow still blew and the sky released *chilling showers*.
The 21st Battalion, along with all four Canadian divisions, had undergone extensive training for a bold plan to capture Vimy Ridge, a heavily
fortified area that had been held by the Germans since the beginning of
the war, and allowed them a great vantage point over allied lines. The
troops below were vulnerable, since everything they did in the daylight
hours could be seen by the enemy. All winter on the *frost-encrusted land*,
the men had practised manoeuvres and studied the ridge in anticipation of the attack, which finally rolled out on April 9. In the hours
leading toward dawn, thousands of men waited in position, utterly quiet.
And then at 5:30, the assault began, the roar of gunfire so loud and so
sudden that nothing else could be heard.

The men moved in a creeping barrage, the artillery like a moving
curtain out front, firing furiously at meticulously timed intervals, and
the attacking infantry following close behind. The approach meant
the enemy had little chance to respond and recover, but also put the
attackers themselves in danger, if the movement wasn't perfectly syn-
chronized. On top of the worry of falling victim to friendly fire, there
was difficult terrain to negotiate—in snow and rain and wind, the men
moved through the darkness, over tangles of barbed wire and slippery
mud torn by shells and mines. They attacked with such relentlessness
that "a rat couldn't live on that ridge."[31]

The four-day battle would mark the first time Canadian troops came
together in their own assault—a major win and a defining moment
for the country, some said, but also a sorrowful loss, with more than
ten thousand casualties. Afterward, the stretcher bearer Ralph Watson
wrote to his wife that the scene was "depressingly desolate.... It's a sort
of dirty pale grey; not a blade of grass or growing thing anywhere.
The ground is littered with rotting French packs and equipment and
German ditto and the more recent stuff of ours. It is a graveyard. Big
shells have uprooted parts of bodies everywhere, and human bones lie
dirty white in the open. Old-fashioned munitions unexploded lie side

by side with the new, half-buried in the drying mud. . . . Tin cans with labels printed in French and English and German are everywhere."[32]

Edward Roberts missed the aftermath. On the very first day of fighting, he received a gunshot wound in his left forearm, where the tattoo of the woman's face was. At first it seemed the wound healed quickly, with no need for surgery, and while recovering in England, Edward had his portrait taken in "convalescent blues," the soft, comfy, pyjama-like suits the men wore, complete with collared shirt and red tie.[33] Flannelette, with no pockets and little shape, they came in only a few sizes, which produced an overall sloppy look when sleeves and pant legs were rolled up. The uniforms were mandatory dress for convalescing soldiers once they were well enough to be up and about, though officers were exempted from wearing them, and instead got silk pyjamas or a dignified arm band embroidered with a red crown. The *Daily Mail* labelled hospital blues "painfully ugly," insisting "it is a disgrace that our wounded privates should be forced to wear clothes that hang on them like sacks, and are the last word in slovenliness. It is suggested that the wretched cut of the uniforms is designed to prevent pressure on wounds. Unfortunately, the apology will not bear a moment's examination, for the War Office manifests no such tender concern for the wounds of commissioned officers."[34]

Judging by the number of photographs taken of men in hospital blues, it would seem they didn't mind wearing them. Photographers often visited hospitals to take portraits of patients, which the men could purchase and send home to their families. This must be what Edward did. Sometimes the photographs were formal shots, despite the informal look of the attire, and sometimes they were playful, candid images, such as one of a group of men lighting each other's cigarettes, or another of two grinning nurses lifting a patient who kicks his legs out toward the camera. There were wedding portraits, too — happy grooms with brides at their sides. Edward's portrait, though, is serious: he appears tense and unhappy. His head is turned and he looks off to the left. His is not a *rugged soldier's face*, but long and thin, and somehow delicate. His hair is brushed carefully back and his tie is neatly knotted, though the suit itself is rumpled, with one tip of the collar turned under. It's a head-and-shoulders shot, so the state of his wounded arm is not evident, but his record reveals that a fractured radius bone required screws and a steel plate.

More than a year passed before he was invalided to Canada, and *the ocean's lazy roll* brought him home on that last westbound run of the *Llandovery Castle*. He spent some time in London with his wife and children, but his arm refused to heal. As with Charles Ellis, his service record includes a ghostly x-ray image, with tiny arrows pointing to the area of concern, and to the screws holding the bone together. By February 1919, a couple of weeks after the DOH opened, he was transferred to Toronto for care, and there he remained through to the following February, when influenza claimed James Campbell and Charles Ellis.

Edward's own symptoms began the day James and Charles died. No one knew it then, despite the medical leaps and bounds, but the virus exploding inside him resembled tiny disk grenades, twirling and spinning. Over the next few days, the awful pattern of *dying moans and painful breath* emerged. His pulse was erratic. His temperature climbed and he became delirious and restless, sometimes so much so that two orderlies had to restrain him. He was at times unconscious, and where he went in those moments is impossible to know. Back to a smoky estaminet, *drinking wine in France,* or to the cacophony of Vimy Ridge where the earth had trembled, or to the English hill he flew down on his bicycle, before the fall that brought his first wound. Back to the day his picture was taken in hospital blues. His record states that he regained consciousness briefly, but whether he spoke or how he acted is not noted. He died at 1:30 in the morning on February 11, 1920. Like Charles's wife Lillian, Edward's wife Mary Kate — already the mother of three — was pregnant at the time, and would give birth to a son in July. The boy would be named for the father he never knew, and in turn would name his own son Edward Martin Roberts.

The hospital blues photograph remains in the family collection, but there's another image too: a hand-drawn copy of the original pose, with curious alterations. Edward's face is fuller, his neck thicker, his hair more smoothly swept back. In place of the flannel suit, the artist has drawn Edward's uniform, complete with the high collar and its 21st

Battalion badges. There's been considerable effort to colour the image in sepia so that it looks at first glance like a photograph, though the buttons glow ever so slightly golden.

According to the *London Free Press*, a military funeral was planned. The death notice makes one other surprising mention: "While in hospital at Toronto, Mr. Roberts saved the lives of two other patients there by giving them blood by transfusion."[35]

By the end of February, the *Star* was still running its daily flu report culled from the details gathered at City Hall, and listing the numbers admitted to hospital and the names, ages, and addresses of the dead. The sickness was hobbling the city in a number of ways: one article claimed "Toronto needs physicians more than policemen," since at least thirty residents had appeared at Police Court in a single afternoon, explaining that they'd not obtained their annual motor licence because either they or their relatives had had the flu.[36] The same page carried a call for more volunteer nurses, and reported that City Hall had received eleven new appeals for care the previous day, but that only four could be answered. Three of the nurses sent had come directly from tending to other cases. How they got from place to place must have been challenging too—late in the month, the Toronto Railway Company placed a notice in the *Star* that read like a plea for patience:

> Almost every business is handicapped by reduction in staff caused by the influenza epidemic. The Street Railway, with its two thousand employees, has not escaped. 243 motormen and conductors have been off duty through sickness in one day. At one division alone, one man in every five was off sick. For comparison, the maximum number off sick at one time in the previous epidemic was 173. The absence of these men seriously retard[s] the Company's efforts to give the maximum service at the rush hours. The Company has taken special measures to cope with this unusual condition,

and it has been possible to give a service at the rush hour
little short of the maximum, and with more cars in operation than a year ago when there was no epidemic.[37]

Winter pressed on and added its own obstacles. The road to St.
Andrew's Military Hospital grew thick with snow because staff who
usually handled snow clearance were overrun with duties inside the
hospital. "Up to date," wrote the medical officer in his request for assistance, "the personnel of the Hospital has been able to cope with the
situation, but with the increased work in the wards, due to the present
epidemic, it is no longer possible to do so. This morning an ambulance
car got stuck in the snow and is still unable to proceed. The same would
happen," he warned, "in case a fire engine was needed on the premis-
es."[38] Neither St. Andrew's, which had been a school, nor Christie Street
were purpose-built hospitals, and the need for appropriate facilities to
care for veterans was far from over.

With spring, the weather warmed, and the city came alive again.
You could hear *the foolish noise of sparrows* chittering in hedges. *The cherry
trees bent over and shed their petals*, and on the rooftop of Christie Street,
patients soaked up the sunshine. The artists Anne Savage and Dorothy
Coles earned another nod in the newspaper as they left the hospital
and travelled to St. Paul, Minnesota, to chart the facial cases there, war
and art once again leading them to unexpected places and experiences. Anne's half-brother, home from France, had died of influenza a
couple of months earlier, and though this powerful strain of flu that
had surged during and after the war was morphing and fading, it would
go down in history as part of the greater conflict: "Spanish flu," "war
plague," "Flanders grippe," "Hun flu," and even "after-war disease."
Some believed "the blood of the dead caused this great sickness," or
that the violence of war had so thoroughly "poisoned the air" that wind
alone had sent the virus drifting through the world.[39] Everywhere, the
loss was staggering. *Add what name you will, and multiply by thousands.*

Minds

In April 1920, a mysterious soldier sailed from England on a mail and cargo ship. News of his arrival at St. John, New Brunswick, went out across the country. "Unidentified Man Back From Front," read a Montreal *Gazette* headline.[1] He thought his name was Frank Hall and that he came from Brantford, Ontario, the paper reported, but he'd been badly wounded at Passchendaele in 1917 and had lost his memory. Maybe he'd worked at Massey-Harris, making farm machinery? He wasn't sure, but he thought he had a sister whose husband was a jeweller, and a son who'd died in the war. He himself had left Canada with the first contingent, and he had vague memories of the fighting at Saint-Omer, Poperinghe, and the Somme. Of medium build, he appeared to be about forty years old, with grey eyes, grey-streaked black hair, and sharp features. The small clues he could offer about himself didn't match any Frank Hall from Brantford, and no Frank

Hall had enlisted there, so the possibilities widened, and people with missing sons, brothers, and husbands of different names were anxious to see if the man was their own loved one, alive, more or less well, and back on home ground.

In every town and city, *someone was missing*, whether a *youth of the countryside*, or *the man who trimmed the garden*. For the people who loved these men, the ache of uncertainty rivalled the cold hard news of death, for there was no body to bury, no *grave for him, that he might better rest*. There were no pockets to empty, which might hold scraps of poems or an unfinished letter, or a picture not yet sent. There was only a faint hope that withered but never quite died as the weeks and months wore on. A missing soldier might have been swept up into the wrong battalion, or captured by the enemy and taken prisoner—and even if he didn't turn up when prisoners were repatriated, there was the chance that he was still out there somewhere, lost, and trying to find his way home. Long after the war had ended, grieving families placed ads in personal columns, searching for sons still missing: "any information will be gratefully received." Throughout the 1920s, articles periodically appeared about men turning up in hospitals around Europe, unsure of who they were and where they came from. "Another mother's hopes aroused," read a 1926 piece in England. "Relatives of missing soldiers are advised not to build up too much hope on the discovery." But it was hard not to have hope when there was no proof of death. For one Toronto family in 1923, the absence of clues as to their son's fate made it seem as if "the earth had swallowed him up"—which of course was a horrible possibility.[2] Countless men were buried by explosions, never to be unearthed. Or they were blown into so many pieces there was nothing left to identify. *A group of laughing comrades—then a shell.* The records of these men, numbering some five thousand in Canada and tens of thousands more elsewhere, held a series of notations that ended in "presumed to have died." But when stories like Frank Hall's surfaced, hope swelled for people like Fred Gullen, whose brother Roy had gone missing in 1917.

The *Globe* reported that the mystery man appeared weak as he posed for the photographer, and that he'd been put on a train to Toronto. Hall's likeness had not yet been published, but Fred felt sure the physical descriptions matched Roy—and Roy had enlisted in Brantford, and worked for Massey-Harris. "Mr. Gullen's brother," wrote the *Globe*, "was last seen lying in a shell-hole near Fresnoy on May 1, 1917, by members of the First Battalion, the unit to which the unidentified soldier is understood to have been attached."[3]

A year after Roy's disappearance, officials had written to his wife Mary in Echo Place, near Brantford, acknowledging her correspondence, but regretfully stating that "exhaustive enquiries have failed to discover any grounds which would justify the assumption that the marginally named soldier may still be alive. Owing, therefore, to the length of time which has been allowed to elapse since he was reported 'missing' his death must now be reluctantly accepted."[4] But without a body, the family hadn't given up. Both Fred and Mary had a cache of letters from Roy's time overseas, a family heirloom preserved to this day. In some of the letters to Fred, Roy inserted a code to reveal his whereabouts: dots under certain letters that could be unscrambled to spell "Vimy Ridge."[5] There were emotional revelations too. Roy told Mary, at home with the couple's seven children, "I am very sorry I have made this part of our life so miserable. [I] did not know anything could be like it.... [I am] sorry for all I have done & left undone. May our Father forgive me my big pile of mistakes. The dandy boys that are over here do not all think like me. I tell them a little once in a while.... I am sorry I did not talk more to some before it was too late but what we know not now we will know again." In his final letter to Mary, he wrote "You are doing great without the old man & will not need to worry very much if he never gets back. Hope to get through though.... will try hard to live."[6] Two days later, the Battle of Fresnoy began, and the letters stopped. Mary wrote:

> We have not had any letters from you for more than a week. Am hoping to get one tomorrow. Dear Old Honey, how I wish this would end.... I was looking out the window at the moon tonight when I put the children to bed, it is full, and [I was] wondering if you could see it too. Now the warmer weather is coming we will get another picture of all of us taken for you.... Well, Bye Bye Dearest, Oceans of Love.[7]

The letter was returned from the front, as was one Roy's brother Fred had written. "Have been looking for word from you every day. Hope you are alive and well, not wounded, and not a prisoner.... I wonder where you are and what you are doing every night, and wonder if you are fighting in those terrible battles that are taking place."[8]

Three years later, Fred's heart was surely racing as he waited at the train station. News reports had said Frank Hall would arrive on the 6:45 a.m. troop train, and "a large crowd of anxious and curious folk" had gathered, only to discover that the subject of interest had actually come on an earlier train and been whisked to the Christie Street Hospital.[9] The crowd followed him there, Fred Gullen among them, but as soon as he entered Ward 304, he knew the man lying there wasn't his brother Roy. In fact, everyone in the crowd was disappointed, and the *dull-sensed loss* in each of them deepened.

It was hard to determine the man's height and body type as he lay in bed, "but he possesses a keen face," the *Star* reported. "His hair is dark and very thick. He has lean features, showing evident signs of suffering." The best clue was a clear connection to Brantford. When a Brantford-born patient came to view the man causing such a commotion, Hall recognized him, and though the man could not reciprocate, the two talked at length about the little city southwest of Toronto, its streets, shops, and hotels, and some mutual acquaintances who worked for Massey-Harris. But when the *Star* photographer suggested a picture for the paper, Hall objected, and said he didn't want the attention. "He preferred that all efforts made to connect him with his friends should be done as quietly as possible." Yet he was somehow convinced, for three photographs accompany the article: the first, taken at the port in New Brunswick, is a full-length portrait that shows Hall in army cap and great coat, leaning on a cane. The other two are headshots taken in his hospital bed, and reveal his features more clearly.

Once the pictures had been published, several people came forward. Men employed by Massey-Harris did indeed recognize Hall as a former co-worker, but said that his name was George Densham, a single man who, as far as they knew, had never enlisted. A Brantford woman spoke up and said she knew George Densham not just from Brantford, but from their shared hometown of Exeter, England, and she had pictures

from their lives there long ago. And finally an immigration official recognized him as a thief he'd deported five years earlier. He still had
documents from that time, and mugshots from several prisons, and
these were forwarded for comparison. The story ballooned now, and
appeared in papers in England and the US as well, for if the accusation
was correct, the man had lived in all three countries under a number
of aliases.

Christie Street buzzed with excitement as Charles McVicar led a team
of officials to interview the man. The press came too, and described
Hall sitting in a wheelchair in a khaki uniform, the general service
ribbon pinned to his jacket. "We want to have a talk with you," McVicar
told him. He was shown the mugshots and the deportation papers, but
after inspecting them, he said, "That's not me," though he claimed he
felt he'd seen the man somewhere before. "In the looking-glass," mut-
tered one of the officials.[10] He was taken to City Hall to be thoroughly
examined, weighed, and measured, and shook continually throughout
the procedure. The size of his ears, nose, and mouth corresponded to
Densham's, as did a scar on his elbow, and the measurements of his
legs, feet, and toes. The fingerprints proved a match, and he was taken
into custody.

George Densham was deported by June, but fragments of his story
turn up in British papers for years afterwards. In 1922, he was arrested
for posing as a Canadian veteran. "Walks very lame," according to the
Police Gazette, "and complains of shell shock and loss of memory; dress,
khaki uniform, and badges of Canadian Infantry." He claimed he'd
been wounded after lengthy service in France, and that "he was always
mistaken for George Densham who was his double." Two years later,
charged with obtaining money under false pretenses, he claimed his
hardship stemmed from the fact that he had served in the Canadian
army, and the government of that country hadn't paid him. The detec-
tive on the case said Densham was "one of the biggest liars and twisters
I have ever met."[11]

Meanwhile, Fred Gullen's grief for his missing brother Roy stretched
on. Mary and the seven children were left with letters that, when reread,
brought Roy to life again, and took him away when the paper was folded.
"I had a fine dream of you Mary last night," he wrote from "somewhere

Roy and Mary Gullen and children (Courtesy the Gullen family)

in France" in 1917. "Could see you walking & you came in and you had
not been well for you were tired & looking tired so I kissed you on the
mouth. In the dream we had been apart for some reason, but felt we will
never be parted again."[12]

The soldier-patients' response to news of the impostor among them is
not recorded in the many articles written about "Frank Hall," but jail
was likely a safer place for him than Christie Street. For men whose uniforms had become like a second skin, worn while sleeping and fighting
and marching and sloshing through the trenches, the disguise must
have seemed both pathetic and despicable. Quaking and feigning illness
in the company of wounded veterans was still more appalling, for many
of the men knew soldiers who'd actually experienced shell shock, or
they'd had the horrible symptoms themselves. Van Buren Whetsel—the
leg patient who'd worn a black tie in later years to remember his fallen
friends—had had a nervous breakdown shortly after his amputation

surgery. Before his leg wound at Amiens, Charles Harrowsmith was buried and hospitalized for shell shock. And before the tuberculosis diagnosis that led him to the Christie Street rooftop, Bob Mills of the *Hamilton-Mills Weekly* was a shell-shock patient too. Like Harrowsmith, he'd been buried by a shell burst and had "collapsed under fire" the next day.[13] "Two years' service in line," a doctor noted in April 1917. "Nerves deteriorating since Somme."

Sometimes men who'd been buried felt panicky and claustrophobic long afterward; when they closed their eyes, desperate for rest, the *smothering dreams* came surging. For others it was the trembling earth and the constant roar of ammunition that haunted them, or the image of *a man's brains splattered on a soldier-bearer's face*. Often the men were just physically exhausted and undernourished, and a week or two at a rest station was enough to set them right again so they could return to their units. Further from the fighting, surrounded by nurses and their aides, washed and well-fed, they could be tucked into bed and *be still; for a time be one with all escaped things*. But some were so badly debilitated they were shipped to England and admitted to shell-shock wards, like the one where May Bastedo and Mabel Lucas had worked. Service records contain a range of descriptions: the patients were extremely nervous and easily startled; they twitched and trembled or walked with a "hysterical gait"[14]; they had terrifying dreams and suicidal tendencies; they had aphasia or amnesia; some wept uncontrollably, or raged and smashed windows; they had visions and heard voices, or felt so despondent they refused food. One man "imagines whole world gone wrong owing to his misdeeds." Another felt sure something was moving in his head, as if the thoughts running through had a physical presence. "He hears voices talking to him saying all kinds of foolish things like 'Watch yourself, Na Poo!' . . . and when he looks around to see who it is there is no one there."[15]

Though some nurses did have psychiatric training, most, like May and Mabel, relied on their war and nursing experience and on common sense. A wartime article by British nurse Dora Vine stressed that care must be threefold, addressing the body, the soul, and the mind.[16] "The patient is physically ill," ran the theory of the time, "and is suffering from what one may term a sudden jarring of the vital machinery." The body needed rest, wrote Vine, but each case was different. Some men couldn't bear lying in a darkened room, and others needed just that. The "chief object" for shell-shock nurses, of course, was the mind:

> If the patient has had a great mental shock of a distressing nature, and can speak of it, do not forbid this. If what one dreads and fears is carried out into the open, one loses one's fear, and so here I should let the painful topic be frankly mentioned (otherwise the patient will certainly brood in secret!), and then I should try to get the conversation into other channels. When such patients cannot cry, and cannot speak of their trouble, and seem simply numbed, it is indeed difficult to give the mind rest, and real sympathy and that psychic instinct that is so invaluable in mental nurses will alone give one the cue.... In all cases I should try to get my patient's confidence, and make sure that I knew the whole state of the case. I should want my patient to feel I was at hand as a helper in case of need, never in the way, never out of it.... Treat body, soul, spirit, [and] be normal—help, don't fuss.

Some men never really got better. Or their troubles returned years later, and they found themselves traumatized and unable to rebuild. Hugh Russell was nineteen when he enlisted in London, Ontario.[17] Like the arm patient Walter Dunn, he'd been a "home child," one among some 250 brought from England in June 1906 by Dr. Barnardo's Homes. Barnardo's had been operating since the 1860s and had already sent around nine thousand "waifs and strays" to Canada, many of whom would lose contact with their biological families forever. Hugh was placed with the Wray family, who were farmers in Wingham, Ontario, and had a two-year-old son named Graham. Nearly a decade on, Hugh was still living with the Wrays when he enlisted with the 18th Battalion, later transferring to the 12th Canadian Mounted Rifles because of his experience with horses after years on the farm. At some point during his time overseas, he had images of a horse's head and a horseshoe tattooed onto his forearm.

His love of horses is evident in his letters home to Graham, some of which were published in the *Wingham Advance*. Early in 1916, from "Somewhere in Belgium," he writes:

> I am longing for a pair of horses to drive. I think I will see
> my CO and ask him if I can transfer into some unit where
> I can get a horse to look after. I always had a great fancy for
> Judy, and I used to take a great interest in her, and paid the
> best attention to her care and comfort. You never knew how
> sorry I was the day your father took her out of the gate for
> the last time. If I ever see her again I will be tempted to buy
> her. I think she would know me.... Well, I had better quit,
> or else I will be thinking there is no war on, and I am back
> in Canada trading horses.
> From your old friend, Hugh
>
> PS—Here is a song we sing in the trenches: Sing me to
> sleep where the bullets fall; let me forget the war and all.
> Damp is my dug-out, cold are my feet, waiting for someone
> to sing me to sleep.[18]

For a horse-lover especially, it must have been dismaying to see up close what war did to these animals. Millions of horses were requisitioned for war work. They were lifted by cranes onto ships that carried them across the ocean. Sometimes they didn't survive that terrifying journey. Those that made it were used in cavalry charges, or to transport messengers, supplies, or equipment, or pull heavy artillery and loads of wounded. Large and vulnerable, truly beasts of burden, they perished in mind-boggling numbers—some sources say eight million died in battle, at sea, or of illness, disease, exhaustion, or poison gas. One soldier wrote that horses, too, suffered trauma, and would sometimes "shiver, tremble all over, and break out in a sweat" when the shelling started. Seeing horses injured was "worse than seeing men cut up. The men have an idea what it is all about but the horses have to take it as it comes and say nothing."[19]

In March, Hugh wrote to Graham:

> Well that was quite an accident you had while you were on
> your way to bid farewell to your old neighbours, I am glad
> to hear you both got off safely. It was certainly a good thing
> that you didn't have [the horse] Pete, or I am afraid it would
> have been the worst for you. It seems a person is in danger
> wherever he is. You make me homesick when you speak of
> dealing horses and cattle and of someone getting married.
> I often dream I am back there working at one thing or
> other, and it all seems real, and I forget there ever was a
> war until a big gun firing or mine blowing up awakens me,
> and I remember I am still here in Flanders and the enemy
> is still there. . . . Well I guess this is all I can say this time,
> hoping to see you all soon. I will say good-bye.
> Your loving friend, Hugh"[20]

In August, another letter arrived, saying "we have been up against
it pretty hard this last three months," but "I am getting used to these
Belgian horrors now."[21] Even the time out of the trenches was gruelling,
he told Graham, "for they keep drilling us all the time." But he got great
joy out of a horse show put on for the men a few days before writing.
"Just think," he wrote with wonder, "a real horse show within range of
the German guns," and went on to describe the events and the prizes
in detail. There was "a Charlie Chaplin" in the ring too—presumably
someone impersonating the popular star, and who brought some much-
needed comic relief. He closed the letter with his regular refrain, "so
hoping to see you all some day soon," and included a drawing from the
trenches, which unfortunately was not reproduced for readers of the
Wingham Advance.

Together the letters from Hugh to Graham form a picture of a bright,
thoughtful, articulate young man who'd developed close attachments
not just to the family who'd taken him in, but to his wider community
of Turnberry and Wingham in Huron County. So it's no surprise that
in September, during the Battle of the Somme, the paper reported
"Turnberry Boy Falls," as though Hugh was one of their own.

Word was received here that Pte. Hugh W. Russell 54180
had been admitted to 2nd Western General Hospital, Bristol,
England, suffering from severe shell shock. Hugh had made
his home for some time with Mr. and Mrs. Jas. Wray, 6th
con. of Turnberry and no parents could be kinder or think
more of him. He went to London from Wingham on Feb. 1st,
1915, and enlisted with the 18th Batt....At the time he was
wounded he had served over a year in the trenches....Hugh
was well liked by a wide circle of friends who hope he may
recover and come back to old Huron again.[22]

His record shows that he "went sick" after being buried in a mound
of earth, right around the same time Charles Harrowsmith had the
same frightening experience. His case was indeed severe. He was unconscious for three days, and when he woke, he couldn't speak or walk. He
was invalided to England, where the doctors had a low opinion of his
overall intelligence, which seems at odds with his letters and must have
been due to his trauma. He received various forms of treatment to help
him regain his speech, but the words didn't come.

According to the British psychiatrist Frederick Mott, the treatment
of mutism from shell shock was often quick and simple.

The patient, after a careful and thorough examination, is
assured that he will be cured of his disability....he is asked
to produce sounds, to cough, to whistle, to say the vowel
sounds, which he will probably not be able to do. The voice
may return by suggestion only. But a more rapid method
is to reinforce suggestion by the application of the faradic
current to the neck by means of a roller electrode or brush.
The current is increased in strength and very often the
patient immediately recovers his voice and speaks.[23]

Early notes from Hugh's time at a hospital in Bristol suggest that
these methods were attempted, and eventually he could walk again, and
whistle "a trifle," and place his lips into the shapes necessary to form
sounds. But though he understood all that was said to him, he shook his

head when asked to speak. "Lies half asleep most of the time—is not
anxious to communicate with anyone." He had ferocious headaches and
insomnia, and then nightmares when he did manage to sleep. Notes in
his file show that treatment included anaesthesia, hypnotism, and electric shock therapy, but that there was "no effect except to terrify him."

Theories varied as to what was at the root of these men's troubles,
and changed over time. Were their symptoms a result of a physical shock
to the system brought on by heavy bombardment—a "sudden jarring
of the mental machinery," as Dora Vine put it? Or were these men of
cowardly, weak stock to begin with, and so made poor soldiers? Or were
they suffering mental trauma from prolonged exposure to stressful conditions? Approaches to curing them ranged from gentle and nurturing
to shockingly harsh, and doctors often disagreed with each other about
what patients needed. Canadian psychiatrist Lewis Yealland, working in
England during the war, described electricity as "the great sheet anchor"
in cases of mutism, and claimed a 100 per cent success rate. In his 1918
book *Hysterical Disorders of Warfare*, he laid out the case of a twenty-four-
year-old patient who'd been mute for nine months.

> Many attempts had been made to cure him. He had been
> strapped down in a chair for twenty minutes at a time, then
> strong electricity was applied to his neck and throat; lighted
> cigarette ends had been applied to the tip of his tongue
> and "hot plates" had been placed at the back of his mouth.
> Hypnotism had been tried. But all these methods proved to
> be unsuccessful in restoring his voice. When I asked him if
> he wished to be cured he smiled indifferently. I said to him:
> "...You appear to me to be very indifferent, but that will not
> do in times such as these."...In the evening he was taken
> to the electrical room, the blinds drawn, the lights turned
> out, and the doors leading into the room were locked and
> the keys removed. The only light perceptible was that from
> the resistance bulbs of the battery. Placing the pad electrode
> on the lumbar spines and attaching the long pharyngeal
> electrode, I said to him, "You will not leave this room until
> you are talking as well as you ever did; no, not before." The

mouth was kept open by means of a tongue depressor; a
strong faradic current was applied to the posterior wall of
the pharynx, and with this stimulus he jumped backwards,
detaching the wires from the battery. "Remember, you must
behave as becomes the hero I expect you to be," I said.
"A man who has gone through so many battles should have
better control of himself." Then I placed him in a position
from which he could not release himself and repeated, "You
must talk before you leave me." A weaker faradic current was
then applied more or less continuously, during which time
I kept repeating, "Nod to me when you are ready to attempt
to speak." This current was persevered with for one hour
with as few intervals as were necessary, and at the end of that
time he could whisper "ah." With this return of speech I said:
"Do you realise that there is already an improvement?...You
will believe me when I tell you that you will be talking before
long." I continued with the use of electricity for half an hour
longer, and during that time I constantly persuaded him to
say "ah, bah, cah," but "ah" was only repeated. It was difficult
for me to keep his attention, as he was becoming tired; and
unless I was constantly commanding him his head would
nod and his eyes close. To overcome this I ordered him
to walk up and down the room, and as I walked with him
urged him to repeat the vowel sounds. At one time when he
became sulky and discouraged he made an attempt to leave
the room, but his hopes were frustrated by my saying to him,
"Such an idea as leaving me now is most ridiculous; you
cannot leave the room, the doors are locked and the keys are
in my pocket. You will leave when you are cured, remember,
not before."[24]

As the treatment went on, the patient wept and finally whispered for
water, which was denied until a louder sound could be made, brought
about by the use of a stronger current. "I don't want to hurt you,"
Yealland's recounting goes, "but, if necessary, I must." After four hours'
continuous treatment, the man was deemed cured.

It's impossible to know the specifics of Hugh Russell's treatment
now, and one can only hope he endured nothing as horrible as laid
out in Yealland's book. By the time he was moved to another hospital
in February 1917, he was still not speaking, but gradually he began to
improve in other ways. He slept and ate well, and began "regaining
confidence," though he still had headaches and nightmares. "Is now
employed about the stables," a doctor wrote in April. "General condition
is good. His general nervousness and fear of MO's is disappearing." As
an aside, presumably to explain the fear of medical officers, the doctor
added, "(He was frightened of former methods to)..." but the sentence
is unfinished, and the following page, if there was one, is missing from
Hugh's file. "Has been to several horse races," the doctor wrote a month
later. "Did not speak even under excitement."

Whatever happened to Hugh with the aim of curing him, he wanted
no more of it. When he arrived back in Canada in the summer of 1917
and entered the mental hospital in Cobourg—an asylum taken over
for military purposes—his picture appeared in the *Wingham Advance*,
surely submitted by the Wrays. "As soon as was possible," the paper
reported, "he received a week's leave in order to visit with Mr. and Mrs.
Jas. Wray..., with whom he made his home before enlisting. They have
been all to him that parents could be to any boy."[25] The visit must have
been rejuvenating. At the end of the week, the paper reported that
a group of neighbours and friends gathered at the Wray farm "to do
honour to Private Hugh Russell." He was presented with a watch, chain,
and locket—just like Charles McVicar when he returned from the Boer
War—and one of the guests read out an address:

> We, your neighbours and friends...bid you a cordial wel-
> come back to the land of your adoption. We are proud of
> every loyal son but our hearts go out more particularly
> to you [whom] we have known and respected, and would
> therefore ask you to accept this watch and chain as a slight
> token of our esteem for you. While we are overjoyed to
> have you with us again, we all sympathize with you in your
> great affliction, but trust that An-all-wise-Providence will
> see fit to restore your speech to you. Although for lack of

forethought we did not acknowledge your bravery when you
enlisted alone and went to London to train yet we followed
you with our prayers and best wishes and our fervent prayer
now is that you may long be spared to enjoy the comforts of
life....[26]

Hugh stayed at Cobourg until December, silent all the while. "At
present his only trouble is complete loss of voice," the doctor there wrote,
"and he refuses any treatment for this, says he was tortured enough in
England by treatment.... This man is anxious for his discharge.... He
should pass under his own control."

And so Hugh was discharged from the army. He returned to the
Wingham area and was working for farmers related to the Wrays in
September 1918, when again he made the pages of the *Wingham Advance*
with the headline "Speech Returns." It was almost two years to the day
since he'd been buried. He'd been bringing a horse to the exhibition
grounds in Toronto, and during transport, the horse became frightened. "Whoa!" Hugh shouted, trying to calm the animal, and at the
same time surprising himself, finally, with the sound of his own voice
again.[27]

On the 1921 census, he appears with another family in the Wingham
area, employed as a labourer on their farm, but after this there's a long
gap in what remains of Hugh's story. In 1937, twenty years after his shell-
shock diagnosis, he was living at another farm when he went missing
one Sunday in July. The paper described him as forty-two years old,
very thin, with jet black hair, horn-rimmed spectacles, and a swarthy
complexion. He'd acted strangely at dinner, the farmer said, and after
finishing his meal, had walked in the direction of the nearby swamp.
The farmer thought he was suffering from a bout of melancholia, but
called the police when he didn't turn up the next day, fearing Hugh
was experiencing memory loss and "a recurrence of shell shock." The
day after that, the *Windsor Star* reported that police had found evidence
that "Former Barnardo Home Boy Had Bedded Down in Bog."[28] So as
in his soldier days, he had slept outside, *under the stars*, where all was
quiet except perhaps *an owl's cry, shaken out long and clear*. Before long,
he turned up at the Wray home. What happened after that only raises

more questions, for when Mrs. Wray saw him, she called police, and he immediately disappeared again. When police finally caught up with him a day later, he claimed he wasn't Hugh Russell, then "broke for a nearby bush and disappeared. The bush consists of more than 1,000 acres and will, it is believed, afford him a haven until he re-appears of his own accord."[29]

What was Hugh running from? What prompted Mrs. Wray to call the police? Had he suffered from melancholia, memory loss, and "recur- rence of shell shock" at other times through the postwar years? What, if anything, brought relief? He never married, and he had no children, but Wray family members recall that Graham tried to stay in touch with "Hughie," and thought of him as an older brother. A photograph in the family's possession shows Hugh with a huge grin, meeting Prince Philip, Duke of Edinburgh, on a 1962 royal visit to London, Ontario. The happy image gives no hint of the troubles Hugh experienced in his later years. His pension record reveals that Graham lost track of Hugh for a period of time, and eventually found him in the late 1960s, living in small, dirty quarters in a rooming house in London, and subsisting on a diet of candy and chocolate bars. He'd been working as a janitor at St. Joseph's Hospital, but now his physical and mental condition were deteriorating, and Graham brought him to Westminster Hospital, which managed veterans' cases, "looking for some care for this little man." His record states that he trusted no one, and believed people were always laughing

Hugh Russell with Prince Philip,
Duke of Edinburgh, May 1962
(The *London Free Press* Collection of
Photographic Negatives, Archives and
Special Collections, Western Libraries,
Western University, London, Canada)

at him and trying to steal his money and papers. He threw his food and lashed out at nurses and periodically complained of the "torture" he was receiving, and "the strange things that are going on." And yet one report stated: "[he] seems like a lovely soul who talks in riddles."[30]

Hugh lived out his last days at a psychiatric institution, but after his death in May 1970, he was brought back to Wingham for burial in the Wingham Cemetery. The *London Free Press* ran a spare obituary with one poignant detail: "Survived by a close friend, Graham Wray."[31]

Searching through newspaper archives for phrases like "recurrence of shell shock" turns up a number of stories through the 1920s and '30s, hinting at how war's long-term damage remained in the public consciousness. A bride in Montreal was left waiting at the altar because her veteran-groom had been taken to hospital for loss of memory. In British Columbia, a veteran who'd found work selling gramophones to farmers was caught in a storm while on delivery; a tree branch crashed down on his automobile, and though he escaped unhurt, he was so shaken by the incident that he lost his ability to speak. A woman in rural Saskatchewan begged police to search for her missing husband, an ex-soldier who'd recently lost his job. "Owing to a chronic state of disability, worry over financial difficulties, and acute depression, it is feared he has had a lapse of memory, and may now be in some hospital or home, and that he does not know who he is."[32] Another veteran was on board an ocean liner, playing cello in the orchestra, when a violent storm damaged the ship. A rush of water swept past him, carrying with it an injured man, and the sight was "so alarming that [the veteran] became temporarily deranged and had to be strapped down." Men went missing, or committed tragic acts of violence against themselves and others, or drank *to drown the memory* of *the hurricane of war*. A doctor in Britain believed "many thousands of neurotics were created by war, but peace has produced a more dangerous type.... Only fear of punishment will keep the after-war neurotic on a straight course." An opinion piece in an American paper went further, raging against "popular explanations

for all kinds of misdemeanors and crimes on the part of the boys who
served in the war." The writer claimed that shell shock and gas poisoning were no excuse for "pure cussedness super-induced by rotten
whiskey. It is quite the fad...to find fancy names for crimes caused by
the slopping over of original sin in the members of the human family."[33]

In its early years, Christie Street didn't have a psychiatric ward.
Mental patients went to Cobourg, like Hugh Russell did, or to any
number of military asylums across Canada if the mind was the sole
focus of their treatment. But for many Christie Street men still recovering from physical wounds and illnesses, despair also plagued them.
John Armitage was one such patient.[34] Like the spinal TB patient
Tom Ronaldson, he'd been gassed at Ypres, and like Hugh Russell,
he'd suffered severe mental breakdown, and he was still dealing with
repercussions of both those injuries in the mid-1920s.

Another English-born soldier, John had gone overseas with the first
contingent in 1914. Tall, blue-eyed, with sandy hair and a fair complexion, he was a career soldier who'd served with the Royal Canadian
Regiment since his arrival in Canada in the early 1900s. The gas attack
had seen him hospitalized at Wimereux, on the coast of France, where
Connie Bruce and Win Hammell were nursing, and when he didn't
improve, he was sent on to England, eventually returning to Canada
early in 1916. Stationed at Camp Aldershot in Nova Scotia, he was scheduled to go back overseas, but at the end of June, plans changed. The
details in his record are sketchy, but one note from a superior officer
stands out:

> Early in the morning of the 29th...it came to my notice
> that Lieut. Armitage was suffering from a form of nervous
> breakdown which apparently would be relieved if he could
> get away from camp for a little while. As the case seemed
> so urgent he was told to go to Kentville and try to get some
> rest, as he...had not been able to sleep in Camp. He is
> much improved today and will very shortly be able to report
> for duty again.

By September, he'd been promoted to captain, but deemed unable to return to the front. He stayed on in Nova Scotia, and in the spring of 1917, married a woman named Emma Munn, the day after her arrival from England. How this relationship came about is a bit of a mystery, since John had emigrated years before. He was the son of a musician, and had grown up in Hastings, Sussex, and Emma was distantly related and had been living in London, so perhaps their romance had begun when John was convalescing in England. They were married at St. George's Round Church in Halifax, by the minister Henry Ward Cunningham, but John's troubles continued. His pension record references "occasional emotional disturbances" in June of that year, and states that he "cries for hours about once in six weeks, following exceptionally hard work." His complaints were like those of so many other men: nightmares, nervousness — *I feel I cannot sleep*. Between these bouts of emotional turmoil he felt "quite well," though the skin on his right buttock was hardened and marred with scars. The wound had apparently been sustained at Ypres during the gas attack, though there was no record of it made by doctors at that time.

Although John was stationed at Camp Aldershot near Kentville during this period, and also in the sanatorium there for a time, his service record places Emma at a Halifax address. Judging by the dates scrawled on a form, it appears the couple was still in Nova Scotia in December 1917, when two ships collided in the Narrows, just north of Halifax Harbour. One of the ships had been loaded with munitions, and the collision caused a fire on board that soon saw the vessel engulfed in flames. Within twenty minutes, the ship exploded, spewing debris and toxic fumes over a wide area on both sides of the Narrows. The blast was so enormous that blocks of buildings were decimated, and windows shattered as much as eighty kilometres away. A tsunami washed the second ship ashore, and devastated an old Mi'kmaw village situated along the Dartmouth waterfront, home to some seventeen families.

The dead and injured lay among the ruins. More than two thousand people perished, and nine thousand were wounded. For soldiers, it must have looked as though war had swept through the region as vehemently as at Passchendaele or the Somme, snapping trees and lamp posts and obliterating people's homes. Almost immediately, soldiers were put to work in the *desolated waste*, gathering the dead and searching through rubble for survivors. If John Armitage was among this band, it must have been gruelling work indeed, the kind that traumatized mentally healthy people let alone those who were already struggling. Afterward, according to personal accounts collected for the Halifax Disaster Record Office, one officer recalled seeing "a trail of blood" as refugees streamed away from the hardest-hit areas. As he directed soldiers in the work of removing bodies, he noticed in the distance "patches of white scattered all over" on Citadel Hill.[35] The image puzzled him until someone explained that these were cloths laid over the faces of the dead.

Reverend Cunningham, the man who'd married John and Emma at the Round Church, likewise offered his recollections of the terrifying event.[36] He had just finished his breakfast, and his wife was handing him a cup of coffee when a deep boom thundered, as if a bomb had burst on the church lawn. All at once, a "mighty rush of air" smashed the windows and blew in glass with the curtains, and he was thrown under the table, bleeding from a cut in his neck. He looked for his wife, who had run to the basement, and from outside he heard children at the local school screaming. For a couple of hours, until it was certain no further explosions would occur, he and his neighbours were crowded into the Halifax Common not far from the church, but as soon as he could, he went to check on parishioners. The devastation was everywhere. "He had the impression," his interviewer wrote, "of being in a strange country—that he had never been there before." He saw homes destroyed to nothing more than "a pile of bricks and a bath-tub," bodies covered with burlap bags, fires blazing. One woman told him that when the vessels had first collided, she'd called to her children to "come out and see the beautiful sight of the burning ship," and then was thrown three hundred feet when the blast occurred, her clothing torn from her body. Some people's faces were covered with soot from the fine black rain that had fallen after the explosion. And then, the following day, a blizzard blew in, *the mantling snow* hampering clean-up and rescue efforts.

There are few traceable details about John and Emma's life after the explosion through to the end of the war, but in January 1921, they sailed from New Brunswick to England, and if the ship's ledger is correct, they intended to stay there. Emma was listed as "wife," and John as "pensioner," so he was not yet working. They were destined for a London address in the area where Emma's sister lived, but by September, they'd returned to Canada. Though John's brother and his wife lived in Toronto, John and Emma settled on a small farm in Malton, just outside the city, probably on the advice of doctors who would have wanted John to work outdoors because of his ongoing medical issues. Just like the beekeeping taken up by Tom Ronaldson, the work was meant to be healthy, invigorating, and useful. As with Tom, the gas had damaged John's lungs, and he was regularly examined at Christie Street to determine his level of disability and how much of a pension he should receive. Through the early 1920s, he was downgraded from 100 per cent disability to 70 per cent disability, and though his overall health appeared to be worsening after his return to Canada, his pension did not increase again. He had "some chest disability... [but] no further emotional attacks," and then at the next exam he had "evidence of bronchiectasis with much sputum" but still appeared fairly healthy. In February 1923, he was "rather anaemic," and "looked older than age 41.... Slight tremor of fingers.... Debility fairly marked." In August of that year, he "complained of cough and sputum" but "looked healthy." And then in October 1924, "complained of severe attacks of bronchitis." His skin was sallow, he'd lost weight, and his general appearance was poor. "Referred for chest report."[37]

Two days later, in a tiny article at the bottom of the page, the *Star* reported:

> Sad circumstances attended the death of John Armitage, an ex-soldier, who has been suffering from the effects of shell shock and gas, and who was found at Malton this morning with a bullet hole through his head. Armitage, who is a married man with no family, was conducting a small chicken farm at Malton and was down at Christie Street Hospital on Thursday for examination. He did not return home as expected, and Rev. H.O. Hutcheson made a prolonged search for him, finding the remains on a small clump of trees not far from the school house.[38]

An investigation followed, summed up in John's pension record. Back in the spring, not long after the pension board examination had noted marked aging and "tremor of fingers," a local civilian doctor had been called to John's home to address an attack of bronchitis and asthma. When the doctor saw that he had a loaded revolver at his bedside, John told him, "You never know what may happen and you may need it any time." The doctor believed John seemed not just "depressed and despondent," but "mentally unbalanced," though he did not notify anyone about his concerns at the time. "The man's physical condition was such that it would employ him a mental case," the investigator wrote, "as he impressed the Doctor of having a feeling of despair and helplessness." Later on, in the summer, the doctor forwarded a prescription for bronchitis and asthma, but did not personally check on him again.

The wife of Reverend Hutcheson, the man who'd found John's body, stated that she knew John well, but "had never heard any comment regarding him being mentally unbalanced, nor had she noticed anything herself." Perhaps the meaning of the term was in question, for she added that there was no doubt he was despondent, and Emma had told her that whenever he returned from examinations in Toronto, "he was very much depressed."

The agent at the Malton train station was also interviewed, and stated that he knew John well, since he'd come to Malton three years earlier and regularly travelled to the city for his medical appointments. He kept two cows and some chickens, the man said, but his wife did most of the farm work. He described John as "very nervous," and also "depressed" the day he went for his final examination at Christie Street.

On the day of John's death, Reverend Hutcheson had received a letter from him, asking that he look after Emma's interests because he was going on a long journey. The letter also said that "he had been sick for a long time and lately he had met with a great disappointment and was greatly upset." To Emma, John wrote that he was "fed up with the pension business." He had closed his bank account and issued money orders for the full amount—about $1,000—in her name. He was "mentally sick," he told her, and did not know when he would be home again. The bullet had released him. He could now *be still and send his soul into the all.*

John Armitage's sad story bears some similarities to that of Jack Hoar, the double amputee who'd killed himself in Chicago in 1920. Both men linked the *troubled mind* not just to their war injuries but to their pensions, and their certainty that a bleak future loomed. Both left childless widows who likely suffered their own form of anguish that they had not been able to assuage a husband's pain. John had been a career soldier, and the chicken farm seems to have held no sense of promise for him. While many men appeared to recover and adjust after having been wounded, others sank deeper into a misery that was steadily worsened by the evidence of life moving on without them.

Back in February 1919, when the hospital on Christie Street had first opened, there was still plenty of coverage about returned soldiers and how the general public could assist in their reintegration, and what sorts of accommodations should be made in the workplace. The Canadian Pacific Railway, which hired disabled veterans for retraining, drafted "Rules for Treating Returned Soldiers," reminding civilian employees that "most returned soldiers' constitutions are broken down. They have been gassed, shell shocked, and tortured by wounds, and consequently, are highly strung and nervous and will be for some time to come. What they make of themselves depends on you.... The greatest tact, care and attention that you can give these men in helping them to become useful employes is what the company expects, and moreover—you owe it to them."[39]

But increasingly through the 1920s, there was a general feeling among veterans that their concerns had fallen out of the limelight. A British writer claimed that thousands of wounded men still lay in hospital beds, but that "now nobody looks at them." At a rally protesting unemployment, he'd seen a sign that read "Wanted 1914, Forgotten 1920."[40] Here in Canada, on Christmas Eve in 1921, several papers reported on the "scores of unemployed, penniless ex-soldiers...soliciting aid for themselves and for their starving companions. The tags they are today selling are inscribed with the words: 'Help keep the man who fought for you from starving.'"[41] As returned men pushed for progressive changes for themselves, "aliens"—especially those from wartime enemy countries—were maligned for taking valuable jobs, and many women returned to their traditional roles, giving up careers and independence. In 1920, Winnipeg's mayor was incensed by the idea that women were taking jobs for "pin-money" while family men were out of work.

All of these social issues knotted and tangled in a world that had been upended by war. Even before the fighting was over, the Great War Veterans' Association was pressuring government to give "Indian land" to soldiers who couldn't return to their old jobs. There were swathes of land, a Vancouver paper asserted, being put to no practical use. "Young Indians...sometimes come swaggering into town of a Saturday night, buy an ice cream cone, swagger around a little longer and then go back to the reserve, on which they would raise about an acre of potatoes and the rest Scotch thistles."[42] In the end, some eighty-five thousand acres of Indigenous land was seized for veterans who wanted to try farming. Indigenous veterans could apply for the land too, but were less often successful, a racist disparity in keeping with other veteran-related issues. In the early 1930s, the Department of Indian Affairs took over administration for soldiers living on reserves, the thinking being that "as the Indians are wards of the Department of Indian Affairs, this department should be responsible for any assistance that they might be in need of." But when Mohawk veteran Angus Goodleaf applied for additional aid, having suffered pneumonia, neurasthenia, shell shock, and gunshot wounds, his commanding officer received a letter that stated, "We are not in a position to treat returned soldiers as generously as the whites are treated by the...Pensions Board." The letter went on to explain that the department had to consider not only the needs of returned soldiers but the "nature and extent of assistance given to other members of the same band who may be in needy circumstances.... The department is seeking to do its best, not only for returned Indian soldiers but all Indians who may be in distress in these times."[43] Of course the reasons for that distress circled back to the government itself, and its age-old mistreatment of Indigenous people. Newspapers of the day rarely reported that vantage point. Even when the League of Indians held their first convention during the Prince of Wales's visit in 1919, it was framed as "a new movement to see what the Indian can do towards formulating higher plans of social, moral, political and industrial economics."[44] It was thought that Indigenous soldiers who'd returned from war formed "a new and progressive class" on reserves across the country; "their experience has been a broadening one and they are not likely to return to the primitive life of their antecedents."[45]

For many, it was precisely those old ways that would help them heal from the trauma of war, if only they could practise them. Sweat lodges, shaking tents, and other sacred rituals had been outlawed decades earlier in the name of assimilation, though they were still practised covertly in some places. Francis Pegahmagabow, the highly decorated Ojibwe soldier thought to have been one of the most successful snipers of the war, believed adherence with traditional rituals had helped him survive his years on the Western Front. For soldiers returning home, ceremonies led by Elders who knew the songs, stories, and practices associated with each ritual would have restored balance to the mind, body, and spirit, and reconnected the men with their communities. But Pegahmagabow found these old ways had almost disappeared when he arrived back in Georgian Bay.

Men of all demographics struggled, and the inevitable march of the years passing, combined with the economic downturns, only made their situation harder—people kept moving on and growing less mindful of veterans' plights. In 1931, a frustrated veteran named Edward Chesley wrote a scathing piece called "The Vice of Victory," and claimed that "There is no one more sick of the seemingly endless plaint about the 'returned soldiers' rights' and 'returned soldiers' problem' than are the very men of the Canadian Expeditionary Force who wandered back to Canada about 12 years ago."[46] But society was forgetting them, he said; government was letting them down. The general public believed that men were granted pensions in accordance with their injuries, and that, through regular examinations, pension amounts were adjusted as an injury worsened or healed. And in a time when ordinary citizens paid out of pocket for their own medical care, designated military hospitals looked after the men free of charge, so people asked themselves, "What could be fairer than that?" and drew conclusions that grumbling veterans were just "trouble-makers and malcontents." Newspaper accounts often suggested life in a military hospital was fun and even a bit glamorous—the silent screen star Mary Pickford visited Christie

Street several times, and her swashbuckling husband Douglas Fairbanks was snapped doing chin-ups on the roof ward. The hospital had grown into a "unique and gallant little community," according to *The Hospital World*, complete with tennis courts in summer and a skating rink in winter.[47] So what was the problem? And why were there so many down-and-out veterans begging on the street or abusing alcohol? People were baffled and annoyed, Chesley wrote, by "the multitude of draggle-tail men who peddle from house to house and from office to office and even accost you on the street with requests to buy three cakes of soap." They had lost touch with the fact that "the joy of living was killed in the souls of tens of thousands of the pick of Canada's youth who marched away to fight the war to end war so long ago."

Chesley claimed that men were kept from medical assistance by "great masses of departmental red tape." He recounted the story of an ailing veteran who'd been refused admission to a military hospital because his illness couldn't officially be connected to his war service. "He had a wife and family; no money; and his legs were rapidly growing dead and damnably painful, just as they did to a lesser extent when trenchfeet caught them in the cold mud and water years before. But he had not reported sick in France—one did not always squeak at the first pinch of hardship—and without records of disability overseas our overlords could not find it within their power to admit him to hospital or confer a pension. But the problem of this fellow was nicely solved. He died while the debating went on."

These were the sorts of stories that further embittered veterans. Chesley believed that almost every one of them had come back from war "thoroughly disillusioned" and "burned out....You cannot go through four years of such a war and come out unscathed." It was true for the medical staff too. War had changed them, and returning from it meant figuring out what they'd been through, and who they were once it was over.

When stationed in a hospital at the front, nurse Nettie Howey was given a canary in a cage.[48] She kept it with her as she worked her ward, so that she and the patients could hear its beautiful singing. Once, during an air raid, the corner of the cage was shot off, but the bird survived. Sometimes men from other wards would come and ask if they could borrow the bird for the afternoon, to spread the music around. When the war ended, Nettie had had the bird for more than three years, and thought, "I'm not going to leave it behind me." One of the soldiers made the bird a little travelling cage she could carry easily, and in this way the canary accompanied her across the ocean back to Canada. "On the train going from Toronto to Owen Sound, I had my little bird in the cage sitting on the seat beside me. I never had a word said to me about it [until] the conductor came through and said, 'No birds or animals allowed in this coach.' I said, 'This is a war hero, and if you put that bird off, you put me off too!' So he let me take it on to Owen Sound."

And yet, in its new environment, the bird stopped singing. Nettie kept it at her parents' place and returned to Toronto for nursing work at St. Andrew's hospital, but whenever she visited, the bird seemed to know her, and though silent, would dance around in its cage. "That was a wonderful bird," she recalled years later, "but one night after a year or so, it was forgotten and left out and in the morning the cage had been knocked down and the bird was gone! I must say I shed a few tears over that bird. Sounds foolish, but really, it was part of my life. Those things are crazy, but they're all ... [well,] 'tis the war."

Bellies

By 1920, its second year, the hospital had become a fixture on Christie Street, plain in design but large enough to dominate the slope on which it sat in Toronto's west end. With the warm days of spring, the vines clinging to the red brick had begun to glow green, and patients appeared more frequently on the grounds, soaking up the sun or preparing for a group trip to High Park. There was always a certain amount of camaraderie, for many of the patients and staff knew each other well by now, but the population at Christie Street was also continually revolving: patients dying off or happily discharged; new ones entering; and nurses, doctors, and staff coming and going.

Around the time that "Frank Hall" was admitted, with camera flashes popping and anxious visitors seeking him out, a patient named Leslie Chadwell was on the brink of his release from the hospital.[1] After nearly two years of treatment for gunshot wounds, he was almost ready to go west to Saskatchewan, where a plot of prairie farm land awaited him.

He was twenty-five years old, tall, with a fresh complexion, dark hair, and blue eyes. Life as a soldier had given him a T-shaped scar on his shoulder, and another scar on his jaw, but he was fairly healthy and had come through his operations well. Once his final dental work was completed, his only complaint was that, for the past three or four years, he'd had trouble digesting meat. Two hours after a meal, he'd have sharp pains and "a feeling of distress."

The pains in his abdomen prompted doctors at Christie Street to delay his release in order to search out the source of his discomfort, and by the end of April, he'd had his gall bladder removed and was suffering from shock and hemorrhage following the operation. Over the next few days, his condition worsened. His temperature soared and he had diarrhea and vomited large quantities of bile. The bowel movements stopped but the vomiting continued over the next few days, and then the incision made to remove the gall bladder reopened, and "intestinal viscera" pushed through it. He was rushed to the operating room, where it was found that "old blood" had hardened and pooled inside him, and adhesions had formed, triggered by the initial abdominal surgery. These fine, filmy bands of scar tissue looped and twisted around his intestines, kinking them so furiously as to cause an obstruction. The adhesions were broken down to allow the intestines to function again, but over the next few days his condition kept deteriorating, and toward the middle of May he was given a blood transfusion. Was it a fellow soldier lying beside him, donating blood? Or his brother Ernest, who was with him at the time? Immediately afterwards he seemed "much improved," but by the next day he was failing again. "Not well," the notes say. "Very emaciated." He died early in the morning on the fifteenth, with Ernest at his side.

Had Ernest come to accompany Leslie on his release from the hospital? What was it like, then, to instead have to inform the rest of the family that their shot-up soldier had recovered but died of another cause? And what had prompted Leslie Chadwell's ailments in the first place? Since the problems began "three or four years" earlier, they coincided with his war service. Gastric complaints were common enough among soldiers, and doctors often noted that men were underweight or had poor appetites. A man suffering from some sort of mental distress might refuse

food altogether, his nervousness shutting down his ability to take in
nourishment. A poor diet, dirty water, and life in the trenches amid
rats, flies, and corpses could have lasting effects on the digestive system.
Depending on where a man had served, he might have come down with
yellow fever, malaria, or dysentery.

The same was true, of course, for the doctors and nurses who treated
the men. May Bastedo — the travel-loving nurse who'd seemed so formidable early in the war, recording the ship "rolling finely" while everyone
else on board was seasick — had severe, recurring attacks of enteritis in
Salonika, and though she worked at Christie Street after her return to
Canada, she left the job in December 1919, unable to meet the demands
of her long-time occupation. Her wartime letters and diaries suggest she
had loved being a war nurse, and though she was older than most of
her colleagues, she'd possessed extraordinary energy and enthusiasm.
When she took on a hospital ship posting, *out where the white seas toss*,
she wrote to her mother that it was an honour to be chosen. "We had a
rough time the other night and about four of us were the only ones not
seasick. I had to stay on night duty after being on from 2 o'clock and in
the smelliest ward in the place. I stuck it out, wasn't sick even with both
orderlies ill. They all thought I was a wonder." Later, on land, she was
put in charge of infectious-disease patients who were kept in isolation
tents, with her own "duty tent" in the centre, and she sloshed around
the field from one tent to the next in rubber boots. "The mud is jolly
sticky," she told her mother. "You lose your rubbers every second step, if
you stand still they stay there." At one point, she wrote about having her
portrait taken to capture this new person she'd become. "You wouldn't
know me. I'm like a tough; dirty skirt, two sweaters, raincoat, old gloves
and a sou-wester on, tied under my chin, mud on everything."[2]

The challenges seemed to invigorate her. "I am well and fat.... I live
in the open air," she wrote, adding that it was a good thing she didn't
feel the cold much and that she'd had all the regular bouts of sickness
as a child, toughening her up for this mission. It was chilly and damp
through the winter — "as cold as in Canada" — with rain and wild gales
and blizzards, and some of the patients had not just war wounds but
frozen toes, nasty colds, and aching rheumatism. Many were desperately
ill with dysentery. The nurses had chilblains on their hands and feet,

May Bastedo, 1915 (Photographic Collection of Nursing Sister
May Bastedo, 19780041-006, George Metcalf Archival Collection,
Canadian War Museum)

and sometimes their tents collapsed in the miserable weather. They went
to sleep at night—wind howling, *shadows wildly blown*—not knowing if
the tents would stay upright until morning. "They are to build huts for
us," May wrote, "but I don't mind the tents....We are allowed two oil
stoves but we burn them pretty hard and it makes very little impression
when the wind blows. It isn't so bad at night but in the morning—I have
the stove near me and turn over and light it as I am always first awake."

She'd made fifty dollars a month as a wartime nurse, a good living
in those days, especially for a woman. But she was getting older, and the
work and her illnesses had tired her out. At the time of her discharge
from the army, a medical examination found that she was frequently in
pain, and that her body couldn't handle the "ordinary food supplied"
at Christie Street. She couldn't do more than a few hours' work before
weakness set in. "Patient is rather pale," the doctor wrote, "has worn,

tired expression. Musculature in debilitated condition.... Has general appearance of malnutrition."[3]

But her wanderlust hadn't dissipated. Though Toronto was home, her pension record shows that after leaving Christie Street, she went south to California, and spent several months there recuperating and presumably pondering what she'd do next, with nursing no longer an option. She was fifty years old by this time, and unmarried, but also seemingly an independent intelligent woman determined to continue making her own way in the world. In the spring of 1920, while Leslie Chadwell suffered out his last days, May Bastedo travelled north from California to Victoria, having learned that the vocational training branch of the Department of Soldiers' Civil Re-establishment was offering a course there in poultry and fruit farming for veterans who needed a new start. The deadline to apply for the course had passed at the end of January, but she did so anyway, explaining that she'd been "in the South for my health... [and] took the first opportunity to put my application in on my return to Canada."[4]

Her application was quickly rejected—she was too late, officials wrote without apology, and being away was no excuse, since the course had been advertised in the States as well. The letter was firm, but May persisted:

> I have been very miserable with stomach trouble and
> attack of gastritis and do not feel that I will be able to
> nurse for sometime.... I believe other nursing sisters have
> had Vocational Training given them who have applied
> since [the deadline]. Would it be possible for you to give
> me a short course as the Drs all advocate an open life. I was
> overseas with No. 4 University of Toronto Unit for nearly
> four years and was on duty in Canada on my return.... If
> you could see your way to giving me a Vocational Course,
> I would be very much obliged and ever so grateful.

She closed the letter with strategic mention of high-ranking army men she'd come to know in her years of service, who also wrote to the department on her behalf. "This officer," one of them stated, "is a woman of the highest efficiency and character....I will be very pleased indeed if her application is accepted." Next came the news that the department would be "only too pleased" to include May in the program: "You are advised that special consideration is being granted in your case due to the fact that you were in the United States and were therefore unable to apply for training within the time limit."

That it was still a man's world she was navigating also came through in the correspondence that followed: "Please be advised that the marginally named man was taken on the strength of the Training branch of this department...." And later, "the marginally named man...completed his course in Poultry & Small Fruits." Whoever filled in the medical report for her application took the trouble to x through a mention of "man" and replace it with "lady."

Vocational retraining was open to nurses who could prove their need for it, but was largely undertaken by ex-soldiers who could no longer work at their old jobs, so it seems likely that the first half of the course—three months' study at the University of British Columbia—was spent in the company of men. Following that, May had several months' practical training on farms, a period that was extended twice so that she could receive additional instruction. She may not have been in a rush to finish the course, for vocational training paid well. She got sixty dollars a month while the course lasted, plus an additional ten dollars for her dependent mother in Toronto, which totalled more than she'd made as a nurse in service. Afterward, her income would dwindle significantly.

But what a feeling it must have been to *grow apples and flowers in the valley,* to don rubber boots again and work the soil of her own land. There were so many joys in an "open-air" life: *bluebells swinging; blackbirds singing on a moss-upholstered stone.* Certificate in hand, she acquired her own small farm on Old West Saanich Road just outside Victoria, and there she remained for nearly twenty years, tending a flock of poultry, fruit trees, and a garden.

On the eve of the Second World War, she sold the farm and moved to a small house nearby. When a pension board investigator visited to assess her needs, he discovered "a small, husky, grey-haired lady who scarcely appears her years and who is active." An official had also inspected the family bible in Toronto to verify her age. Though healthy,

May was "obviously unfit for work," and living on just over twenty dollars a month, plus a $7.50 veterans' allowance. Totting up her expenses, he pointed out to her that she had nothing left over for maintenance or emergencies. "She admitted that," the man wrote, "and stated that she is indebted to friends who were good to her when she lived a most frugal life." The board upped her allowance a couple of dollars more each month, but in 1947 May wrote to request the money stop coming. "It's only right I give up my war allowance you so kindly gave me. It has certainly been a great help in these days of increased cost of living & I thank you very much." The board concurred, and told her she could apply for the funds to be reinstated should she find herself in need again.

By 1950—truly elderly now, and paying room and board at a friend's house—she made that request, and was again visited by a pension board investigator to ensure the authenticity of her claim. Once more, the official was struck by May's vitality. "She is very active both mentally and physically. She is quite short and slim, has a deeply lined face, small eyes and wears glasses. States her health is fine....Miss Bastedo is a remarkable woman for her 81 years."

She lived two years longer, and even after death some small part of her carries on. Her wartime diary can still be thumbed through in the quiet rooms of the Canadian War Museum, its pages thin and soft, the tiny compass embedded in the cover flickering. Prefacing her own entries are several colourful pages depicting the funnels of ocean liners and the flags of the world. There's a chart listing international time differences and another showing how long it takes to sail from one port to another. Pages heavy with text are decorated with ropes, anchors, shells, and fish, and go into great detail explaining buoys, beacons, and lighthouse lights, as well as the meanings of whistles and bells sounded on board a steamship. With these rules for navigation in hand, May Bastedo embarked on her great journey, recording her impressions as she went. These and her handwritten letters, saved for a lifetime, suggest an awareness that in the years to come, someone, somewhere, would want to know a little of what it was like to be her: the "first awake," "a good sailor," and a "tough" in a dirty skirt.

That May Bastedo could not stomach the "ordinary food supplied" at
Christie Street fits with the complaints some patients made to the *Star*
in the hospital's early days. "A number of the boys go downtown every
little while to buy a square meal," one patient told the *Star*, and to have
a break from "hash under...fancy names" regularly served at the hospital.[5] The hospital maintained its meals were of excellent quality, and
that men at Christie Street were better fed than at any other hospital
in Canada. Visiting one mealtime in 1919, the *Star* went even further:

> There is a marked contrast between the 'grub' that was
> served on active service, and the meals that daily delight
> the souls of the patients of the Dominion Orthopaedic
> Hospital....As for variety, no meals in Blighty or France
> during the last few years of the war could rival the daily
> menu at the hospital. There are more ways than one of
> restoring the badly wounded men to health, and for this
> reason the hospital staff, from Col. [C.S.] McVicar down,
> spends almost as much time in planning the recreation
> and meals of the men as is given to medical attention.[6]

McVicar and his successors certainly had help with these huge tasks.
The *Illustrated Souvenir* contains a striking photograph of a woman
seated in the hospital's dining hall. Dressed in the veil and crisp white
uniform of a dietitian, her hands are folded in her lap, and she gazes
into the distance as if she has all the time in the world for idle contem-
plation—highly unlikely given the hundreds of men fed at the hospital
each day. She sits alone at the edge of the frame, dwarfed by the vast
space and the tables stretching *row on row* behind her, each place set with
plate and cup and saucer. The room looks like a factory cafeteria, with
exposed beams and ductwork and pipes zigzagging along the ceiling.
Someone has hung plants from the beams in an attempt to make the
space homey, much in the way nurses decorated hospital huts overseas
with gathered flowers and branches. The bench seating at long tables
must have been awkward for men with crutches and artificial legs, but

here they came three times a day if they were "up" patients well enough to move around on their own. Hospital rules stipulated they be properly dressed and arrive and clear out in a timely fashion. No wonder, really, because as soon as one meal had been served, preparations for the next one began.

In 1919, Violet Ryley, the woman who oversaw food services for all of Canada's military hospitals, wrote that "suitable food is second only to efficient medical and surgical treatment, as without it the latter fails to secure adequate results."[7] As a rule, these hospitals placed trained dietitians rather than superintendents in charge, having discovered that dietitians could save institutions thousands of dollars a year through what Ryley called "wise and intelligent menu building." An efficient dietitian knew how to choose the best food from a nutritional and aesthetic perspective, but also from an economical one. She was able to manage her department using fewer people who worked with greater efficiency. She understood food safety issues, as well as the science of nutrition and digestion, and the necessity of carefully interpreting a prescribed meal plan, for in some cases, "the very life of a patient may depend on correct diet to suit the disease."

Ryley insisted that if a dietitian was to properly do her job at the hospital, she must be given full authority over the kitchen and dining-room staff, for she was held to account for everything from consumption levels to broken crock pots. The returns each hospital's dietitian submitted to Ryley, as General Organizing Dietitian, were so detailed that they included total costs per meal and also any losses incurred "through wear and tear in equipment, silver, linen, and china."[8] In this way, head office could compare efficiencies as well as the quantities consumed in hospitals across the country—though of course the costs varied with the types of diet the patients required. The tuberculosis patients on the roof ward at Christie Street, for instance, cost more to feed, because they needed bulking up with greater quantities of rich food like milk, eggs, and butter.

Dietetics was a career just coming into the public awareness—another "progressive profession for girls" according to a *Maclean's* piece by Gertrude Pringle, who'd likewise profiled the "girls in green" working in occupational therapy. In 1919, *Maclean's* ran a piece written by newly

minted dietitian Doris McHenry, under the telling title "What Is a
Dietitian?"[9] She was twenty-two at the time, and had recently graduated
from the University of Toronto's household sciences program. "Justly
proud" of her profession, she took exception to the fact that seemingly
intelligent acquaintances—even those in the health-care field—didn't
know what a dietitian was:

> It is true that the dietitian is comparatively an innovation,
> and that our forefathers throve fairly well on meals planned
> in ignorance of the great scientific laws of feeding. Yet, now
> that an increasing number of young women elect to spend
> four arduous years in grappling with this vital problem, it
> is advisable that the world at large should at least be able
> to attach some significance to the term 'dietitian.' Having
> once mastered the difficulties of the meaning of the word,
> it is our fond hope that the world will advance one step
> farther, and endeavor to assimilate some of the rudimentary
> lessons connected with the science of dietetics.[10]

By at least February 1921, Doris had another degree and had become
the chief dietitian at Christie Street. A newspaper article headed "Girl
Dietitian at Big Hospital" pegged her as an "important executive [of]
big housekeeping." She and her assistants Marjorie Cooper and Bertha
Monaghan—"three remarkable women"—oversaw the nourishment
of 700 men gobbling 2,100 meals per day: "perfectly 'balanced'" and
"daintily served."[11] The women worked in shifts and together were
responsible, just as Violet Ryley had laid out, for the buying and the
bookkeeping related to their department, for the management of all
the staff in the kitchen and dining room, and also for the supervision
of the nurses' residence, a separate building on the hospital grounds.
They planned the meals for the men who ate in the big basement dining
room, and also for the TB patients on the roof ward. Everyone between
those two floors also came under their jurisdiction, for many were bedridden or had to be fed by an orderly or nurse.

It would seem the women grew close over the years. When Doris
eventually married, her colleague Marjorie served as a witness. In those

days, marriage still normally meant a woman gave up her career, so Doris went from managing a "family of 700" to overseeing an ordinary little household, where a grocery list could be jotted on a scrap of paper. After Doris left, Marjorie and Bertha stayed on at Christie Street, proud of their work and the education that had landed them their jobs. A 1919 photograph shows Marjorie on the U of T campus, beaming in graduation cap and gown and holding an armload of flowers. A year later, she was one of several speakers at the University Women's Club, discussing the various career options open to women who were college graduates.

Bertha, the eldest of these three dietitians, was accustomed to trios. As her son and granddaughter tell it, she was the middle of three sisters and had grown up on a farm in Prince Edward County. Her mother died when she was eight years old, and her father remarried to a widow who helped him raise the girls. Unusually for his time and circumstance, Bertha's father insisted his daughters be educated and able to support themselves, so by the time the war began in 1914, twenty-four-year-old Bertha had been teaching in a schoolhouse for several years. But war caused a shift in demographics—fewer children were being born, and those who were in school often left at a younger age to work on farms or otherwise help their families while so many men were overseas. In the early 1920s, Bertha joined the team at Christie Street, a move that would shape her future more than any other, for it was there that she met William Wishart, the amputee who demonstrated prosthesis use in "limb parades" arranged by the DSCR.[12] They married—yet another Christie Street romance—and over the years, William's work for the DSCR morphed into arranging entertainment for the soldiers. Both he and Bertha worked at Christie Street until at least the late 1920s.

Bertha, Marjorie, and Doris were working as hospital dietitians when some of the most exciting research took place using Christie Street's diabetic patients in experiments with insulin, under the supervision of Dr. Frederick Banting. When the war was still underway, Banting's eventual involvement with diabetes couldn't have been guessed at. A graduate of the University of Toronto's medical school, he'd had little awareness of the disease, and no idea about how widespread it was. "Diabetes was a disease that people did not talk about," he later wrote. "It was usually a family secret known only to the doctor."[13]

Banting's studies had been condensed because of the war and the great need for doctors, and in 1917, he arrived in England as part of the Canadian Army Medical Corps. One of his first jobs was research-based, working at the Granville Canadian Special Hospital for the esteemed Toronto surgeon Clarence Starr, where he recorded the details of patients undergoing nerve sutures due to problematic re-amputations or ununited fractures. He had to describe the limb's condition in detail before the operation, record the steps taken during the operation, and then describe the limb again once the work was done. The idea was that these cases would be followed for years to come, so that surgeons could acquire a deeper understanding of the long-term effects of a relatively new procedure. Banting considered it "extremely important" work, but soon he was moved to the front line with a field ambulance, where his skills became a more immediate matter of life and death. He later wrote of having a profound understanding, at this time, that his training and work were of real value to his fellow man. "It is on only rare occasions that a doctor can honestly feel that his skill has saved or prolonged a human life. A Battalion medical officer has this experience sometimes frequently.... The great disadvantage in this type of work was that the wounded men passed on to base hospitals and one never knew the results of [one's] work or what became of the men."[14]

Work with the field ambulance brought him close to *the mad alarms of battle,* so he was seeing not just the wounds but some of the action, too, and understanding the philosophy that many soldiers resorted to in the chaos of war: *there was nothing to do but keep on.* The wounds he was treating were brand new. To be the first doctor addressing them was a great responsibility for a young man recently graduated from medical school with a truncated education. Banting himself was wounded during this time. In the Battle of Cambrai, shrapnel from an exploding shell pierced his forearm, and though he kept working for many hours after being struck, the wound was a "blighty" that saw him shipped back to England.

Back in Canada after the war had ended, he was posted to the Dominion Orthopaedic Hospital for six months in 1919, and spent some of this time following up on the research he'd done for Dr. Starr at

Granville a couple of years earlier. Some men had fared remarkably well after their nerve sutures, though for others, the results had been disappointing. Still others couldn't be traced at all, so nothing was known of what had become of them. Conducting research seems to have been more interesting to Banting than the day-to-day treatment of patients, which, at Christie Street, was much like it had been at Granville. Notes on his army experience written years later mention a project undertaken with Robert Inkerman Harris, sun-god doctor to the roof ward patients, and how the two spent many hours in the pathology building at U of T experimenting with cartilage implants — the kind of work that might have helped rebuild Stewart Colquhoun's nose.

    After he was discharged from the army, Banting left Christie Street, just as many other staff members did, and he likely didn't imagine himself returning there. The war was over, and he was now a young civilian doctor embarking on his career. The following year, in London, Ontario, he began in private practice but had trouble earning a living, and often couldn't bring himself to charge for his services because his patients were usually poor. But lecturing at the university there was stimulating, and the reading he had to do in preparation for his talks furthered his own education. One of the articles got him thinking about the role of the pancreas in diabetes, and he became fixated on the idea of investigating the possibilities in a laboratory setting. The disease affected the body's ability to control blood sugar, which in turn harmed the organs, blood vessels, and nerves. There was no known cure, though newspaper ads sometimes suggested otherwise. One testimonial claimed, "I am sure I would be in my grave today, but for Dodd's Kidney Pills.... [They] have done so much for me that I feel like recommending them to everybody."[15]

    Visiting Toronto for the wedding of Clarence Starr's daughter, who'd been a nurse overseas and at Christie Street, Banting asked some medical colleagues who were also in attendance what they thought of him giving up private practice to embark on his research. "They all advised against such a radical move," he later recalled.[16] All of these men, like Banting and the bride, had strong connections to the Christie Street Hospital, and some of their photos show up in the *Illustrated Souvenir*.

They had all turned a corner in their careers because of war, and by now
had probably participated in more surgeries than the previous generation would have seen in their entire working lives. Against their advice,
Banting pushed his plan forward, and by the spring of 1921, his famous
work with Charles Best and a series of ill-fated dogs had begun at the
University of Toronto.

It was already understood that the pancreas played a role in process-
ing sugars, and that when a person became diabetic, something must be
amiss with that organ. The goal was to isolate what researchers suspected
was an internal secretion—some "mysterious substance"—within the
pancreas that regulated metabolism, and use it to treat dogs who'd
been rendered diabetic by pancreatectomy.[17] In the early experiments
by Banting and Best, dogs' pancreases were removed and ground up
to make a serum that hopefully contained the secretion. Having an
adequate supply of dogs was a problem and eventually, the pancreases
were obtained from cows and pigs at slaughterhouses.

Walter Campbell, a specialist in diabetes and a colleague of Banting's,
later wrote that "before the First World War, there were only two types
of diabetics, those who died quickly and those who stuck around
deteriorating for a long time."[18] Dietary controls were the main form of
treatment, but by no means a cure. People slipped into comas or died
of starvation—the most effective approach was a liquid diet that essentially starved the patient until the sugar disappeared from the urine.
The patient could begin to eat again in small but increasing quantities,
with all food strictly weighed and recorded, until the sugar reappeared.
This determined the patient's glucose tolerance level, and the diet that
would need to be followed.

The doctor Joe Gilchrist, a friend and classmate of Banting's during
medical school, would have understood his prognosis better than the
average patient when he was diagnosed with diabetes in 1917. By then
he was part of the Canadian Army Medical Corps, having reported for
duty, like Banting and the rest of their class, immediately after graduation. His yearbook entry states that he "plodded through the darkness
of Arts into the light of Medicine, where he will bask when the war is
o'er."[19] But Joe never made it overseas. Around the time that Banting set
sail, in March 1917, Joe experienced his first symptoms: extreme thirst,

frequent and abundant urination, a craving for sweets, weakness, and weight loss. Tests showed sugar present in the urine, and though his symptoms cleared up quickly when carbohydrates were removed from his diet, they came raging back when he returned to eating normally. "Immediately after eating even a slice of bread," one doctor noted in his record, "he shows 2% sugar in the urine." The recommended treatment was rest, fresh air, exercise, and an "anti diabetes diet" that quickly turned him gaunt and rangy.

So Joe Gilchrist's postwar condition saw him following these principles and heading "slowly downhill" on a nearly sugar-free diet until October 1921, when he contracted severe influenza that "shattered his tolerance."[20] The pounds began to fall away. He was thirsty and hungry. He grew steadily weaker and found it hard to work. The sugar was always present in his urine samples, and sometimes his breath smelled of acetone—a sharp, acrid, rotting fruit scent that was a clear sign of dangerously increased acidity in the blood and a poorly functioning metabolism.

At first he had no idea his illness coincided with his old classmate's current obsession, but shortly after his bout with influenza, news of Banting and Best's research began burbling in medical circles. They gave a talk at U of T in November and another at Toronto General Hospital in December, so perhaps Joe Gilchrist was in attendance, hanging on every word. As a 1923 account puts it, he approached Banting around this time "in a fit of despair...to beg for a shot of the new preparation."[21] Even if he hadn't been diabetic, he would have thought the work exciting, but his own medical history added a profound layer to his interest in the research, and he was eager to be what he called a "human rabbit" for the cause. Joe was given an oral dose, probably because the extract hadn't been tried on humans yet, and injection was considered too risky. All involved were no doubt anxious to see what would happen. But the outcome was disappointing. Fred wrote in his notes, "Dec 20. Phoned Joe Gilchrist—gave him extract that we knew to be potent.—by mouth. empty stomach. Dec 21—no beneficial result."[22]

Within a month, though, there was major progress when the extract —tinkered with and vastly improved by a biochemist named James Collip—was given by injection to a teenage boy wasting away at Toronto

General Hospital. Weighing sixty-five pounds on admission, the boy was considered so near death that even the wildest experiment gave him more of a chance than doing nothing. To see a body so utterly transformed was astonishing. It was as though a magic potion had travelled through him and brought him back to life. As the serum was tried on more patients in more places, the amazement spread, and pressure mounted to make the medicine widely available. American diabetes specialist Elliott Joslin likened the serum's effect to "near resurrections," and had high hopes for his own patients, who were wasting away on starvation diets in a diabetic clinic in Boston.

These were thrilling times for people involved in the development and production of insulin. The sense of urgency around the affair sparked plenty of collaboration, infighting, selflessness, and ego as the work evolved and various doctors and scientists helped perfect, produce, and deliver the treatment. A hundred years later, the spotlight still shines brightest on Fred Banting, though he was far from the lone player: along with doctors, academics, and pharmaceutical companies, the drama enfolded nurses, orderlies, dietitians, patients, and patients' families—and also veterans newly returned from the First World War.

By the spring of 1922, a clinical trial at Christie Street had been arranged, and diabetic soldiers were being recruited into the ward. Joe, with Banting, was a supervising doctor as well as a patient participant. The men were lucky the illness had surfaced in wartime, if "luck" can be used in connection with such a damaging disease. Those who'd fallen ill during service were entitled to free health care, so this group was in the right place at the right time to receive ground-breaking treatment that had taken on the qualities of a miracle. As ordinary soldiers, they knew what it was like to be *hungry, cold and tired*, and then to have that discomfort compounded by illness. And yet, knowing the treatment was experimental may also have made them wary. Each patient signed a declaration stating that the treatment had been thoroughly explained to him, and that he understood it hadn't yet reached "a stage of finality" —that the work involved an element of risk, and that "it is not yet fully known just what the treatment will do."[23] But for the most part the men at the Christie Street clinic were severe diabetics, like Joe Gilchrist, and therefore faced either "a downhill progression to a diabetic coma, or a slow starvation."[24] *They did not wish to die.* One man was already in a coma when admitted, and another weighed a frightening seventy-six pounds.

The men ranged in age from twenty-five to fifty-three, and as on the rooftop, there seems to have been a cheerful camaraderie in their ward. Following a complete physical and the establishment of the proper diet and insulin levels for each patient, they were monitored closely by the medical staff and the dietitians. Ideally, the men received their injections three times a day, though at this early stage, there were still major challenges in producing enough of the extract and obtaining a pure, effective product. When they could get their shots, many of the patients "suffer[ed] horribly with large abscesses in the hips-buttocks," according to a colleague of Banting's who visited the ward.[25] A strong brew of the extract caused more severe side effects, but a weaker strain meant large doses that were more painful to receive. As the doctor-patient, Gilchrist took the first sample of each batch, according to Banting, and followed up with regular blood sugar examinations. "I doubt if there is a person in the world who has had his veins punctured so many times. He had abscesses at the site of injection on many occasions, but he took his injections regularly and persistently."[26] The inconsistency of the treatment, and the pain involved with the injections, seems to have made men reluctant to join the study as it inched forward. "But then an event occurred," wrote Banting, "which surprised and encouraged everyone.... One of the faithful lads asked for leave. This was a most unusual request. He also wanted insulin to take with him. He was intelligent and could look after himself & his requests were granted. On the following Monday morning he returned all smiles, 'For the first time in three years I am a man again,' he told everyone. Severe untreated diabetics lose all sex desire. With insulin the desire and power returned. By night every diabetic in the hospital was asking for insulin."

Jim Ostrom was one of the younger patients.[27] After the *shrapnel screams* at Vimy Ridge in April 1917, *when spring came around again and the first meadow-flowers appeared,* he entered hospital in Boulogne with an illness that doctors couldn't quite pinpoint. He was nervous and tired—not surprising considering his placement at the front and his rank of signaller. Signallers kept the communication flowing to and from the front lines, laying cables in the trenches and constantly repairing them when they were blown apart by shellfire or broken by soldiers' boots. Signallers also encoded and decoded messages, or they carried them in person, travelling through the trenches when technological means of communication failed. For defensive purposes, trenches were dug in a zigzag pattern, making short distances much longer. Sometimes these missions took a soldier into the wide open, where he risked sniper fire or being buried by a shell explosion; or he travelled further afield, *through deep night under a cloudy, moonless sky*, crossing territory he didn't know and memorizing the landscape for the return trip. Even the shortest journeys overland put a man at great risk, so it was common that two or three soldiers were sent out with the same message but travelling different routes, "so that one at least will be certain to arrive."[28] The men had to have stamina and good instincts for such potentially dangerous missions, just like the dogs and pigeons who were their counterparts in the communications realm.

Fit and healthy when he'd enlisted, now Jim experienced palpitations, vertigo, and dyspnea—also known as "air hunger," meaning he gasped for breath on the slightest exertion. He was invalided to England, where he was diagnosed with "disordered action of the heart," sometimes called "soldier's heart," an ailment thought to be brought on by stress and exhaustion rather than organic disease.[29] He was moved to a couple of different hospitals before landing in a convalescent home in Bushy Park, a park with royal designation that neighboured the splendid Hampton Court Palace on the outskirts of London.

If he felt well enough to enjoy it, this was surely a wonderful place to be, with a river that fed cascading pools and a waterfall, deer roaming beneath huge chestnut trees, and birds chirping in the woodlands. One patient, convalescing at Bushy Park around the same time as Jim, wrote to his family back home that "we could not be situated in a prettier or more interesting place."[30] The palace sat just south of the park, along the River Thames, and soldiers could visit for free whenever it was open. It was a popular destination for soldiers recovering at other hospitals in and around London as well, or for troops passing through, and great numbers turned up for tours of the historic site. The hospital grounds

Jim Ostrom and Grace Parliament, early 1920s
(Courtesy the Ostrom family)

were quieter, but there were bursts of excitement, as when a buck with
a "magnificent pair of antlers" leaped over the railing and onto the
verandah, and just as quickly was gone again, into the woods of the park.

The hospital specialized in heart cases, which was what Jim Ostrom
was thought to be at that time, and according to the war diary, patients
mostly responded well to treatment, which involved convalescing on
the verandah and engaging in physical therapy. But after forty days
at Bushy, Jim had not improved. "General condition not good. He has
not reacted well to exercises." He was returned to Canada, and back in
Toronto, an examination revealed "Man cannot walk one mile without
resting at intervals." Running for a streetcar set his heart racing and
his lungs heaving for air. These were surely symptoms of what was later
determined to be diabetes. There's no record of exactly when Jim was

diagnosed, but a family story says that he was a young, fit man when he went to war; that he was buried in a shell explosion; and that after this his rapid decline began, so it seemed to him that war had somehow caused his illness.

By 1921 he was living a little west of the Christie Street Hospital and working as a mail clerk. His health was poor at this point, and his thirst was insatiable. He'd fill a big glass milk bottle with water each night before bed, and by morning it was empty. There was nothing other than the restrictive diet to control his symptoms, but even with the illness, the period must have been somewhat joyful, for he'd fallen in love with a young woman named Grace, who lived in the Christie Street neighbourhood as well and worked at Eaton's department store. There's a feeling among Jim's descendants that Grace's family didn't approve of the match, perhaps because Jim was unwell and his future therefore in question. But you wouldn't guess at his frailty on seeing a photo of Jim and Grace from the time: Jim wears a flat cap and civvies, his sleeves rolled up; he's lifted Grace on to one shoulder, and she perches there, smiling and leaning into him, with her hands folded at his collarbone. They married about a week after the emaciated boy, Leonard Thompson, received his transformative injection of insulin. It isn't known whether Jim volunteered to be part of the trial at Christie Street or if the doctors brought him in, already aware of his condition and knowing he'd be a good candidate. Either way, he and Grace must have felt hopeful that what the press was calling "one of the most important discoveries in modern medical research" would make a difference in their lives.[31] Even as medicine for a debilitating disease, insulin seemed miraculous, but many believed it might be a permanent cure—that with enough injections, the body might relearn the ability to regulate blood sugar.

The dose was hard to get right, especially at that time, when the qualities of insulin being produced were variable. Just before Christmas in 1922, Joe Gilchrist delivered a lecture describing a case of hypoglycemia brought on by the administration of too large a dose. The man—Jim Ostrom—had received his injection in the late afternoon, as usual, then gone down to the hospital dining room and eaten a hearty meal, "but by 8 o'clock he evinced a strong desire to climb up the walls of the ward."[32] It must have been an awful sensation. The first sign of a hypoglycemic reaction was "an unaccountable anxiety and a feeling of impending trouble associated with restlessness." After that, the patient would start to sweat and then feel an overwhelming craving for food—"bulk of any kind" would do.[33] Then the trembling would start, the skin would turn pale, the pulse would race and the pupils dilate. As the blood pressure dropped, the patient would feel faint and lose the ability to concentrate and call up names and ordinary words. Without the ingestion of glucose to relieve the symptoms—which Jim quickly received at Christie—convulsions and coma could follow.

Some of this was known because of experiments on animals. When the *Star* reported on Joe's lecture, it also detailed experiments done on rabbits that had been intentionally sent into convulsions with overdoses of insulin. They grew so hungry they devoured wood shavings; their eyes bulged; they panted and jerked themselves around; they grew rigid and comatose. The experiments confirmed that sugar was an effective antidote. When news of the story reached an animal rights activist, she contacted the local Great War Veterans' Association and urged them to join the antivivisectionist fight and protest the inhumane treatment of soldiers at the hospital, which in turn prompted the *Star* to investigate.

Joe Gilchrist invited the reporter to visit the Christie Street clinic and meet the patients for himself, nine of them at that time. One—a man named Doherty—claimed that he'd been close to comatose when he'd entered the hospital, and "almost literally a mass of skin and bones." The doctors thought that he'd die within a few days, but since then he'd gained twenty-five pounds, and his skin, once "dry and brown like that of a mummy," was now fresh and pink. "His eyes sparkle, and he declares that he is fit for anything."[34] All of the men spoke of weight gain and renewed energy, but also a sense of hope. Said one: "It's given me a chance for my life."

Jim Ostrom had been discharged from Christie Street by this time, and carried on as an outpatient, but the *Star* reporter went along to his home with Grace just a few blocks away from the hospital to ask about the overdose that had sent him climbing the walls of the ward. "Mr. Ostrom admitted having had certain pronounced reactions, but added: 'I would be willing to climb the CPR building if I could get the benefit that I got from the treatment.'"

In the specially equipped laboratory at Christie Street, the men were taught how to test their own blood and urine for sugar levels, check the strength of the insulin, and administer their own doses. They knew to always carry a bit of candy, and to carefully monitor their diet; they even took turns preparing meals with the dietitians. The diabetic menu at the hospital—presided over by Bertha, Marjorie, and Doris—was something like oatmeal, bacon, and eggs at breakfast, then beef, cauliflower, tomatoes, and a salad at lunch, with "orange snow" for dessert, and then poached eggs for dinner, with string beans, rhubarb, and "diabetic jelly." Before they left to marry, Marjorie and Doris published a cookbook called *Diabetic Diet*, which offered seventy-five simple recipes as well as details about how to weigh food and determine its nutritional value and where to find unusual ingredients. It was a printed and bound version of the material that Christie Street soldiers received when they were ready to leave the diabetic clinic, and included a preface—or perhaps a seal of approval—by Joe Gilchrist and Fred Banting.

The work of the dietitians was "intimately allied with treatment," according to the doctors in charge, and seems to have been appreciated, though the women were very much in the background as the discovery shone in the press and researchers fought for the spotlight.[35] What was it like to participate in this medical miracle, calculating nutrients and watching the patients grow steadily fatter and happier, "rescued from a lingering death"?[36] Doris McHenry's step-grandson says she always spoke with pride of this brief, exhilarating period, believing she'd had "a direct relationship" with the work, the researchers, and their subjects. It remained a high point in her long life to have witnessed such change in the patients. Those who'd struggled to climb a flight of stairs could now walk two or three miles a day with no trouble. With the other men at Christie Street, they took part in workshops and tried to outdo each other with their creations. The effect of the insulin was so noticeable that strangers who visited the ward—medical experts from other cities and countries—said they could tell at a glance which patients had begun receiving injections and which ones hadn't started their treatment.

But as on the roof ward, there were losses. Some of the men were so unwell when they arrived that there was just no saving them. They had

weakened hearts or tuberculosis, or other complications that persisted
even when the insulin successfully regulated their blood sugar. The deaths
must have been a blow to both the caregivers and the fellow "rabbits"
—Jim Ostrom, doctor Joe, and the rest—who would have worried about
their own chances for survival.

Jim's fellow patient Ogden Besserer was twenty-eight when he was
conscripted in 1917.[37] He'd been managing the fur department of a
popular shop in Ottawa; he wasn't married, and he was young and relatively fit, according to his medical examination. On his paternal side, he
was of German extraction, but his family, mixed with French Canadians,
had been in Canada for generations, and his grandfather had owned
great swathes of land in Ottawa and named streets after family members. By the First World War, the area that had once been Besserer
property was a bustling neighbourhood called Sandy Hill. When his
younger brother Theodore voluntarily enlisted in 1915, Ogden kept
on with his job, perhaps because he knew his health was fragile. At age
twenty-two, just before the war began, another brother had died in a
diabetic coma; and a family history of diabetes was noted in Theodore's
service record. The first great loss had happened in Ogden's childhood,
when his mother, also a diabetic, died at thirty-two.

Ogden travelled overseas early in 1918, and after training in England
he proceeded to France in September, when the war was close to ending.
He was a driver, charged with delivering ammunition to the front
line, and though he made it through the war unscathed, just before
Christmas in 1918, when he was still overseas, he entered a casualty
clearance station, complaining of double vision. The problem had come
on suddenly and persisted. In medical terms, it was called "diplopia,"
and while it was sometimes noted in shell-shock cases, especially those
with concussion, it can also be a symptom of diabetes, when damage to
circulation causes a sort of palsy in the muscles that control eye movement. The muscles of one eye stop working, and the two together can't
align and send a cohesive message to the brain. If Ogden was still working as a driver at this time, his job would have been impossible, and if
the symptoms came on when he was behind the wheel, they would have
been especially alarming. But "with treatment"—probably rest and a
patch over the eye—the symptoms subsided during the next six weeks,

and Ogden returned to Canada. It's impossible to know if he suspected diabetes, but it seems likely. During his time in the army, he requested a portion of his earnings, separation pay usually reserved for wives and family, go to a woman named Laura Blake, listed only as "friend" in his record. Laura was a single woman who worked as a government stenographer. Did they hesitate to marry because of Ogden's illness?

After his discharge from the army, he returned to his old job at the furrier's, which he'd begun at the age of fourteen. But over the next year, he developed sores on his chin and the back of his neck, and he grew weak and thin. Doctors diagnosed diabetes, and he was hospitalized in Ottawa as his disease quickly progressed. At one point he received less than four hundred calories a day, "obviously way below his body requirements," but necessary, the doctors thought, to control his metabolism.[38] He suffered recurring attacks of diarrhea and edema, a swelling in his face, legs, and ankles. His symptoms were so persistent that one doctor wondered if someone was sneaking in food for him, since "the mathematics of diabetic feeding" just didn't add up. The doctor added that "the man's morale is badly shaken and this idea should not militate against him." The Ottawa doctors felt they couldn't offer him the specialized care he needed, nor monitor his condition closely enough, but there was little improvement after a stay in Elliott Joslin's Boston clinic. Joslin would go on to become a world leader in the treatment of diabetes, but at this time he, too, implemented the starvation treatment, training patients to manage their condition by diet. The work was heartbreaking, and he followed news of encouraging developments in Toronto from the earliest days. "Naturally if there is a grain of hopefulness in these experiments which I can give to patients," he wrote in a 1921 letter to Banting's supervisor that "it would afford much comfort, not only to them, but to me as well, because I see so many pathetic cases."

By the spring of 1922, Ogden Besserer was "markedly undernourished" and weighed 110 pounds, 40 pounds less than when he'd left the army a few years earlier. News of the insulin trials must have offered a welcome spark of hope. "Arrangements are being made," states his record, "to have this man admitted to Christie Street Hospital, Toronto, so that Dr. Banting's treatment may be tried."

In June, Ogden joined the rest of the men on the diabetic ward. He was in rough shape upon admission, with clusters of boils, skin infections, and abscessed gums. Though he was emaciated, the swelling in his legs and face persisted. To add to his discomfort, the hospital's proximity to a railway meant that the building shook when trains went past. He didn't sleep well, and sometimes suffered night sweats that soaked his pyjamas and made him cold and clammy. Despite his placement in a pioneering trial, he continued to falter. Joe Gilchrist jotted down that Ogden's muscle mass had diminished, and that he experienced "loss of memory, loss of interest in things generally." Doses of the extract seemed to help some days but not others, and by September he was so unwell that injections were stopped, and he was moved to a private ward. He ached all over. His vision blurred. He was unable to distinguish between people he knew, though the record doesn't specify if family or the friend named Laura were among his visitors. By the time of his death at age thirty-three—around the age his mother had died—he weighed 96 pounds. The secrecy around the illness, which Banting wrote about in later years, shows in the obituary that appeared in the *Ottawa Citizen*: Ogden had been undergoing "special treatment" at the Christie Street Hospital, the piece said, but "died as the result of illness contracted by over-exposure at the front during the war."[39] The word diabetes was not mentioned.

Ogden was the last of four diabetics to die at Christie that month. Of the earlier deaths, two were recent admissions to the hospital; the third, a brewer's labourer, left behind a wife and five children living in poverty. Following a sweltering city summer with major problems in insulin production, these losses must have demoralized the whole diabetic team. That first summer during the clinical trials at Christie Street, Banting wrote to Best that "worse than the heat as a disturbance is that diabetics swarm around from all over and think that we can conjure the extract from the ground."[40] Desperate souls even showed up at the lab, hoping to get insulin, though at that time the sporadically available doses were all going to the veterans. Soon the trials expanded further, to Toronto General Hospital and the Hospital for Sick Children, and the work continued at Christie Street, with Joe Gilchrist in charge and Banting and Best in high demand elsewhere.

By the summer of 1923, insulin was being used in the United States, England, the Netherlands, China, and Australia. There were articles raving about patients being "brought back from the very threshold of death," so it was not surprising when, later that year, Banting and John Macleod, his supervisor at the University of Toronto, received the Nobel Prize in Medicine, and in turn shared the award with Charles Best and James Collip.[41] The discovery made the men famous, and could have made them rich, too, but rather than profit personally, the team sold the patent to the University of Toronto for one dollar, and the university set up committees that would oversee its use internationally, avoiding monopolization and ensuring the drug was affordable and widely available. The system remained in place until the 1950s. Today, even in Canada, many diabetics can't afford the full cost of their treatment, and ration their use of insulin.

Banting didn't live to see the changes. In 1941, he died in a plane crash, making headlines once again as a hero and a "great benefactor of mankind."[42] In 1934, he'd been knighted for his accomplishments—a doctor, a Sir, and a Nobel laureate all at once. One wonders how Joe Gilchrist felt during Banting's glory days, remaining in the shadows, yet having played such an integral part in the development of a medicine that would save so many lives worldwide. "It was on him," Banting himself had written shortly before his death, "that we tried not only new batches of insulin . . . but also many experiments that had to be carried out, for example, the time in relation to meals, the distribution of dosage, the treatment for overdose."[43]

In 1951, Joe was admitted to Sunnybrook Hospital, which had by then replaced Christie Street. He was in his late fifties, his legs, arms, and buttocks scarred from years of insulin injections. His pension record states that he'd controlled his diabetes well on his own until shortly before his admission, when he started having chest pain and shortness of breath that caused him to speak "in gasps."[44] The record also notes a separation from his wife, and an ongoing battle with mental illness following his years at Christie Street. "Since the early 30s, he has been over active mentally and physically having an obsessive-compulsive behaviour with grandiose ideas. . . . He is very talkative and keeps on referring about his research he did back in the early 30s. He has the true mental activity of a manic depressive. His thought processes are disjointed and mixed with delusions of importance and influence with occasional paranoidal ideas." Joe rallied for a time and was discharged, but returned to Sunnybrook that same year, "in gross cardiac failure." He died soon after, of heart disease caused by diabetes. A *Globe and Mail* obituary acknowledged that he'd been "the first walking diabetic patient to receive the insulin treatment," and also "a personal friend of Sir Frederick Banting and Dr. C.H. Best."[45] But there was no mention of the clinic he'd run at Christie Street, and his vital role as both patient and doctor.

Unlike his doctor, Jim Ostrom lived a relatively long life, raising two sons with Grace in a pleasant neighbourhood in the east end of Toronto. *The years had given them kindness.* He continued to work as a postal clerk, and took excellent care of his health, eating well and rising early each morning to boil his single insulin needle. His son Ron, now in his nineties, recalls that his father always carried butterscotch candies when they went on drives, and that he had his own mini lab in the basement of their home: as taught at Christie Street, he'd pee into a test tube, heat the urine and a chemical reagent over a Bunsen burner, and measure his glucose level by colour the solution turned, which told him how much insulin he needed. Despite scrupulous self-care, he sometimes went into diabetic shock: as the family sat at the dinner table, "the knife and fork would start rattling," Ron recalls, and Grace would have to get Jim to the floor and "get the o.j. into him." Half an orange usually sufficed when he had an insulin reaction, but occasionally he worsened and slipped into a coma and had to be rushed to hospital.

And yet, Jim outlived Grace, who suffered two massive strokes and died in her fifties. He stayed on alone in their home for a while, but once, in the throes of an insulin reaction, he started hammering on the wall shared with his neighbour, who called Jim's son Lloyd in a panic. After that, Jim had a live-in caregiver for a time, and eventually moved into Sunnybrook, like his doctor Joe. He remained there until his death at almost eighty years old. By then, Walter Dunn, Arwood Fortner, and Tom Ronaldson had also died at Sunnybrook; and Stewart Colquhoun, recognizable by his ever-present bandage, had made regular visits from northern Ontario over the years. When Jim entered the hospital, the old nurse Win Hammell was living out her last demented days, with regular visits from the sister who always wore hat and gloves for the occasion. Did the aging patients of Christie Street sometimes recognize each other at Sunnybrook, where the wards were named after battlefields and fighter planes, just as the trenches had been named for places back home? What did it mean to be nostalgic for a period in your life that contained so much horror and tragedy? Jim's granddaughter Anne says that like most vets, he didn't really talk about the war to his family. But perhaps he did at Sunnybrook, where the memories had a different context. Every Saturday Anne's father, Lloyd, would travel out to Sunnybrook, pick up Jim and bring him home for a roast beef dinner and a game of cribbage. "I think of him whenever I smell a cigar or have an Orange Crush," Anne remembers. And when asked if she knew of Jim's early involvement with insulin, she answers yes: "I would not be alive if not for the discovery."

The Last Post

As the years rolled on, the "temporary" hospital became a fixture in the urban landscape, but its origins as a factory were not forgotten, and the building and the people in it grew older. Though many of the doctors and nurses who'd been an instrumental part of the hospital's beginnings left in those first years—Charles McVicar, Win Hammell, Mabel Lucas—others settled in for a long career. Charles McMane, who'd taken over from McVicar in the early 1920s, stayed on until retirement in 1945, and the long-time matron of the hospital, Annie Hartley, stepped down from her post after fifteen years in the position, relinquishing her role only when she had to. Highly decorated from her long war service and holding the rank of captain, she was "forced by ill health to resign," according to the *Globe*'s tribute. "Her breakdown is attributed, in part, at least, to the tirelessness with which she—herself a war hero—has pursued her work on behalf of men broken in war.... Miss Hartley devoted thirty-seven years to nursing, twenty-one of them on behalf of war wounded."[1]

Some of those wounded never left the hospital, and began to resemble the cartoons that soldiers had drawn years earlier, depicting themselves as perpetual patients with long beards and wrinkles. Patients who had been discharged came back periodically for lengthy stays. Others were outpatients from far and near. In the summer of 1925, when Field Marshal Douglas Haig visited the Christie Street Hospital, his photo was taken on the rooftop with a bedridden patient wearing a visor to keep the sun out of his eyes. The caption reads "Earl Haig chatting with Ojibway Indian."[2] John Spaniel comes to mind, though this man is certainly not him, and looks rounder and younger than John does in the *Illustrated Souvenir* photos. Whoever he is, what was it like to be at Christie so long after the war, with Earl Haig at your bedside? Haig had been commander of the British Expeditionary Force during those lethal battles where so many men had died: the Somme, Arras, Passchendaele. What was it like to have him lean in close to you and lock eyes as he asked after your health? An honour and a privilege? A fright? Or just another day in the sunshine back on Christie's rooftop ward?

A little more than a year later, in 1926, a man returning to the institution for a slight operation on an old wound found it to be a nostalgic experience in a cheerful atmosphere, despite so many patients there fighting a long and ultimately losing battle. Upon reporting, he had his bath, climbed into his regulation pyjamas and dressing gown, and got into bed. An orderly appeared, loaded him on to the "agony wagon," and wheeled him up to the operating theatre, where his stump was shaved and washed with green soap, and then "anointed with turpentine." He returned to bed to await his operation the following morning, and over the next hours he observed the "merry repartee that was bandied to and fro round the room." Any man taken out for his operation was "jollied along" by the others, who offered advice freely and jokingly inquired how to dispose of the fellow's belongs should he not return. "The routine is practically the same as in the old war days, and the Sisters are just as devoted to their charges as they were then. The same back rubs with alcohol, the same baths in bed.... The same old routine when the dressing or agony wagon comes around, the same irrigations, carrell's tubes and all the other paraphernalia of wound dressing, and the same old MO looking over the cases and deciding what is to be done."[3]

Whenever the facial patient Stewart Colquhoun travelled south from Krugerdorf for his appointments at Christie Street through the 1920s, '30s and '40s, he visited with his old friend Percy Rimmell.[4] The hospital was home for Percy, something he never would have imagined when he was first discharged from the army. At Ypres, in the frenzy of a bayonet charge, he'd been wounded by a machine-gun bullet, and as he lay waiting to be found by stretcher bearers, he was "overcome with gas poison." His record suggests a thorough recovery from these wounds, and also from a bout of Spanish flu contracted in the third wave. He was a survivor, and he declared "no disability" when he left the army in the spring of 1919.

That June, when the hospital patients were lining up for their panoramic portrait at Christie Street, Percy was a free man. He placed an ad in the *Toronto Star*, distinguishing himself as not just a returned soldier but one who'd signed up in 1914, an "old original" of the first contingent who now wished employment as either a warehouse clerk or a timekeeper. He was a tall, well-developed man with good hearing and good vision, and he found work with the Hydro-Electric Power Commission not long after he placed the ad. The demand for electric power had rapidly increased during the war, and a massive generating station was being constructed in Niagara Falls. A visiting reporter described the startling spectacle of clamshell dredges sinking into the water and pulling out great bites of riverbed, as well as boulders that were broken down by a stone crusher. On land, huge electric shovels scooped up the mud and clay, swinging it through the air and depositing it into boxcars, and the trains in turn carried the load off to a dump nearby. The gangs of men at work on the busy site painted a "striking picture" that only briefly included Percy Rimmell. Shortly after starting the job, he was jammed under a boxcar, his head and knees rammed together, fracturing his spine just below the rib cage and causing complete paralysis from there down. Early on, it was obvious that he would need care for the rest of his life. He entered Euclid Hall, the convalescent hospital located in a mansion on Jarvis Street, which since 1917 had looked after a small number of men considered "almost completely helpless,"[5] and who would continue to require more constant care than men in other military hospitals.

Within a couple of years he was moved to Christie Street, where eventually all the Euclid men would go, but since his wounds were not war-related, an arrangement was made with the Hydro-Electric Power Commission to cover the cost of his care. A string of entries in his record made by medical staff over the years shows he was usually "doing well" and that his condition rarely changed, though there were sometimes flare-ups in the original wound or short bouts of illness. "He leads a fairly comfortable life," one doctor wrote, noting that he was up and about in a wheelchair. Later entries even mention a specially rigged automobile that he could take out for drives. He seemed "contented and happy," and sometimes took short leaves at Christmas or Easter, probably to visit family, and always in the company of a nurse. For two years in a row, he went to the Toronto Islands in summer, travelling over by ferry and spending a couple of months in a convalescent home set up at the lakeside especially for so-called incurables. Given Christie Street's proximity to the train tracks and to surrounding industry, the fresh breeze and the slow pace of the island, *ringed about with shining waters*, must have been a welcome change.

The constant sameness was perhaps the most difficult thing for long-term patients. In the mid-1920s, a writer in *The Fragment*, a magazine published by the War Amputations Society, acknowledged the misery of such men. Though there were fewer patients now, and though the writer believed they were getting great care, "The [military] hospitals are no less painful institutions than they were during the great peak of 1920. Christie Street Hospital is lonelier and more cut off from the world than it ever was. Faithful societies, organizations and individuals still serve the veterans who have borne their wounds and their virtual imprisonment for ten years or more. But no amount of visitors can create even the illusion of freedom."[6]

What was it like, then, another twenty years on, when a new generation of soldier-patients had filled up the empty beds, and the original patients, by contrast, looked like old men? By the autumn of 1947, Percy Rimmell was nearly sixty, a fringe of white hair ringing his bald spot. Physically, he was showing more frailty. He had repeated kidney

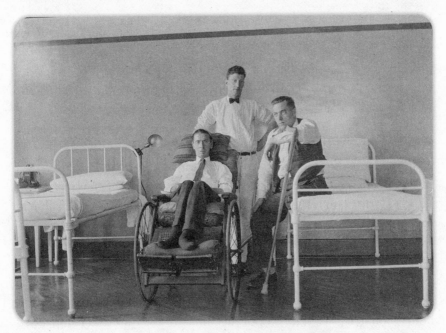

Christie Street patients and orderly, 1930
(City of Toronto Archives, Fond 1256, Item 19056)

infections and frequent, painful bed sores, and the fracture in his spine was breaking down again. He sometimes went mysteriously comatose. Suspicions raised, a nurse reported that on several occasions she'd gone to waken Percy between 7 and 8 a.m. and couldn't rouse him, "even by the most vigorous efforts." An orderly claimed the same, and said that when Percy did wake up, his speech was slurred and his pupils widely dilated; he soon lapsed back into unconsciousness while being readied for the day. He perspired freely during these incidents, his coronary reflex was absent, and his breathing was "of the Cheyne Stokes type," a cyclical pattern of deep, fast breathing sinking to slow, shallow inhalations or periods of apnea where no breaths were taken at all. When a doctor examined him he found nothing untoward, and Percy denied anything unusual had happened and claimed "the Orderlies were trying to pin something on him."

By the following spring, his health continued to decline, and another round of suspicious symptoms occurred. "He is deeply stuporous with starey eyes and is only partially able to follow simple instructions.... There is some question of this patient taking analgesic and hypnotic drugs on his own with procurement from an orderly who comes in from the outside to fix him up." Percy denied taking anything, but five capsules were found in his wallet and another stuck in his armpit, and over the next weeks his condition continued to cause increasing concern. "This morning he is mildly confused, speech is slurring and extremities are cold. He states that pills and capsules have been brought to him; but he will not reveal the source. However, he volunteers the information that he will not, in the future, take any drugs not ordered by the staff of this ward. It is difficult to determine how much of his mental state is due to barbiturate intoxication and how much is due to organic deterioration." It was hard to know *why* he was taking the drugs as well: to assuage physical pain or depression?

Despite the staff watching him closely, somehow the pills kept coming. "White pearls" were found in his bed, and a small bottle of pills in his room. He was "semi-stuporous" much of the time and complained of pains all over his body. He began to refuse food and drink, and it became clear that he was terminally ill, and that death would come in a matter of days. When he died on April 30, 1948, *released from time and sense of great or small*, there were only trace amounts of barbiturates found in his system. Death was due, in the end, to kidney failure, paraplegia, and fracture of the spine.

Not all of the so-called incurables lived out their days in the hospital. Like Percy, Curley Christian had been a patient at Euclid Hall before moving to Christie Street, but in his wife Cleo he had a steadfast advocate who helped him change the trajectory of his life.[7] They met when Curley was still in hospital, recovering from multiple wounds sustained in the Battle of Vimy Ridge.

Curley was a Black man, born in the United States, who'd travelled widely throughout South and North America by the time he enlisted with the Canadian Army in November 1915. He was about thirty, and had worked a number of different jobs as he'd wandered: he'd been a cook, a hairdresser, a hotel porter, a bricklayer, and even a semi-pro baseball player, but listed chain-maker as his occupation when he joined up in Selkirk, Manitoba. Since the war's first days, many Black men had been turned away when they tried to enlist in the army. Racism was widespread, and as with Indigenous and Asian recruits, it was thought that white soldiers wouldn't want to fight and live out the war with non-whites; that mixed-race units would look like "a chequer-board army."[8] So many young, fit, and capable Black men were being turned away that eventually an all-Black battalion was raised to put the men to good use — this "construction battalion" wouldn't participate in battle, but instead dig trenches, build and repair infrastructure, and retrieve bodies from the battlefield. But Black soldiers did fight. Since there was no official policy against particular races, "the final approval of any man, regardless of colour or other distinction, must of course rest with the officer commanding the particular unit which the man in question is desirous of joining."[9] Curley was among a small number of Black soldiers who were folded into "white battalions."

On the first day of the battle, he and a group of fellow soldiers were charged with picking up supplies. According to a family story, he joked with the others that he could get to their destination faster on foot than they could by supply truck. A bet was made, and Curley was off running. He did beat them — but then he was struck by shellfire and buried in a trench. "The earth caved in on me," he later said, "and I was planted like a tree in the ground."[10] The sound of war was muffled, then, so it seemed that even *the birds, like secret thoughts, lay still.* Trapped beneath rubble, he lost consciousness and slept through *a slow-gathering darkness overhead.* For two days, all four of his limbs were crushed, impeding his circulation, and the gunshot wounds in his hands and feet began to fester. When stretcher bearers finally found him, dug him out, and began to carry him off for treatment, they themselves were struck and killed, and again Curley lay helpless, his wounds worsening. Another team retrieved him, but gangrene was already spreading so furiously that Curley lost part of all four limbs. He is thought to be the only quadruple amputee to have survived the war.

More than 7,000 Canadians were wounded at Vimy Ridge, and more than 3,500 died. That Curley survived first the injuries, then the attack that killed his rescuers, and then the surgeries to his traumatized body is astonishing. Years later, a *Star* reporter would call him "the man who refused to die."[11] But Curley himself would probably say that the most fortuitous event of his life happened after all of that, when he was back in Toronto in the hospital.

There are differing versions of how Curley Christian met Cleo MacPherson. One, conveyed by a reporter in 1936 as the couple travelled by ship to attend the unveiling of the Vimy Ridge memorial, says that theirs was a "war romance" — that Cleo was a young woman working in Toronto, happy going to parties and dancing in her spare time, when a friend invited her to visit Curley in the hospital, just as Florence Leggett and her friends had visited patients like Stewart Colquhoun. Born in Jamaica, Cleo had come to Canada with her family via England a year before the war began. When she met Curley, she "felt sorry...for the man who had not seen his colored folks in the south for nearly a score of years," and she began to visit him regularly. They were married in 1920. "I knew when I married Curley what I was doing," Cleo told the reporter. "But I've never regretted it. I alone look after him. Everything that's done for him, I do, shaving, bathing, dressing, and even driving his car. But we're so happy."[12]

Cleo's work on Curley's behalf actually had a profound effect on the lives of other veterans too, according to Cliff Chadderton, long-time CEO of the War Amps.

> [Curley] was in Christie Street Hospital in Toronto, costing the government a fair amount of money to keep him there. His wife went to the director of the hospital and she said, "Curley is very unhappy. Now," she said, "I can take him home and I can look after him, but it would mean that I can't do anything else." And she was a scrub-woman. That's how she earned her living, you see. They were not wealthy people. But she said, "I can take him home, but...somehow or other, the government has got to pay some money for this." Well, the director of the Christie Street Hospital immediately wrote a memorandum to the then-minister. ...and he said, "This sounds like a good financial deal."

The Attendance Allowance, as it came to be known, is still in place today, an impressive legacy for a working-class couple who were immigrants to Canada. But there are sparks of magic about Curley and Cleo's story that somehow make their accomplishments unsurprising. In retrospect, it seems a given that they would withstand *the world's darkness*, that their lives would be rich with *lovely, joyful things*. "Blithe and gay of spirit," wrote one reporter at a convention for amputees, "they are the centre of attraction in every group of Amps in which they mingle."[13] In July 1936, they were among a crowd of fifty thousand when King Edward VIII officially unveiled the Vimy memorial, a mournful stone structure soaring up from the old battlefield and visible for miles around. Edward had become king earlier that year—a short-lived reign that would be over by December—and was still beloved by veterans who'd appreciated his presence at the front. Fond of informal encounters with his subjects, like the one he'd had at Christie Street years earlier, he moved through the massive crowd, greeting people before delivering his speech. Curley stood two rows deep in the throng, behind a double line of guards, but Edward spotted him, and said to the army general next to him, "I know that man." He pushed through the rows, toward Curley, and grasped his arm. "Hallo! I saw you in Toronto eighteen years ago!"[14] A reporter described the exchange, and how Curley was "obviously delighted" at the king's recognition. "The King then asked him how he had been getting on. Before the conversation could be carried any further, however, the Canadians round about the King had lost all semblance of order. Pressing eagerly around his Majesty, they strove to exchange a word with him. It was with some difficulty that the King could move at all." But Curley managed to hold his attention. He told the king that just behind him there were twelve blind soldiers, and he led him to them, so that each man's hand could be gripped by Edward's. Reporters described it as a moving scene, no doubt more so for the blind soldiers themselves, who'd come all this way to witness a spectacle they couldn't see.

Curley made the papers frequently on that trip. One article claimed that he'd sat on the grass "on the identical spot"[15] where he'd been buried almost twenty years earlier, and while it's highly unlikely an exact location could be determined, it still must have been strange to revisit the site of such enormous death and destruction, and in the company of so many others who'd been through the battle. The place bore little resemblance to the wartime scene, and the same was true all along the old front line. As the veterans had made their way across Belgium and France toward Vimy—traversing "our own land of war,"[16] as one writer put it—they'd seen rich, emerald fields and gentle hillsides. Pastoral countryside in which "no traces of war remained"—except, of course, the cemeteries, great expanses of green striped with rows of pristinely placed tombstones.

Back at Christie Street, the wonders of technology enabled patients and staff to listen to the memorial service by radio, in a broadcast that offered "a graphic word-picture of the stirring scene." Afterward, 150 or so patients moved outdoors to gather on the grassy quadrangle for a service of their own. One hundred and fifty more remained inside, unable or perhaps not wanting to join in. Guests arrived in great numbers, and a band played patriotic songs. A chaplain stood and spoke about the men who'd "laid down their lives," as it was often put, and pronounced peace "the only religion for today.... We pay homage to peace, but peace must get into the very fibre of our living, our thinking, until war is unthinkable."[17]

As the bugler sounded the "Last Post," who among them would have guessed that the period of *light after darkness* would be so fleeting? Three years after this Vimy ceremony, another "world war" would begin, as great or greater than the first, and numbers would be needed to distinguish between the two. New waves of young men would arrive at Christie Street, missing legs, arms, noses, minds sick with the same trauma, hearts forever heavy with loss.

As the second war progressed, the hospital grew crowded again, and the original inhabitants took on a new role. Curley—who could walk on his artificial legs, who'd designed knife-and-fork attachments for his arms, and who could write—would advocate for other amputees for the rest of his life. "It's not a question of bravery," he'd tell them, "but of facing the situation. It's a matter of looking forward, not back....You've got to be wary of sympathy and you've got to have patience and a sense of humour."[18]

But there were stories, too, of help going in the other direction. In 1949, a few months after Percy Rimmell died and the hospital had only a small number of patients who hadn't been transferred to the newly built Sunnybrook, a young pilot from the Second World War named Bill Wheeler took a job as a part-time speech therapy instructor while he finished up his university studies. Though he had next to no training for the work, he took on twelve patients, all around age seventy, who could no longer speak due to stroke that had affected the right side of their bodies. Not really sure how to proceed, he started by encouraging the men to communicate by a nod or a shake of the head. It took a month for a man named George to say "hello," and the same length of time for another man, Fred, to remember his own name. But by spring, Fred was singing "Cruising Down the River on a Sunday Afternoon," his voice ringing out along the hospital corridor.[19] Bill's work with the veterans expanded: a man named Bert approached him and somehow conveyed that he'd like to learn to write again, using his left hand, since his right had been rendered useless by the stroke. The work with Bill allowed him to write his own letters to his wife in Owen Sound.

George, Fred, Bert — these aging men were among the last patients at Christie Street. Some of them had known the hospital from its busy early days, through the quieter interbellum, and then through the next wave, when the new generation of wounded joined the old. Once upon a time soldiers had *pottered over small fires, cleaning their mess-tins*, and now they were still together, a family cobbled from war. The hospital had never been intended as a permanent institution, but it had taken in a second onslaught before it had managed to release its first. In the early days of the Second World War, it still felt, in many ways, like "an old boiler factory," as one report called it, poorly located, under-facilitated, and, to some minds, "a disgrace." One doctor claimed the noise of the trains clanging past made it difficult to hear his patients' heartbeats. "It was a factory," a patient from the second war later stated. "I was in there with a bunch of old WW1 guys who had been there since [1919]."[20]

In 1941, a patient described the environment for the hospital's own publication, *The Christie Street Incision*:

> There is a "battle royal" every time a train passes. At night
> you have just dropped off into a deep sleep, when there is
> a violent shaking and rumble, whereupon everything in
> the room commences to vibrate and rattle. The windows
> start first, then your locker...finally the beds. By this time
> your bed is shaking like an egg beater and you feel as if any
> minute you will end up on the floor. There is a racket which
> sounds like all Hell's been let loose in a grand concert
> orchestra and you strongly suspect that a passing train is
> the cause of it all. Sure enough, the damn thing is panting,
> snorting and blowing past your window now, like a mad
> beast. You're awake now; you just lie there, waiting for it all
> to end. It seems like it's going to last for an hour. Rattle....
> rattle....rumble. Finally the monster is gone, and every-
> thing is quiet once more. You get to sleep again, only to
> be wakened by a recurrence of the same thing, a half
> hour later.[21]

Four years into the Second World War, in the autumn of '43, a new site was announced as the home for a permanent, purpose-built military hospital. It would go up in the northeast corner of Toronto, on Sunnybrook Farm, a pastoral acreage that had been bequeathed to the city for use as parkland. The Don River wound through the property, which was rich with woodland and rolling meadows, and all through the 1930s city dwellers had picnics there, or studied birds and butterflies. The city sold the property to the federal government on the condition that work would begin on the hospital right away, rather than after the war had ended. Construction of such a large facility would take time, though, and meanwhile, Christie Street and its outbuildings were growing increasingly overcrowded. With hundreds of beds urgently needed, and civilian hospitals unable to handle the overflow, renovations for a new wing were begun on the factory, a sort of band-aid solution that stirred anxieties: proponents of an entirely new space feared the renovations would mean more delays at Sunnybrook.

The "frightful conditions" at Christie Street and the slow progress of the new build got more and more attention in the press, but it was a group of women who drew the greatest publicity and managed to frame the controversy in human terms. Headed up by a doctor, Minerva Reid, and bolstered by influential, wealthy women like Lady Flora Eaton, the Women's Emergency Committee gathered signatures from across the country, demanding prompt, adequate care for veterans, and "positive abandonment" of Christie Street.[22] "The building is old, cockroach-infested and rat-ridden," Minerva wrote in an open letter to the government, "and sick and wounded men are suffering there needlessly."[23]

But by September 1944, only "the barest start" on the Sunnybrook site had been made, and one after another, troubles mounted.[24] Materials were in short supply, and with so many men at war, it was difficult to find skilled and even unskilled labour. The site was far enough from the main part of the city that arranging for transportation for the workers or accommodating them in place added to the logistical hurdles. At one point, a group of twenty-five labourers quit their jobs at Sunnybrook, claiming it was too far to travel to and from work each day—which prompted a veteran to write into the paper, asking just where "this haven Sunnybrook" was located. "Is it really out in the sticks? If so, I would prefer Christie, even with a little noise."[25]

But noise was far from the only issue. The journalist Judith Robinson reported extensively on Christie's decline, offering intimate stories that showed how the delays and the overcrowding affected human beings.

A Canadian paratrooper died in Christie Street Hospital, Toronto, two weeks ago last Sunday. He died in a small room on Third West—one of those that used to be single rooms until the responsible Minister enlarged the hospital's accommodation for the wounded of this war by crowding new iron cots into old, unsafe buildings. There are three beds now in the single room on Third West. Beside the one

where the dying man lay was barely space for a chair. There
was no room for a screen. Without even that poor shelter
for her grief, his wife sat beside him hour after hour while
the soldier died. Sunday is visiting day at Christie Street
Hospital....All the breathless afternoon and most of the
evening he was dying, while the visitors to the other two
in the room came and went, crowding past the chair where
the woman sat to reach the cots beyond.[26]

Shortly after Judith's piece was published, Minerva Reid railed
against the "beauty treatments" going on at Christie and the snail's
pace of the work at Sunnybrook. "Gangs of workmen were busy on every
floor of the old hospital," she told the *Globe*, "working over and around
the patients, painting, putting in false ceilings to mask girders, wires
and wooden boarding overhead, patching partitions and covering the
old brick walls of the factory with plasterboard."[27]

A week later, pensions minister Ian Mackenzie travelled to Toronto
to meet with the mayor and members of the women's committee and
veterans' organizations, and hear their concerns in person. As the dis-
cussion went on inside the posh Royal York Hotel, Lady Eaton and a
"small army" of women marched outside, carrying huge photos of the
hospital and signs that read "Get Our Wounded Out of Christie St."[28]
Promises were extracted that Christie Street would never again be overcrowded, and that work at Sunnybrook would speed up. But as in the
first war, the second war had ended by the time the new hospital took
in its first patients in September 1946, and nearly two more years passed
before the official opening ceremony was held. In comparison with
the glittering new Sunnybrook, it was hard to recall, now, that in 1919
the Dominion Orthopaedic Hospital on Christie had been described as
"the best of its kind on the continent."[29] Sunnybrook had taken its place
as a "hospital Shangri-la," impressive to staff, visitors, and patients alike.
When a writer for *Maclean's* toured the massive facility, a nurse confided
to him, "I wish they'd let me bring my bicycle." The reporter recorded
an enthusiastic exchange with a patient:

In the swankest bathroom I have ever seen,...I met a
veteran of the First World War. Surrounded by pink-tiled,
chromium-plated elegance, he was shaving. Razor in mid-
air, he paused and turned to me. "Pretty swell setup, eh?"
he beamed. "I've served time in half a dozen hospitals but
never one like this. I'm going to stay here the rest of my life
if I can."[30]

A formal memorial to the old hospital was held in the *pale cold days*
of winter, in January 1949, almost thirty years to the day after opening. People gathered in the auditorium and listened to speeches and
sang songs. It was the same space where all the wonderful shows had
happened—stars performing skits and Shakespeare plays and double-
edged songs like "Oh, It's a Lovely War."

   Some who'd posed for the panoramic picture in front of the hospital back in 1919, or who'd graced the pages of the *Illustrated Souvenir*,
chomping watermelon and playing the mandolin, were likely in attendance now too—or they were upstairs, tucked in their beds, and the
voices and music drifted up through the floors, vague fragments of
revelry in a building that would soon fall silent. Though the hospital
was officially closing and the majority of its patients had already gone,
the most infirm requiring "domiciliary care" stayed behind: old First
World War men, for the most part, who were living out their final days.[31]
As the "Last Post" was blown for the hospital, a solemn silence accompanied those notes of farewell. Outside, on the rooftop where the sun
worshippers had once lain, pigeons rested, puffed up for warmth in
the winter air. A train rolled past, and the grey birds lifted in unison,
soaring in a circle over *the glowing earth* and then landing again. It was
a brief flight, and *the hills, the sun, the winds, the clouds, the trees* were just
where they'd left them.

Acknowledgements

This would have been a very different book if not for the rich detail and numerous surprises that came to me from the generous family members of my "characters," or from others who'd researched their fascinating lives. My thanks to the following people for sharing what they knew, and for trusting me with the information: J. Bud Colquhoun, Ivan Cragg, Gordon Brock, Armand Garnet Ruffo, Andy Thomson, Hugh Thompson, Mary Ann Whetsel Bixler, Gay Haar, Tom Woelfersheim, Normand Bourdon, Carol Wilson, Jean Zazelenchuk, Dawn McNea, Ed Roberts, Robert Alldritt, Antonia Nelson, Sally Anne Blunt, Christopher and George Gullen, Karen Wishart and family, James Cambridge, the Wray family, Lori McCulloch, Donna Norman, Sharon Williams, Kath Grant, Anne, Dorothy, and Ronald Ostrom, Connie Mason, Neil Prior, John A. Vila, Elizabeth Vila Rogan, Eric Edwards, Janet Tobin, Yvonne Fenter, Debbie Cameron, Vincent Stuart, and my fellow sleuths at the Imperial War Museum's Lives of the First World War.

Thanks also to Jeff Winch, Sara Angelucci, Shannon Anderson, Tracy Kasaboski, Heidi den Hartog, Jim den Hartog, Marilyn Charbonneau, Marcel Fortin, Anne Fortin, Kelly Payne, Gerry McLoughlin, Rosie Connor, Mark Joithe, Nellie Winch, Linda Pruessen, Jess Shulman, and everyone at Goose Lane Editions.

The First World War has been written about in all kinds of ways by all kinds of people. The many newspapers, histories, diaries, and memoirs I quoted from are cited in the endnotes. But there were other books that also helped me understand the times. These are just some of those stories:

Charlie Connelly, *The Forgotten Soldier* (London: HarperElement, 2014).

Collingwood Ingram, *Wings Over the Western Front*, eds. Ernest Pollard and Hazel Strouts (Oxfordshire: Day Books, 2014).

Cynthia Toman, *Sister Soldiers of the Great War* (Vancouver: UBC Press, 2016).

David Macfarlane, *The Danger Tree* (New York: Bloomsbury, 2001).

Jonathan F. Vance, *A Township at War* (Waterloo: Wilfrid Laurier University Press, 2018).

Pat Barker, Regeneration Trilogy (London: Penguin Books, 1991-95).

Stephen O'Shea, *Back to the Front* (Madeira Park: Douglas & McIntyre, 1996).

Tim Cook, *The Secret History of Soldiers* (Toronto: Allen Lane, 2018).

Vera Brittain, *Testament of Youth* (London: Virago Press, 1978).

The following institutions, digital archives, and archivists were excellent resources throughout my years of research:

Ancestry

Australian War Memorial

British Newspaper Archive

Bunker Military Museum, Dan Larocque

Canadian Great War Project

Canadian Letters & Images Project

Canadian Research Knowledge Network

Canadian War Museum

CBC Archives

Chronicling America

Europeana 1914–1918

Family Search

Find My Past

Gillies Archives, Andrew Bamji

Great War Forum

Hathi Trust Digital Library

Huron County Newspaper Archive

Imperial War Museum

Internet Archive

Library and Archives Canada

The Long, Long Trail

Maclean's Archives

National Archives, U.K.

Nova Scotia Archives

ONECA (Ontario Native Education Counselling Association)

Osler Library of the History of Medicine, McGill University, Mary K.K. Hague-Yearl

OurOntario/OurDigitalWorld

Project Gutenberg

The Rooms, Newfoundland Archives

Royal Canadian Legion

Sunnybrook Health Sciences Centre Historical Archives

Thomas Fisher Rare Book Library, University of Toronto, Natalya Rattan

Through Veterans Eyes, Laurier Centre for the Study of Canada

Toronto Archives

Toronto Public Library, *Toronto Star* and *Globe & Mail* archives

Trent University Archives, Karen Suurtaam and Bernadine Dodge

Trove (National Library of Australia)

University of Toronto Archives, Tys Klumpenhouwer

Veterans Affairs Canada

The Vimy Foundation, Canadian Centre for the Great War

The War Amps, Frances Dee

Waterloo at War

Wellcome Library

Western Front Association

Western University Archives and Special Collections

I'm grateful to have received grants from the Canada Council, Ontario Arts Council, and Toronto Arts Council, and to *Geist Magazine* and *Spacing Magazine* for publishing my early articles exploring the Christie Street Hospital.

And finally, my thanks to the poets and their poems:

Frank Smith Brown, 1893–1915
 "Rubaiyat of a Man-at-Arms"; "The Convoy"; "The Veteran"; "Glory";
 "To Sam Hughes"; "Opened by the Censor: The Second"; "The Call";
 "Letters"; "Opened by the Censor: The First"

Wilfred Edward Salter Owen, 1893–1918
 "Spring Offensive"; "Dulce et Decorum est"; "Insensibility"; "Strange
 Meeting"; "Futility"

Julian Henry Francis Grenfell, 1888–1915
 "Into Battle"

Francis Edward Ledwidge, 1887–1917
 "The Lost Ones"; "Soliloquy"; "A Soldier's Grave"; "To One Dead"

Colwyn Erasmus Arnold Philipps, 1888–1915
 "Release"

Charles Hamilton Sorley, 1895–1915
 "XXXVI"; "XXXIV"; "Two Sonnets"

Rupert Brooke, 1887–1915
 "Peace"; "Fragment"; "The Dead"; "Safety"

Isaac Rosenberg, 1890–1918
"Killed in Action"; "Dead Man's Dump"; "Spring"; "Daughters of War"; "Louse Hunting"; "Returning, We Hear the Larks"; "Through These Pale Cold Days"

Philip Edward Thomas, 1878–1917
"The Sign-Post"; "Thaw"; "It Rains"; "The Cherry Trees"; "The Owl"

William Henry Littlejohn, 1891–1917
"Suvla Bay"; "The Hospital Ship"

Thomas Ernest Hulme, 1883–1917
"The Poet"; "The Embankment"; "Trenches: St Eloi"

Leslie Coulson, 1889–1916
"Who Made the Law?"

Robert Stafford Arthur Palmer, 1888–1916
"How Long, O Lord?"

William Noel Hodgson, 1893–1916
"Release"; "Durham Cathedral"

John McCrae, 1872–1918
"In Flanders Fields"; "The Anxious Dead"; "The Unconquered Dead"

George Upton Robins, 1878–1915
"L'Envoi"

Bernard Freeman Trotter, 1890–1917
"Ici Repose"; "Dreams"

Patrick Houston Shaw-Stewart, 1888–1917
"Achilles in the Trench"

Alan Seeger, 1888–1916
"I Have a Rendezvous with Death"

Alfred Victor Ratcliffe, 1887–1916
"At Sundown"; "Into the Night"

Edward Wyndham Tennant, 1897–1916
"Light After Darkness"

Richard Molesworth Dennys, 1884–1916
"Better Far to Pass Away"

Notes

A Factory

1   Fred H. Albee, *A Surgeon's Fight to Rebuild Men* (London: Robert Hale Limited, 1950), 110, https://archive.org/details/b29979080/page/110/mode/2up.

2   *Souvenir of Captivity in Germany* (Münster-Rennbahn: Camp Print. Office, 1917), 10, https://cmhcwm-mchmcg.on.worldcat.org/search/detail/220437514?queryString=rennbahn.

3   "High Park Remains as Hospital Site," *Toronto Daily Star*, November 28, 1917, 13, ProQuest Historical Newspapers.

4   "High Park Remains as Hospital Site," *Toronto Daily Star*.

5   "Buy Cash Register Factory for New Military Hospital," *Toronto Daily Star*, January 28, 1918, 1, ProQuest Historical Newspapers.

6   "Overhauling is Needed," *Globe*, November 9, 1918, 7, ProQuest Historical Newspapers.

7   "Cousins, Frank C. Letter: 1918 September 12th," Canadian Letters and Images Project (CLIP), https://www.canadianletters.ca/document-4298.

8   "Pecover, William Markle Letter: 1917 October 31st," CLIP, https://www.canadianletters.ca/document-63532.

9   "Canada Can Well Be Ashamed," *Globe*, October 25, 1918, 1, ProQuest Historical Newspapers.

10 "Interview with Lieutenant (Nursing Sister) Mabel Lucas Rutherford," by Margaret Allemang, 1978, Canadian War Museum, 20080087-013, https://www.warmuseum.ca/collections/archive/3174587. Unless otherwise noted, all quotations from Mabel Lucas Rutherford are taken from this source.

11 "Dear Mother," October 20, 1915, Letter Collection of N/S May Bastedo, Canadian War Museum, 19780041-009, https://www.warmuseum.ca/collections/archive/3143425; May Bastedo service record, Personnel Records of the First World War, Library and Archives Canada, RG 15, accession 1992-93/166, box 496-37, 28431, https://www.bac-lac.gc.ca/eng/discover/military-heritage/first-world-war/personnel-records/Pages/item.aspx?IdNumber=28431.

12 "Interview with Katharine Van Buskirk," by Jean Murtaugh, 1980, Canadian War Museum, 20080087-015, https://www.warmuseum.ca/collections/archive/3174589.

13　Clare Gass, *The War Diary of Clare Gass*, ed. Susan Mann (Montreal: McGill-Queen's University Press, 2000), March 2, 1916, 106.

14　Frances Upton, quoted in Cynthia Toman, *Sister Soldiers of the Great War* (Vancouver: UBC Press, 2016), 144.

15　"Letters and Diaries of Helen Fowlds," Trent University, September 15, 1915, https://digitalcollections.trentu.ca /exhibits/fowlds/fdiary-1.htm and https://digitalcollections.trentu.ca /exhibits/fowlds/.

16　Sister Anne Donnell, quoted in Cynthia Toman, *Sister Soldiers of the Great War* (Vancouver: UBC Press, 2016), 145.

17　"Strikers Object to the Cost Unit System," *Toronto Daily Star*, January 28, 1919, 4, ProQuest Historical Newspapers.

18　"New Superintendent for Limb Factory," *Toronto Daily Star*, January 31, 1919, 4, ProQuest Historical Newspapers.

19　"New Orthopedic Hospital Now Open," *The Hospital World* XV, no. 3 (March 1919), 83, https://archive.org/details /hospitalworld1516torouoft/page /82/mode/2up.

20　"Big New Hospital Will Be College, Too," *Toronto Daily Star*, December 4, 1918, 18, ProQuest Historical Newspapers.

21　"New Hospital Opens with Fifty Patients," *Toronto Daily Star*, February 4, 1919, 8, ProQuest Historical Newspapers.

22　Charles McVicar service record, South African War, 1899–1902—Service Files,

Medals and Land Applications, Library and Archives Canada, RG 38, 10930, https://www.bac-lac.gc.ca/eng/discover /military-heritage/south-african-war -1899-1902/Pages/item.aspx?IdNumber =10930&.

23　"Ailsa Craig," *Exeter Advocate*, November 6, 1902, 4, Huron County Newspaper Archive.

24　"Orthopedic Patients Complain About Food," *Toronto Daily Star*, March 18, 1919, 8, ProQuest Historical Newspapers.

25　"Duke Too Sensitive to See Operation," *Toronto Daily Star*, February 24, 1919, 2, ProQuest Historical Newspapers.

26　"Sgt. W. Mackintosh Writes," *Toronto Daily Star*, February 27, 1919, 5, ProQuest Historical Newspapers.

27　Classifieds, *Toronto Daily Star*, February 27, 1919, 17, ProQuest Historical Newspapers.

28　*Illustrated Souvenir: Dominion Orthopaedic Hospital*, compiled by F.W. Coyne, YMCA, 1920, https://archive.org/details /illustratedsouve00coynuoft. All quotations from the *Illustrated Souvenir* in this chapter are taken from this source.

29　*Canadiana*, https://www.canadiana.ca /view/oocihm.9_90214/15.

30　*Canadiana*, https://www.canadiana.ca /view/oocihm.9_90214/47

31　*Canadiana*, https://www.canadiana.ca /view/oocihm.9_90214/91

32　*Canadiana*, https://www.canadiana.ca /view/oocihm.9_90214/99

Legs

1　"Patients & Administrative Staff of the Dominion Orthopedic Hospital, Toronto ONT 9-6-19," Toronto Archives, fonds 2, series 411, item 48, http:// jpeg2000.eloquent-systems.com/toronto _arch.html?image=/webcat/systems /toronto.arch/resource/fo0002/ser0411 /s0411_it0048.jp2.

2　*Illustrated Souvenir: Dominion Orthopaedic Hospital*, compiled by F.W. Coyne, YMCA, 1920, https://archive.org/details /illustratedsouve00coynuoft. Unless otherwise noted, all quotations from the

Illustrated Souvenir in this chapter are taken from this source.

3　"Mothers and Wives Enjoy Banquet," *Toronto Daily Star*, February 21, 1919, 11, ProQuest Historical Newspapers.

4　"Dull Care Begone," *Toronto Daily Star*, February 21, 1919, 4, ProQuest Historical Newspapers.

5　"Army Doctors Agree About Shell Shock," *Toronto Daily Star*, February 28, 1919, 4, ProQuest Historical Newspapers.

6　"Army Doctors Agree About Shell Shock," *Toronto Daily Star*.

7   "War Diaries—3rd Canadian Infantry Battalion," July 1915, Library and Archives Canada, RG9-III-D-3, vol. 4914, file 356, https://recherche-collection-search .bac-lac.gc.ca/eng/home/record?app =fonandcol&IdNumber=1883208&q =3rd%20canadian%20infantry%20 battalion. Unless otherwise noted, all quotations from the unit's war diary in this chapter are taken from this source.

8   Andrew Macphail, *Official History of the Canadian Forces in the Great War 1914– 19: The Medical Services* (Ottawa: National Defence, 1925), 76, https://archive.org /details/medicalservices00macpuoft /page/76/mode/2up.

9   Charles Thomas Harrowsmith service record, Personnel Records of the First World War, Library and Archives Canada, RG 150, accession 1992-93/166, box 4115- 23, 445990, https://www.bac-lac.gc.ca /eng/discover/military-heritage/first -world-war/personnel-records/Pages /item.spx?IdNumber=445990. Unless otherwise noted, quotations regarding Charles Harrowsmith in this chapter are taken from this source.

10   "Transcript Extracts of the Diary and Letters of Ronald Alison McInnis, 1915– 1919," Australian War Memorial, PR00917, https://www.awm.gov.au/collection /RCDIG0000887?image=37#display -image.

11   "Wounded Second Time," *Toronto Daily Star*, August 16, 1918, 2, ProQuest Historical Newspapers.

12   "An Invitation," *Toronto Daily Star*, February 25, 1915, 15, ProQuest Historical Newspapers.

13   "Business is Booming," *Globe*, November 3, 1915, 7, ProQuest Historical Newspapers.

14   "The Late Mr. C.T. Harrowsmith," *Surrey Advertiser*, July 22, 1944, 2, British Newspaper Archive.

15   "Revealed: The 18th-Century Guide to Amputations, Operations and Medical Tips," *Daily Mail*, January 28, 2009, http://www.dailymail.co.uk/news/article -1130463/Revealed-The-18th-century

-guide-amputations-operations-medical -tips.html.

16   Almroth E. Wright, *Wound Infections* (London: University of London Press, 1915), 1, https://archive.org/stream /woundinfectionss00wrigrich#page /n11/mode/2up.

17   "Interview with Lieutenant (Nursing Sister) Mabel Lucas Rutherford," by Margaret Allemang, 1978, Canadian War Museum, 20080087–013, https://www .warmuseum.ca/collections/archive /3174587.

18   Woods Hutchinson, *The Doctor in War* (Boston and New York: Houghton Mifflin Company, 1918), 135–36, https://archive .org/details/doctorinwar00hutcuoft /page/134/mode/2up.

19   William Wishart service record, Personnel Records of the First World War, Library and Archives Canada, RG 150, accession 1992-93/166, box 10509-39, 319655, https://www.bac-lac.gc.ca/eng/discover /military-heritage/first-world-war /personnel-records/Pages/item.aspx ?IdNumber=319655.

20   John Patrick Hoar service record, Personnel Records of the First World War, Library and Archives Canada, RG 150, accession 1992-93/166, box 4395- 2, 462318, https://www.bac-lac.gc.ca/eng /discover/military-heritage/first-world -war/personnel-records/Pages/item .aspx?IdNumber=462318.

21   "War in All Its Grimness," *Rock Island Argus*, August 14, 1917, 10, Library of Congress: Chronicling America.

22   Gerald Hanley service record, Personnel Records of the First World War, Library and Archives Canada, RG 150, accession 1992-93/166, box 4014-10, 444166, https://www.bac-lac.gc.ca/eng/discover /military-heritage/first-world-war /personnel-records/Pages/item .aspx?IdNumber=444166.

23   "Spencer Square," *Rock Island Argus*, August 16, 1917, 7, Library of Congress: Chronicling America.

24   Van Buren Whetsel service record, Personnel Records of the First World War,

Library and Archives Canada, RG 150,
accession 1992-93/166, box 10272-28,
308973, https://www.bac-lac.gc.ca
/eng/discover/military-heritage/first
-world-war/personnel-records/Pages
/item.aspx?IdNumber=308973.

25 W.L. Kidd Collection, Library and
Archives Canada, R13007-0-2-E, 1974-137
NPC, http://central.bac-lac.gc.ca/.redirect
?app=fonandcol&id=10773&lang=eng.

26 Excerpt from Elsie Tranter's diary
found at Through These Lines, http://
throughtheselines.com.au/2010/research
/etaples.html. Tranter's original diary was
published as J.M. Gillings & J. Richards,
eds., *In All Those Lines: The Diary of Sister
Elsie Tranter 1916–1919* (self-published,
Newstead, Tasmania, 2008).

27 Wayne Larsen, *AY Jackson: The Life of a
Landscape Painter* (Toronto: Dundurn
Press, 2009), 29.

28 Wilfred Owen, *The Poems of Wilfred Owen*
(London: Chatto and Windus, 1931), 32,
https://archive.org/details/in.ernet
.dli.2015.505111/page/n39/mode/2up.

29 Mabel Clint, Our Bit: Memories of a War
Service by a Canadian Nursing Sister
(Montreal: Alumnae Association of the
Royal Victoria Hospital, 1943), 2, https://
www.fadedpage.com/books/20201201
/html.php#chap01.

30 Quoted in Bruce Davis, *Craigdarroch
Military Hospital: A Canadian War Story*
(2016), https://navalandmilitarymuseum
.org/wp-content/uploads/2019/06
/CFB-Esquimalt-Museum-May-2018
-Craigdarroch-Military-Hospital.pdf.

31 "Scales, Harold Wilcox Diary: 1918 May
20th," Canadian Letters and Images
Project, https://www.canadianletters
.ca/content/document-2326.

32 "Étaples Outrage," *Northern Whig*, May 29,
1918, 3, British Newspaper Archive.

33 S. Weir Mitchell, *Injuries of Nerves and Their
Consequences* (Philadelphia: J.B. Lippincott
& Co., 1872), 348, https://archive.org
/details/injuriesofnerves00mitcuoft
/page/348/mode/2up.

34 "Toronto Hails Peace in Delirium of Joy,"
Toronto Daily Star, November 12, 1918, 5,
ProQuest Historical Newspapers.

35 "Voices of the First World War: Armistice,"
Episode 47, Imperial War Museum,
https://www.iwm.org.uk/history
/voices-of-the-first-world-war-armistice.

36 R. Tait McKenzie, *Reclaiming the Maimed*
(New York: Macmillan Company,
1918), https://archive.org/details
/reclaimingmaimed00mcke/page/n5
/mode/2up.

37 "Hold Fork or Pen with a Dummy Hand,"
Toronto Daily Star, February 9, 1918, 9,
ProQuest Historical Newspapers.

38 "Novelties at GWVA Meet," *Globe*, June 16,
1919, 12, ProQuest Historical Newspapers.

39 "Legless Swimmer Does Stunts at High
Park," *Globe*, September 16, 1919, 11,
ProQuest Historical Newspapers.

40 *Canadiana*, https://www.canadiana.ca
/view/oocihm.9_90214/80

41 "What Every Disabled Soldier Should
Know," 19900076-847, Canadian War
Museum, https://www.warmuseum.ca
/collections/artifact/1027516.

42 *Souvenir of Captivity in Germany* (Münster-
Rennbahn: Camp Print. Office, 1917), 10,
https://cmhcwm-mchmcg.on.worldcat.org
/search/detail/220437514?queryString
=rennbahn.

43 Ernest Hemingway, *Men At War* (New York:
Bramhall House, 1955), xii, https://
archive.org/details/in.ernet.dli.2015
.58488/page/n15/mode/2up.

44 "Part of Hamburg Street is Now Victory
Place," *Chicago Tribune*, April 1, 1918, 5,
newspapers.com.

45 "Pension Cut, He Ends Life," *Washington
Times*, September 4, 1920, 1, Library of
Congress: Chronicling America.

46 "Veteran of Princess Pats, Doomed to
Life as Cripple, Kills Himself When
Government Pension Ceases," *Butte Daily
Bulletin*, September 17, 1920, 1, Library of
Congress: Chronicling America.

47 "Soldier Suicide Not Deprived of Pension,"
Globe, September 6, 1920, 5, ProQuest
Historical Newspapers.

48 "Shell Shock Victim's Tragic Death,"
   Nottingham Evening Post, April 19, 1920, 2;
   "Shell-Shocked and Crippled," *Nottingham
   Evening Post*, September 18, 1926, 5;
   "Glo'shire Farmer Found Shot," *Western
   Daily Press and Bristol Mirror*, February 23,
   1934, 5; "Old Man's Suicide on Railway,"
   Leicester Mercury, August 19, 1929, 1. Both
   newspapers.com.
49 "Editorial," *Hamilton-Mills Weekly* 1, no. 2,
   September 11, 1920, 3, *Canadiana*,

   https://www.canadiana.ca/view/oocihm
   .8_06800_2.
50 Clover Culver, "A Black Tie With Solemn
   Significance," *Morning Herald*, February 3,
   1950, 4, newspapers.com.
51 Letter provided by MaryAnn Whetsel.
52 Glenn Iriam, *In the Trenches, 1914–1918*,
   eBookIt.com, 2011, https://books.google
   .ca/books?id=Nl2AQUqejCAC.

Arms

1 Alfred Caron service record, Personnel
   Records of the First World War, Library
   and Archives Canada, RG 150, accession
   1992-93/166, box 1504-26, 88529, https://
   www.bac-lac.gc.ca/eng/discover/military
   -heritage/first-world-war/personnel
   -records/Pages/item.aspx?IdNumber
   =88529. Unless otherwise noted, all
   quotations regarding Alfred Caron in
   this chapter are taken from this source.
2 Judith Friedland, *Restoring the Spirit:
   The Beginnings of Occupational Therapy
   in Canada* (Kingston and Montreal:
   McGill-Queen's University Press, 2011),
   https://www.mqup.ca/restoring-the
   -spirit-products-9780773539129.php.
3 "Report of the Work of the Department
   of Soldiers' Civil Re-establishment,
   December, 1919," Internet Archive,
   https://archive.org/details/1920v56i5p14
   _1499/page/n35/mode/2up?q=christie.
4 Gertrude E.S. Pringle, "God Bless the
   Girls in Green!" *Maclean's*, February 15,
   1922, 48, https://archive.org/details
   /Macleans-Magazine-1922-02-15/page
   /n23/mode/2up.
5 "Victory Over Wounds, The Soldier's
   Return from 'Down and Out' to 'Up and
   In Again,'" 19900076-843, https://www
   .warmuseum.ca/collections/artifact
   /1027515/; "What Every Disabled Soldier
   Should Know," 19900076-848, https://
   www.warmuseum.ca/collections/artifact
   /1027510; and "The Wounded Soldier's
   Return," 19900076-845, https://www
   .warmuseum.ca/firstworldwar/objects
   -and-photos/archival-documents

   /documents-created-by-organizations
   /the-wounded-soldiers-return/?back=486.
   All Canadian War Museum.
6 "Language Too Strong?" *Toronto Daily Star*,
   June 2, 1919, 9, ProQuest Historical
   Newspapers.
7 "Comradeship, Not Praise," *Toronto Daily
   Star*, April 26, 1919, 4, ProQuest Historical
   Newspapers.
8 "TTC Riders Don't Give Up Seats for
   Veterans," *Toronto Daily Star*, March 4,
   1919, 4, ProQuest Historical Newspapers.
9 "Discipline to Help Veterans Come
   Back," *Toronto Daily Star*, March 4, 1919, 4,
   ProQuest Historical Newspapers.
10 "Kinmel Riots," *Sheffield Daily Telegraph*,
   April 23, 1919, 8, British Newspaper
   Archive.
11 "Explains Rhyl Riots," *Toronto Daily Star*,
   March 29, 1919, 1, ProQuest Historical
   Newspapers.
12 Arwood Fortner service record, Personnel
   Records of the First World War, Library
   and Archives Canada, RG 150, accession
   1992-93/166, box 3221-100, 401538,
   https://www.bac-lac.gc.ca/eng/discover
   /military-heritage/first-world-war
   /personnel-records/Pages/item.aspx
   ?IdNumber=401538. Unless otherwise
   noted, all quotations regarding Arwood
   Fortner in this chapter are taken from
   this source.
13 "The Big Sangerfest," *Globe*, August 14,
   1897, 13, ProQuest Historical Newspapers.
14 "Berlin Council Asks Govt for Alien
   Registrar," *Toronto Daily Star*, February 11,
   1916, 3, ProQuest Historical Newspapers.

15 "Berlin Council Asks Govt for Alien
    Registrar," *Toronto Daily Star*.

16 The Lochead Files, *Waterloo at War*, File 12,
    19, https://move:waterlooatwar.ca
    /wp-content/uploads/2015/11/File-12
    -Marriage-Seperation-Allowance.pdf.

17 "Are You in Favor of Changing the
    Name of This City? No!" (Berlin Record
    clipping), Wikipedia, https://upload
    .wikimedia.org/wikipedia/commons
    /1/16/Advertisement_in_the_Berlin
    _Record_opposing_proposed_name
    _change%2C_1916.jpg.

18 "Curtis, W.E.—10th Battalion—
    Interview," Fonds of Canadian
    Broadcasting Corporation, Radio:
    Flanders Fields, Library and Archives
    Canada, accession 1980-0123, item
    116947, http://central.bac-lac.gc.ca
    /.redirect?app=filvidandsou&id
    =116947&lang=eng.

19 *Report of the War Office Committee of Enquiry
    Into "Shell-shock"* (London, UK: Imperial
    War Office, 2004), 48, https://books
    .google.ca/books?id=O5_XdP-VSZsC&q
    =48#v=snippet&q=48&f=false.

20 "Wounded and Prisoners Behind the
    Lines on the Western Front, 1917," IWM
    409, Imperial War Museum, https://www
    .iwm.org.uk/collections/item/object
    /1060022869.

21 "Horror on the Battlefield: A Soldier's
    Story," *Canada: A People's History*,
    CBC, https://www.cbc.ca/history
    /EPISCONTENTSE1EP12CH1PA5LE
    .html.

22 Will R. Bird, *Thirteen Years After*
    (Toronto: Maclean Publishing, 1932),
    11, 15, 13, https://archive.org/details
    /thirteenyearsaft0000bird/page/n1.

23 "Victory Over Wounds, The Soldier's
    Return from 'Down and Out' to 'Up
    and In Again,'" 19900076-843, Canadian
    War Museum, https://www.warmuseum
    .ca/collections/artifact/1027515/.

24 "Canada's Method of Facing Debt to
    Soldiers Who Have Lost Limbs in Battle
    is Described," *Reconstruction*, January
    1918, 8, https://archive.org/stream
    /reconstructionbu00cana#page/8
    /mode/2up.

25 R. Tait McKenzie, *Reclaiming the
    Maimed* (New York: Macmillan, 1918),
    113, https://archive.org/details
    /reclaimingmaimed00mcke/page
    /112/mode/2up.

26 "Amputation Cases," *Toronto Daily Star*,
    August 19, 1922, 6, ProQuest Historical
    Newspapers.

27 "Artificial Limbs Should Be Improved,"
    Toronto Daily Star, June 26, 1919, 11,
    ProQuest Historical Newspapers.

28 "The 'Hook' Hand Best for Everyday
    Wear," *Toronto Daily Star*, July 4, 1919, 7,
    ProQuest Historical Newspapers.

29 Walter Dunn service record, Personnel
    Records of the First World War, Library
    and Archives Canada, RG 150, accession
    1992-93/166, box 2754-1, 366967, https://
    www.bac-lac.gc.ca/eng/discover/military
    -heritage/first-world-war/personnel
    -records/Pages/item.aspx?IdNumber
    =366967. Unless otherwise noted, all
    quotations regarding Walter Dunn in
    this chapter are taken from this source.

30 "The Catholic Children's Protection
    Society," *Liverpool Mercury*, December 22,
    1899, 8, British Newspaper Archive.

31 "An Interesting Institution," *The True
    Witness and Catholic Chronicle*, June 6, 1894,
    3, Google News.

32 "A Young Wanderer," *Ottawa Evening
    Journal*, January 26, 1899, quoted in
    Immigration Program: Headquarters
    central registry files C-4733, page 775,
    Canadiana, http://heritage.canadiana
    .ca/view/oocihm.lac_reel_c4733/775;
    Miss Brennan's comments, page 778,
    Canadiana, http://heritage.canadiana.ca
    /view/oocihm.lac_reel_c4733/778.

33 "Why don't they come?...join the 148th
    Battalion," Montreal and Toronto:
    J.J. Gibbons Limited, between 1914 and
    1918, Library of Congress, https://www
    .loc.gov/resource/cph.3g12398/; and
    "Why don't I go? The 148th Battalion
    needs me," Montreal: J.J. Gibbons Ltd.,
    1915, Library of Congress, https://
    www.loc.gov/item/2005695756/.

34 "Wounded in the Big Push," *Ripley and Heanor News*, August 4, 1916, 3; "Letters from Clarion Soldiers and Sailors," *The Clarion*, September 3, 1915, 5, British Newspaper Archive.

35 "Blighty," Christmas 1916 edition, https://www.nationalarchives.gov.uk/pathways/firstworldwar/military_conflict/p_blighty.htm.

36 "Wounded soldiers and graffiti," fonds 1244, item 726, https://gencat.eloquent-systems.com/city-of-toronto-archives-m-permalink.html?key=52168; "War wounded and graffiti," fonds 1244, item 736, https://gencat.eloquent-systems.com/city-of-toronto-archives-m-permalink.html?key=52181. Both City of Toronto Archives.

37 "Voting for Soldiers Not Yourselves," *Gazette*, December 7, 1917, 7, newspapers.com.

38 "'Crucifixion' Punishment," *HC Deb*, November 2, 1916, vol. 86, col. 1804-5, https://api.parliament.uk/historic-hansard/commons/1916/nov/02/crucifixion-punishment.

39 "Army Notes: Field Punishment and How the Serving Soldier Views It," *The People*, November 12, 1916, 6, British Newspaper Archive.

40 "Field Punishment," *Ottawa Citizen*, December 14, 1916, 16, newspapers.com.

41 Bulletin found in "26th Battalion, Discipline," Library and Archives Canada, RG9 III-C-3, vol. 4121, folder 2, file 6, https://www.bac-lac.gc.ca/eng/discover/military-heritage/first-world-war/canada-first-world-war/Documents/field-punishment-no1.pdf.

42 "'24th Canadian Infantry Battalion' diary entry for August 1918 p. 9," Canadian Great War Project, https://canadiangreatwarproject.com/diaries/viewer.php?u=24th_canadian_infantry_battalion&m=08&y=1918&i=e000965458. All quotations from the battalion diary in this chapter are taken from this source.

43 Robert Bates, Ministry of the Overseas Military Forces of Canada, courts martial records, 1914–1918, T-8664 image 1896, *Canadiana*, http://heritage.canadiana.ca/view/oocihm.lac_reel_t8664/1896?r=0&s=1.

44 "Read Fresh Meanings into Twelfth Night," *Toronto Daily Star*, December 2, 1919, 3, ProQuest Historical Newspapers.

45 "Soldiers Forget Pain When Fair Julia Comes," *Toronto Daily Star*, December 6, 1919, 27, ProQuest Historical Newspapers.

46 "Playmate's Death Not Fault of Boy," *Globe*, March 15, 1920, 8, ProQuest Historical Newspapers.

47 "Daddy What Did You Do in the Great War?" 19720028-007, https://www.warmuseum.ca/collections/artifact/1026215/; and "My Dad is at the Front" button, 20030334-006, https://www.warmuseum.ca/collections/artifact/1358160/?q=children&page_num=1&item_num=20&media_irn=5198023. Both Canadian War Museum.

48 Katherine Hale, *Grey Knitting and Other Poems* (Toronto: William Briggs, 1914), Internet Archive.

Spines

1 "Visit of His Royal Highness, the Prince of Wales," from "Dominion Orthopaedic Hospital," Library and Archives Canada, RG24-C-8, vol. 4299, file MD2-34-1-54-25, part 2, http://central.bac-lac.gc.ca/.redirect?app=fonandcol&id=1092041&lang=eng.

2 Rupert Godfrey, ed., *Letters From a Prince: Edward, Prince of Wales to Mrs Freda Dudley Ward, March 1918–January 1921* (London: Little, Brown and Company, 1998), 94 and 96.

3 "The Prince Qualified for Life Membership in GWVA of Canada," *Ottawa Citizen*, August 28, 1919, 11, newspapers.com.

4 "Canada's Capital Welcomes the People's Prince," *Ottawa Citizen*, August 28, 1919, 10, newspapers.com.

5 Godfrey, *Letters From a Prince*, 175.

6 "Feather From Hat, But Prince Wore It,"
Toronto Daily Star, August 23, 1919, 12,
ProQuest Historical Newspapers.

7 "Enthusiasm of Vets Was at Highest Pitch,"
Toronto Daily Star, August 28, 1919, 5,
ProQuest Historical Newspapers.

8 "Prince Awards Honors to Heroes in
Hospital," *Toronto Daily Star*, August 26,
1919, 1, ProQuest Historical Newspapers.

9 "Prince Awards Honors," *Toronto Daily Star*.

10 "Prince Awards Honors," *Toronto Daily Star*.

11 Godfrey, *Letters From a Prince*, 183.

12 Jessie E. MacTaggart, "Christie's Roof
Ward Now Belongs to Past," *Globe*,
December 24, 1937, 3, ProQuest Historical
Newspapers.

13 "Honor Dr. R.I. Harris at Veteran
Banquet," *Toronto Daily Star*, February 19,
1934, 17, ProQuest Historical Newspapers.

14 MacTaggart, "Christie's Roof Ward."

15 "Honor Dr. R.I. Harris," *Toronto Daily Star*.

16 R.I. Harris, "Heliotherapy in Surgical
Tuberculosis," *Canadian Medical Association
Journal* 12, no. 11 (November 1922): 802,
Europe PubMed Central.

17 F.W. Coyne, *Illustrated Souvenir:
Dominion Orthopaedic Hospital*, YMCA,
1920, https://archive.org/details
/illustratedsouve00coynuoft/page
/58/mode/2up.

18 Jessie MacTaggart, "'Original' at Christie
St. Chappie's Happy Life Ends," *Toronto
Daily Star*, October 12, 1939, 17, ProQuest
Historical Newspapers.

19 F.W. Coyne, *Illustrated Souvenir*,
https://archive.org/details
/illustratedsouve00coynuoft
/page/60/mode/2up?q=chief.

20 John Spaniel service record, Personnel
Records of the First World War, Library
and Archives Canada, RG 150, accession
1992-93/166, box 9169-18, 242840,
https://www.bac-lac.gc.ca/eng/discover
/military-heritage/first-world-war
/personnel-records/Pages/item.aspx
?IdNumber=242840. Unless otherwise
noted, all quotations regarding John
Spaniel in this chapter are taken from
this source.

21 James Morrison, Treaty Research
Report—Treaty No. 9 (1905–1906),
Treaties and Historical Research Centre,
Indian and Northern Affairs Canada,
1986, https://www.rcaanc-cirnac.gc.ca
/eng/1100100028859/1564415209671
#fn111 (which cites its source as "James
Phipps to the Superintendent General
of Indian Affairs, 5 February 1885").

22 James Morrison, Treaty Research Report.

23 Diary of Daniel G. MacMartin, 1905, 30,
Daniel George W. MacMartin Collection,
CA ON00239 F00149, Queen's
University Archives, http://db-archives
.library.queensu.ca/daniel-george-w
-macmartin-collection.

24 The full text of the treaty is quoted at
Treaty 9, *Canadian Encyclopedia*, https://
www.thecanadianencyclopedia.ca/en
/article/treaty-9.

25 F.W. Coyne, *Illustrated Souvenir*,
https://archive.org/details
/illustratedsouve00coynuoft
/page/98/mode/2up?q=spaniel.

26 John Spaniel pension record, provided
by Veterans Affairs Canada.

27 Karl S. Hele, "League of Indians'
Founding in Sault Reflected Region's
Role in Resisting Colonialism," *Sault Star*,
August 14, 2020, https://www.saultstar
.com/opinion/columnists/league-of
-indians-founding-in-sault-reflected
-regions-role-in-resisting-colonialism.

28 "When the Prince Fished in Canada,"
Gazette, September 6, 1924, 12,
newspapers.com; and "Prince Is Off
to Wilds after Elusive Trout," *Gazette*,
September 6, 1919, newspapers.com.

29 "When the Prince Fished in Canada,"
Gazette.

30 Thomas Shirreff Ronaldson service
record, Personnel Records of the First
World War, Library and Archives Canada,
RG 150, accession 1992-93/166, box
8446-16, 615908, https://www.bac-lac
.gc.ca/eng/discover/military-heritage
/first-world-war/personnel-records
/Pages/item.aspx?IdNumber=615908.
Unless otherwise noted, all quotations

regarding Tom Ronaldson in this chapter are taken from this source.

31 Archibald James, in "Voices of the First World War: Gas Attack at Ypres," Episode 13, Imperial War Museum, https://www.iwm.org.uk/history/voices-of-the-first-world-war-gas-attack-at-ypres.

32 Jack Dorgan, in "Voices of the First World War: Gas Attack at Ypres," Episode 13, Imperial War Museum, https://www.iwm.org.uk/history/voices-of-the-first-world-war-gas-attack-at-ypres.

33 "A Watsonian Taken Prisoner," *The Scotsman*, May 11, 1915, 6, British Newspaper Archive.

34 "WW1 Prisoner of War Post Card Found," BBC News, April 29, 2013, https://www.bbc.com/news/uk-england-22334217.

35 Letter from W.A. Alldritt to Agnes, May 1, 1915, Canadian War Museum, Fonds of Sergeant William Alexander Alldritt, DCM, https://www.warmuseum.ca/collections/archive/3179640.

36 "Lager Lingo," in *Souvenir of Captivity in Germany* (Münster-Rennbahn: Camp Print. Office, 1917), 2, https://cmhcwm-mchmcg.on.worldcat.org/search/detail/220437514?queryString=rennbahn.

37 "Lager Lingo," in *Souvenir of Captivity in Germany*.

38 H. Sharp and P. Alran, *Echo du Camp de Rennbahn*, February 3, 1917, 4, https://cmhcwm-mchmcg.on.worldcat.org/search/detail/1232436810?queryString=echo%20du%20camp%20rennbahn&clusterResults=false&groupVariantRecords=true.

39 "Exercise–Rennbahn, Münster–1946," in *Souvenir of Captivity in Germany*, 17.

40 Letter from W.A. Alldritt to Agnes, March 24 1918, Canadian War Museum, Fonds of Sergeant William Alexander Alldritt, DCM, https://www.warmuseum.ca/collections/archive/3179640.

41 Charles Lyons Foster and William Smith Duthie, eds., *Letters From the Front: Being a Record of the Part Played by Officers of the Bank in the Great War* 1 (Toronto: Canadian Bank of Commerce, 1920),

217, https://archive.org/details/lettersfromfront01canauoft/page/216/mode/2up?q=ronaldson.

42 Jessie E. MacTaggart, "Christie's Roof Ward."

43 *Hamilton-Mills Weekly* 1, no. 3, September 25, 1920, 1, *Canadiana*, https://www.canadiana.ca/view/oocihm.8_06800_3/1

44 "Interview with Lieutenant (Nursing Sister) Mabel Lucas Rutherford," by Margaret Allemang, 1978, Canadian War Museum, 20080087–013, https://www.warmuseum.ca/collections/archive/3174587. Unless otherwise noted, all quotations from Mabel Rutherford in this chapter are taken from this source.

45 Ada Winifred Hammell service record, Personnel Records of the First World War, Library and Archives Canada, RG 150, accession 1992-93/166, box 3994-16, 443607, https://www.bac-lac.gc.ca/eng/discover/military-heritage/first-world-war/personnel-records/Pages/item.aspx?IdNumber=443607. Unless otherwise noted, all quotations from Win Hammell in this chapter are taken from this source.

46 Connie's role at the bank isn't known, but Cynthia Toman, author of *Sister Soldiers of the Great War*, muses that "perhaps the bank position was an early form of 'industrial nursing,' as it was called at that time." Cynthia Toman, *Sister Soldiers of the Great War* (Vancouver: UBC Press), 52.

47 Constance Bruce, *Humour in Tragedy* (London: Skeffington, 1918), *Canadiana*, https://www.canadiana.ca/view/oocihm.9_91731/1. Unless otherwise noted, all quotations from Constance Bruce in this chapter are taken from this source.

48 "Letters and Diaries of Helen Fowlds," Trent University, https://digitalcollections.trentu.ca/exhibits/fowlds/fdiary-1.htm and https://digitalcollections.trentu.ca/exhibits/fowlds/, September 15, 1915. Unless otherwise noted, all quotations from Helen Fowlds in this chapter are taken from this source.

49 R.A.L., *Letters of a Canadian Stretcher Bearer*, ed. Anna Chapin Ray (Boston:

Little, Brown and Company, 1918), 241, https://archive.org/details /lettersofcanadia00rall/page/240/mode /2up?q=%22good+place%22.

50 *Hamilton-Mills Weekly* 1, no. 3 (September 25, 1920), 2, *Canadiana*, https://www .canadiana.ca/view/oocihm.8_06800_3/2.

51 Both quotes from MacTaggart, "'Original' at Christie St."

52 "Bead Bags," *Hamilton-Mills Weekly* 1, no. 2 (September 11, 1920), 4, *Canadiana*, https://www.canadiana.ca/view/oocihm .8_06800_2/4.

53 Carolyn Macdonald, "Summary of Use of Occupational Therapy in Military Hospitals," 20110028-066, Canadian War Museum, https://www.warmuseum .ca/collections/archive/3174480.

54 MacDonald, "Summary of Use."

55 "Editorial," *Hamilton-Mills Weekly* 1, no. 2 (September 11, 1920), 3, *Canadiana*, https://www.canadiana.ca/view /oocihm.8_06800_2.

56 "Sensational Discovery," *Hamilton-Mills Weekly* 1, no. 1 (August 28, 1920), 1, *Canadiana*, https://www.canadiana.ca /view/oocihm.8_06800_1/3.

57 George Hollett service record, Military Service Files database, The Rooms Provincial Archives, GN 19, https://www .therooms.ca/sites/default/files/hollett _george_2304_0.pdf. Unless otherwise noted, all quotations regarding George Hollett in this chapter are taken from this source.

58 "Awful! Terrible!!" *Hamilton-Mills Weekly* 1, no. 3 (September 25, 1920), 1, *Canadiana*, https://www.canadiana.ca/view/oocihm .8_06800_3/1.

59 Sophie Hoerner letter to Mollie, June 8, 1915, found at "Letter - 04/06/1915 to Mollie - Page 2," Sophie Hoerner fonds, 1915–1917, Library and Archives Canada, http://central.bac-lac.gc.ca/.redirect?app =fonandcol&id=102570&lang=eng.

60 Clare Gass, *The War Diary of Clare Gass* (October 22, 1915), ed. Susan Mann (Montreal: McGill-Queen's University Press, 2000), 147.

61 K.G., "The Perils of Peace," *Souvenir of Captivity in Germany*, 10.

62 Ada Winifred Hammell pension record, provided by Veterans Affairs Canada.

63 Thomas Shirreff pension record, provided by Veterans Affairs Canada.

Faces

1 Wayne Larsen, *AY Jackson: The Life of a Landscape Painter* (Toronto: Dundurn Press, 2009), 84.

2 Anne McDougall, *Anne Savage: Story of a Canadian Painter* (Montreal: Harvest House, 1977), 85.

3 McDougall, *Anne Savage*, 35.

4 McDougall, *Anne Savage*, 34.

5 "How New Faces are Made for Soldiers at US Hospital Here," *St Louis Star and Times*, 23 May, 1919, 3, newspapers.com.

6 H.D. Gillies, *Plastic Surgery of the Face* (London: Hodder and Stoughton, 1920), page x, https://archive.org/details /plasticsurgeryof00gilluoft/page/x /mode/2up.

7 H.D. Gillies, *Principles of Art and Plastic Surgery*, (Boston: Little, Brown and Company, 1957), 10.

8 Fred H. Albee, *A Surgeon's Fight to Rebuild Men* (London: Robert Hale Limited, 1950), 110, https://archive.org/details /b29979080/page/110/mode/2up.

9 Michael William Regan service record, Personnel Records of the First World War, Library and Archives Canada, RG 150, accession 1992-93/166, box 8149-34, 596479, https://www.bac-lac .gc.ca/eng/discover/military-heritage /first-world-war/personnel-records /Pages/item.aspx?IdNumber=596479.

10 Ward Muir, *The Happy Hospital* (London: Simpkin, Marshall, Hamiton, Kent and Company, 1918), 143, Hathi Trust.

11 Francis Derwent Wood, "Masks for Facial Wounds," *The Lancet* 189, no. 4895 (June 1917): 949–951, ScienceDirect.

12 Wood, "Masks for Facial Wounds."

13 Muir, *The Happy Hospital*, 150–1.

14 R. Tait McKenzie, *Reclaiming the Maimed* (New York: Macmillan, 1918), 123, https://archive.org/details /reclaimingmaimed00mcke/page /122/mode/2up.

15 McKenzie, *Reclaiming the Maimed*.

16 "Pickard, Joseph (Oral History)," Imperial War Museum, IWM 8946, https://www .iwm.org.uk/collections/item/object /80008738, Reel 18. Unless otherwise noted, all quotations regarding Joseph Pickard are taken from this source.

17 "War's Shattered Faces Rebuilt at Sidcup," *Toronto Daily Star*, July 29, 1919, 10, ProQuest Historical Newspapers.

18 "Social Events," *Globe*, December 8, 1919, 12, ProQuest Historical Newspapers.

19 Quoted in Marjorie Gehrhardt and Suzanne Steele, "Frederick Coates: First World War 'Facial Architect,'" *Journal of War and Culture Studies* 10, no. 1 (2017): 7–24.

20 McDougall, *Anne Savage*, 52.

21 Edgar Andrew Collard, "Of Many Things...," *Gazette*, November 8, 1975, 8, newspapers.com.

22 Larsen, *AY Jackson*, 156; and McDougall, *Anne Savage*, 119.

23 Stewart Colquhoun service record, Personnel Records of the First World War, Library and Archives Canada, RG 150, accession 1992-93/166, box 1890-39, 11106, https://www.bac-lac.gc.ca/eng /discover/military-heritage/first-world -war/personnel-records/Pages/item .aspx?IdNumber=111096. Unless otherwise noted, all quotations regarding Stewart Colquhoun in this chapter are taken from this source.

24 "Wonderful!! Day of Miracles Not Yet Past–Doctors Amazed–Astonishing!!," *Hamilton-Mills Weekly* 1, no. 4 (October 14, 1920), 1, *Canadiana*, https://www .canadiana.ca/view/oocihm.8_06800_4/1.

25 "Plan Visits to Hospitals," *Globe*, February 20, 1919, 8, ProQuest Historical Newspapers.

26 Stewart Colquhoun pension record, provided by Veterans Affairs Canada.

Lungs

1 "Boy, Aged 11, Dies of Flu," *Toronto Daily Star*, January 10, 1920, 1; "Fleeing to South to Escape 'Flu,'" *Globe*, January 22, 1920, 7; "Break Record in Number of Cases of Flu," *Globe*, January 26, 1920, 11; "Grip, Influenza," *Toronto Daily Star*, January 13, 1920, 20; "More Than 500 Cases of 'Flu' at the Border," *Globe*, January 28, 1920, 3. All ProQuest Historical Newspapers.

2 "Robertson, John Hill Letter: 1918 July 7th," Canadian Letters and Images Project (CLIP) https://www.canadianletters.ca /content/document-16218; "Moody, Cecil Tyrell Letter: 1918 June 29th," CLIP, https://www.canadianletters.ca/content /document-18481.

3 "Bloor Street Viaduct Opened to Public," *Toronto Daily Star*, October 18, 1918, 11; "Couldn't Get Autos to Attend Flu Cases," *Toronto Daily Star*, October 18, 1918, 1. Both ProQuest Historical Newspapers.

4 Quoted in N.R. Grist, "Pandemic Influenza 1918," *British Medical Journal* Dec. 22–27, 1979, https://www.bmj .com/content/bmj/2/6205/1632.full .pdf?sid=8198bb03-8f5f-44ee-897d -ad3d0fd8a705.

5 "Jane McKee interview," Indian History Film Project, Canadian Plains Research Centre, University of Regina, https:// ourspace.uregina.ca/handle/10294/1954.

6 "Query Origin of Epidemic," *Globe*, October 1, 1918, 8, ProQuest Historical Newspapers.

7 "Coughing in Big Crowd Is Hun Atrocity," *Border Cities Star*, October 10, 1918, 7, Google News.

8 "Be Safe from The Influenza," *Daily Province*, November 1, 1918, 13, newspapers.com.

9 Mace Walton, "Wear a Mask," *Ogden Standard*, December 6, 1918, 7, newspapers.com.

10 "New Flu Veil Is Quite Bewitching," *Leader*, November 9, 1918, 10, newspapers.com.

11 "New Army to Fight Flu," *Globe*, October 15, 1918, 10, ProQuest Historical Newspapers.

12 "Spanish Influenza: General Preparation for Nursing at Home—SOS Lectures Nos 1 and 2," *Globe*, October 16, 1918, 9; and "Spanish Influenza: SOS Lecture No. 3—General Symptoms," *Globe*, October 17, 1918, 7. Both ProQuest Historical Newspapers. All quotes from Dr. Norris Patterson's Sisters of Service lectures are taken from these sources.

13 "Letters and Diaries of Helen Fowlds," Trent University, http://digitalcollections .trentu.ca/exhibits/fowlds/fdiary-3 .htm (early 1918) and http:// digitalcollections.trentu.ca/exhibits /fowlds/f1918-11.htm (Nov 29, 1918).

14 "Interview with Lieutenant (Nursing Sister) Mabel Lucas Rutherford," by Margaret Allemang, 1978, Canadian War Museum, 20080087–013, https:// www.warmuseum.ca/collections/archive /3174587.

15 James Campbell service record, Personnel Records of the First World War, Library and Archives Canada, RG 150, accession 1992-93/166, box 1438-6, 84786, https:// www.bac-lac.gc.ca/eng/discover/military -heritage/first-world-war/personnel -records/Pages/item.aspx?IdNumber =84786. All quotations regarding Campbell's condition are taken from this source.

16 Charles Edmonds, *A Subaltern's War*, (London: Peter Davies, Limited, 1929), 161–162, https://archive.org/details /in.ernet.dli.2015.208835/page/n175.

17 "Premier Borden's Story of His Visit to France," July 28, 1915, *Globe*, 4; "Borden Proud of Spirit of the Canadians," *Toronto Daily Star*, July 27, 1915, 1, ProQuest Historical Newspapers.

18 S.G. Bennett, *The 4th Canadian Mounted Rifles 1914–1918* (Toronto: Murray Print Co., 1926), 18–19, https://archive.org /details/mountedrifles00bennuoft/page /n53/mode/2up.

19 Bennett, *4th Canadian Mounted Rifles*, 20.

20 "My Diary, Official War Photographer Commonwealth Military Forces, 21 August 1917–31 August 1918," item 5 (3 September 3, 1917) in Papers of Frank Hurley, http://nla.gov.au/nla.obj-223193252 /view and http://nla.gov.au/nla.obj -223193377/view.

21 Quoted in Susan Butlin, "Landscape as Memorial: A.Y. Jackson and the Landscape of the Western Front, 1917–1918," *Canadian Military History* 5, no. 2, 1996, 62–70. The article gives the original source as Arthur Lismer, in Preface to *A.Y. Jackson: Paintings 1902–1953* (Toronto: Art Gallery of Ontario, 1953), 6, https://scholars.wlu.ca/cgi/viewcontent .cgi?article=1220&context=cmh.

22 "You Know, Dear Daddy, I Don't Forget," Europeana, 1914–1918, https://www .europeana.eu/en/item/2020601 /https___1914_1918_europeana_eu _contributions_17646.

23 "Photo of Lost Heroes from First World War Discovered in Auchtermuchty," *Courier Evening Telegraph*, April 2, 2013, https://www.thecourier.co.uk/news /local/fife/75998/photo-of-lost-heroes -from-first-world-war-discovered-in -auchtermuchty/; "Frank Findlay, Studio-on-the-Hill, Auchtermuchty, Fife," *St. Andrews Citizen*, August 7, 1915, 8, British Newspaper Archive.

24 "Real Thanksgiving in Military Hospitals," *Toronto Daily Star*, October 14, 1919, 10, ProQuest Historical Newspapers.

25 Excerpts from Elsie Tranter's diary, found at Through These Lines, http:// throughtheselines.com.au/2010/research /etretat.html. Tranter's original diary was published as J.M. Gillings & J. Richards, eds., *In All Those Lines: The Diary of Sister Elsie Tranter 1916–1919* (self-published, Newstead, Tasmania, 2008).

26 "The Murder of 14 Nurses," *Evening Mail*, July 10, 1918, 2, British Newspaper Archive.

27 Kenneth Cummins, "Midshipman," in *Last Post: The Final Word from Our First*

World War Soldiers, ed. Max Arthur (London: Weidenfeld and Nicolson, 2005), 214, https://archive.org/details /lastpost0000arth_g2x6/page/214 /mode/2up.

28 Edward Roberts service record, Personnel Records of the First World War, Library and Archives Canada, RG 150, accession 1992-93/166, box 8330-30, 610236, https://www.bac-lac.gc.ca/eng/discover /military-heritage/first-world-war /personnel-records/Pages/item.aspx ?IdNumber=610236.

29 "21st Infantry Battalion War Diary (1915–1919)," transcribed by Canadian Expeditionary Force Study Group, https://archive.org/details /21stInfantryBattalionWarDiary1915 -1919/page/n149, Internet Archive.

30 "Voices of the First World War: War in Winter," episode 10, Imperial War Museum, https://www.iwm.org.uk /history/voices-of-the-first-world-war -war-in-winter; and "Voices of the First World War: Winter 1916," episode 25, Imperial War Museum, https://www.iwm .org.uk/history/voices-of-the-first-world -war-winter-1916.

31 "The Vimy Ridge Story, Told in 1965 by the Men Who Fought There," Canadian Broadcasting Corporation Archives, https://www.cbc.ca/player/play /903967811861.

32 R.A.L., *Letters of a Canadian Stretcher Bearer*, ed. Anna Chapin Ray

(Boston: Little, Brown and Company, 1918), https://archive.org/details /lettersofcanadia00rall/page/180.

33 Jeffrey S. Reznick, "The 'Convalescent Blues' in Frederick Cayley Robinson's 'Acts of Mercy,'" Wellcome Library blog, June 23, 2010, http://blog.wellcomelibrary .org/2010/06/the-convalescent-blues-in -frederick-cayley-robinsons-acts-of-mercy/.

34 "Uniform of the Wounded," *Grantham Journal*, August 4, 1917, 7, British Newspaper Archive.

35 "Deaths," *London Free Press*, February 13, 1920, 12, London Public Library.

36 "Flu Delays 'Tag' Issue," *Toronto Daily Star*, February 26, 1920, 3, ProQuest Historical Newspapers.

37 "The 'Flu' and the Street Cars," *Toronto Daily Star*, February 21, 1920, 28, ProQuest Historical Newspapers.

38 Letter to Lieut. Col. T.H. McKillip from E.A. Godfrey, "Dominion Orthopaedic Hospital," Library and Archives Canada, RG24-C-8, vol. 4299, file MD2-34-1-54-25, part 2.

39 "Influenza Pandemic," *International Encyclopedia of the First World War*, October 8, 2014, https://encyclopedia.1914-1918 -online.net/article/influenza_pandemic, and Walt Mason, "Rippling Rhymes," *Leader*, March 26, 1920, 4, newspapers. com. All quotations from Harold Phillips are taken from this source.

Minds

1 "Unidentified Man Back From Front," *Gazette*, April 6, 1920, 2, newspapers.com.

2 Personal ad, *Toronto Daily Star*, October 29, 1919, 17; "The Mute Soldier," *Hull Daily Mail*, December 31, 1926, 5; "Missing Soldier Is Not Toronto Gunner," *Toronto Daily Star*, January 15, 1923, 24. All ProQuest Historical Newspapers.

3 "Hopes to Find Lost Relative," *Globe*, April 7, 1920, 8, ProQuest Historical Newspapers.

4 "Gullen, William Roy – Official Letter from the Department of Militia and

Defence Regarding the Presumed Death of Pte. William Roy Gullen April 11, 1918," Canadian Letters and Images Project (CLIP).

5 Vincent Ball, "Great War Veteran's Letters Yield Code," *Brantford Expositor*, September 11, 2018, https://www .brantfordexpositor.ca/news/local-news /great-war-veterans-letters-yield-code.

6 "Gullen, William Roy Letter: 1916 December 17th," https://www .canadianletters.ca/content/document -4854?position=41&list=aCxilZUBc54L

Hsyo7lz9o9OO5xFet9-lxnaL1kPWXIQ;
and "Gullen, William Roy Letter: 1917
May 1st," https://www.canadianletters
.ca/content/document-4919?position
=94&list=MzrCFhL6FIS8XDwLmlOBHC
rsABBSbApMzI4SXAC-Hw4. Both CLIP.

7   "Gullen, William Roy Letter to Roy from
Mary: 1917 May 6th," CLIP, https://
www.canadianletters.ca/content
/document-16600?position=96
&list=MzrCFhL6FIS8XDwLmlOBHCrs
ABBSbApMzI4SXAC-Hw4.

8   "Gullen, William Roy Letter to Roy
from Fred: 1917 May 6th," CLIP, https://
www.canadianletters.ca/content
/document-16599?position=95&list
=MzrCFhL6FIS8XDwLmlOBHCrs
ABBSbApMzI4SXAC-Hw4.

9   "Sought to Identify Man Without
Memory," *Toronto Daily Star,* April 7,
1920, 1, ProQuest Historical Newspapers.

10   "Mystery Soldier Will Be Deported," *Globe,*
April 13, 1920, 1, ProQuest Historical
Newspapers.

11   "Persons in Custody," *Police Gazette,*
September 22, 1922, 5, ancestry.ca;
"'Canadian Hero' Fooled Landladies,"
Victoria Daily Times, November 25, 1922,
21, newspapers.com; "Ex-Canadian
Held," *Windsor Star,* January 12, 1924,
13, newspapers.com.

12   "Gullen, William Roy Letter: 1917
February 11th," CLIP, https://
www.canadianletters.ca/content
/document-4860?position=60&list
=QWEPDznoao6hbYeVcLJDdoiA84Frq
-Fi_qhkZSEC8eU.

13   Robert Mills service record, Personnel
Records of the First World War, Library
and Archives Canada, RG 150, accession
1992-93/166, box 6219-17, 186213, https://
www.bac-lac.gc.ca/eng/discover/military
-heritage/first-world-war/personnel
-records/Pages/item.aspx?IdNumber
=186213, 73 and 75.

14   *War Neuroses Version B Reel 2,* Netley
Hospital 1917 and Seale Hayne Military
Hospital 1918, British Pathé, https://
www.britishpathe.com/asset/75520/.

15   Jacob Andrew Rice service record,
Personnel Records of the First World
War, Library and Archives Canada, RG
150, accession 1992-93/166, box 8222-39,
599119, https://www.bac-lac.gc.ca/eng
/discover/military-heritage/first-world
-war/personnel-records/Pages/item.aspx
?IdNumber=599119; John Patrick Denis
Ryan service record, Personnel Records of
the First World War, Library and Archives
Canada, RG 150, accession 1992-93/166,
box 8580-12, 607912, https://www.bac-lac
.gc.ca/eng/discover/military-heritage
/first-world-war/personnel-records
/Pages/item.aspx?IdNumber=607912.

16   Dora Vine, "How Would You Nurse a
Patient Suffering From Mental Shock?"
British Journal of Nursing LIII, no. 1391
(November 1914): 421, https://archive
.org/details/britishjournalnu53londuoft
/page/420/mode/2up.

17   Hugh Russell service record, Personnel
Records of the First World War, Library
and Archives Canada, RG 150, accession
1992-93/166, box 8556-36, 618022,
https://www.bac-lac.gc.ca/eng/discover
/military-heritage/first-world-war
/personnel-records/Pages/item.aspx
?IdNumber=618022. Unless otherwise
noted, all quotations regarding Hugh
Russell are taken from this source.

18   "Mid the Din of Battle," *Wingham Advance,*
March 16, 1916, 1, Huron County
Newspaper Archive.

19   Quoted in Glenn Iriam, *In the Trenches,
1914–1918,* eBookIt.com, 2011, https://
books.google.ca/books?id
=Nl2AQUqejCAC&pg=PT158.

20   "Letters from the Front," *Wingham
Advance,* April 27, 1916, 4, Huron County
Newspaper Archive.

21   "Letter from the Front," *Wingham Advance,*
August 24, 1916, 5, Huron County
Newspaper Archive.

22   "Turnberry Boy Falls," *Wingham Advance,*
September 28, 1916, 1, Huron County
Newspaper Archive.

23   Frederick Walker Mott, *War Neuroses
and Shell Shock* (London: Hodder and
Stoughton, 1919), 282, https://archive

.org/details/warneurosesshell00mottuoft/page/282/mode/2up.

24 Lewis Yealland, *Hysterical Disorders of Warfare* (London: Macmillan and Co. Ltd., 1918), 7–10, https://archive.org/details/hystericaldisord00yealuoft/page/6/mode/2up.

25 "Lost His Speech," *Wingham Advance*, July 19, 1917, 1, Huron County Newspaper Archive.

26 "Returned Hero Watched," *Wingham Advance*, July 26, 1917, 1, Huron County Newspaper Archive.

27 "Speech Returns," *Wingham Advance*, September 5, 1918, 1, Huron County Newspaper Archive.

28 "Fear Veteran Lost in Swamp," *Windsor Star*, July 20, 1937, 10; "Vet Returns, Leaves Again," *Windsor Star*, July 21, 1937, 15. Both newspapers.com.

29 "Veteran Still Being Sought," *Windsor Star*, July 22, 1937, 20, newspapers.com.

30 Hugh Russell pension record, provided by Veterans Affairs Canada.

31 "Deaths," May 19, 1970, *London Free Press*, London Public Library.

32 "Wife Seeking Husband Who Left March 10," *Leader*, May 1, 1924, 1, newspapers.com.

33 "75 Passengers on *Arabic* Hurt in Great Storm," *Gazette*, August 28, 1924, 13; "Peace Produces More Dangerous Type of Neurotic," *Province*, January 3, 1920, 3; and "Finding Fancy Names," *Caspar Star-Tribune*, December 19, 1924, 10. All newspapers.com.

34 John Armitage service record, Personnel Records of the First World War, Library and Archives Canada, RG 150, accession 1992-93/166, box 220-19, 12461, https://www.bac-lac.gc.ca/eng/discover/military-heritage/first-world-war/personnel-records/Pages/item.aspx?IdNumber=12461. Unless otherwise noted, all quotations regarding Armitage are taken from this source.

35 Memorandum of Lieut. O.B. Jones, 42 Battalion, C.E.F., Archibald MacMechan Nova Scotia Archives MG 1, vol. 2124,

no. 44, https://archives.novascotia.ca/macmechan/archives/?ID=44.

36 "Personal Narrative" given by Rev. H.W. Cunningham, Archibald MacMechan Nova Scotia Archives MG 1, vol. 2124, no. 138, https://archives.novascotia.ca/explosion/personal/narratives/?ID=27.

37 John Armitage pension record, provided by Veterans Affairs Canada. Unless otherwise noted, all quotations regarding John Armitage in this section are taken from this source.

38 "Veteran Visits Hospital, Then Ends Own Life," *Toronto Daily Star*, October 4, 1924, 3, ProQuest Historical Newspapers.

39 "Rules for Treating Returned Soldiers," *Toronto Daily Star*, February 15, 1919, 10, ProQuest Historical Newspapers.

40 "Disabled Men Soon Forgotten," *Vancouver Sun*, March 2, 1921, 6, newspapers.com.

41 "Canada's Best Driven to Beg," *Saskatoon Daily Star*, December 24, 1921, 1; "Men May Take Women's Jobs in City Hall," *Winnipeg Tribune*, January 8, 1920, 1. Both newspapers.com.

42 "Veterans Want Indians' Land," *Vancouver Daily World*, October 24, 1918, 13, newspapers.com.

43 Letter from the Department of Indian Affairs to Colonel Andrew Thompson on February 6, 1933, quoted in Stephen Smith, "Wounded After Vimy, Kahnawake Veteran Found White Privilege Still Ruled Back Home," CBC News, April 17, 2017, https://www.cbc.ca/news/canada/montreal/wounded-after-vimy-kahnawake-veteran-found-white-privilege-still-ruled-back-home-1.4071241.

44 "League of Indians: First Conference Being Held in Sault Ste Marie," *Gazette*, September 4, 1919, 2, newspapers.com.

45 "Indian Ex-Service Men Progressive," *Ottawa Citizen*, January 24, 1924, 3, newspapers.com.

46 Edward Chesley, "The Vice of Victory," in *Open House*, eds. William Arthur Deacon and Wilfred Reeves (Ottawa: Graphic Publishers Limited, 1931), 26–40, https://archive.org/details

/openhouse0000unse_t4x6/page
/26/mode/2up.

47 "Christie Street Hospital," *Hospital
World* XXIV, no. 6 (December 1923):
204, https://archive.org/details
/hospitalworld2324torouoft/page
/204/mode/2up?q=christie.

Bellies

1   Leslie Chadwell service record, Personnel
Records of the First World War, Library
and Archives Canada, RG 150, accession
1992-93/166, box 1594-56, 93952, https://
www.bac-lac.gc.ca/eng/discover/military
-heritage/first-world-war/personnel
-records/Pages/item.aspx?IdNumber
=93952. Unless otherwise indicated, all
quotations regarding Leslie Chadwell
are taken from this source.

2   "Dear Mother," November and December,
1915, Letter Collection of N/S May
Bastedo, Canadian War Museum,
19780041-009, https://www.warmuseum
.ca/collections/archive/3143425. Unless
otherwise noted, quotations from May's
letters are taken from these sources.

3   May Bastedo service record, Personnel
Records of the First World War, Library
and Archives Canada, RG 150, accession
1992-93/166, box 496-37, 28431, https://
www.bac-lac.gc.ca/eng/discover/military
-heritage/first-world-war/personnel
-records/Pages/item.aspx?IdNumber
=28431.

4   May Bastedo pension record, provided by
Veterans Affairs Canada. Unless otherwise
noted, quotations on the following few
pages (including correspondence) are
taken from this source.

5   "Orthopaedic Patients Complain About
Food," *Toronto Daily Star,* March 18, 1919,
8, ProQuest Historical Newspapers.

6   "Play and Good Meals Give Men Back
Health," *Toronto Daily Star,* 14 April, 1919,
10, ProQuest Historical Newspapers.

7   V.M. Ryley, "Report on the Dietary
Branch," from Report of the Work
of the Department of Soldiers' Civil
Re-establishment, December 1919, https://

48 "Interview with Lieutenant (Nursing
Sister) Edna Nettie Howey," by Sharon
Samland, 1978, Canadian War Museum,
20080087-014, https://www.warmuseum
.ca/collections/archive/3174588.

archive.org/details/1920v56i5p14_1499
/page/n59/mode/2up?q=dietitian.

8   Ryley, "Report on the Dietary Branch."

9   Gertrude E.S. Pringle, "A Progressive
Profession for Girls," *Maclean's,* May 15,
1922, 64, https://archive.org/details
/Macleans-Magazine-1922-05-15/page
/n29/mode/2up; Doris McHenry, "What
Is a Dietitian?" *Maclean's,* November 1,
1919, 114, https://archive.org/details
/Macleans-Magazine-1919-11-01/page
/n51/mode/2up.

10 McHenry, "What is a Dietitian?"

11 "Girl Dietitian at Big Hospital," *Calgary
Herald,* February 12, 1921, 25, newspapers.
com.

12 William Wishart service record, Personnel
Records of the First World War, Library
and Archives Canada, RG 150, accession
1992-93/166, box 10509-39, 319655,
https://www.bac-lac.gc.ca/eng/discover
/military-heritage/first-world-war
/personnel-records/Pages/item
.aspx?IdNumber=319655.

13 F.G. Banting, "The Story of the Discovery
of Insulin," University of Toronto
Libraries, W10027,-0041, https://
insulin.library.utoronto.ca/islandora
/object/insulin%3AW10027_0041.

14 Banting, "The Story of the Discovery
of Insulin," W10027_0059, https://
insulin.library.utoronto.ca/islandora
/object/insulin%3AW10027_0059.

15 "She Says She Owes Her Life to Them,"
Edmonton Journal, February 27, 1917,
newspapers.com.

16 Banting, "The Story of the Discovery
of Insulin," W10027_0119, https://
insulin.library.utoronto.ca/islandora
/object/insulin%3AW10027_0119.

17 Michael Bliss, "The Discovery of Insulin,"
    Canadian Encyclopedia, updated
    December 17, 2021, https://www
    .thecanadianencyclopedia.ca/en
    /article/the-discovery-of-insulin.

18 Walter Ruggles Campbell, "Anabasis,"
    Canadian Medical Association Journal 87,
    no. 20 (Nov. 17, 1962): 12, https://insulin
    .library.utoronto.ca/islandora/object
    /insulin%3AT10054_0002.

19 "Faculty of Medicine," *Torontonensis 1917*
    XIX (Toronto: Students' Administrative
    Council, 1917): 79, https://archive
    .org/details/torontonensis19univuoft
    /page/78/mode/2up.

20 Joseph A. Gilchrist, C.H. Best, F.G.
    Banting, "Observations with Insulin
    on Department of Soldiers' Civil
    Re-establishment Diabetics," *Canadian
    Medical Association Journal* 13, no. 8
    (August 1923): 7, https://insulin.library
    .utoronto.ca/islandora/object/insulin
    %3AT10042.

21 Edwin E. Slosson, "The Story of Insulin,"
    World's Work, November 1923, https://
    insulin.library.utoronto.ca/islandora
    /object/insulin%3AT10100_0013.

22 "Note Card Recording the First Clinical
    Use of Extract," University of Toronto
    Libraries, W10011_0001, https://insulin
    .library.utoronto.ca/islandora/object
    /insulin%3AW10011_0001.

23 "Soldier Patients Laud Work of Insulin
    Clinics," *Toronto Daily Star*, March 24, 1923,
    2, ProQuest Historical Newspapers.

24 Gilchrist, Best, and Banting,
    "Observations With Insulin," 6.

25 Quoted in Michael Bliss, *The Discovery of
    Insulin* (Toronto: University of Toronto
    Press, 1982), 271, fn45.

26 Banting, "The Story of the Discovery of
    Insulin," W10027_0217, https://insulin
    .library.utoronto.ca/islandora/object
    /insulin%3AW10027_0217, and W10027
    _0219, https://insulin.library.utoronto.ca
    /islandora/object/insulin%3AW10027
    _0219.

27 James Samuel Ostrom service record,
    Personnel Records of the First World
    War, Library and Archives Canada, RG
    150, accession 1992-93/166, box 7503-22,
    541963, https://www.bac-lac.gc.ca/eng
    /discover/military-heritage/first-world
    -war/personnel-records/Pages/item.aspx
    ?IdNumber=541963. Unless otherwise
    noted, all quotations regarding Ostrom's
    condition are taken from this source.

28 "Over There," *Kingston Whig-Standard*,
    December 29, 1917, 12, newspapers.com.

29 Arthur F. Hurst, *Medical Diseases of the
    War* (London: Edward Arnold, 1918),
    6, https://archive.org/details
    /medicaldiseaseso00hursuoft/page
    /6/mode/2up.

30 "Turner, Arthur Lawrence Letter:
    1917 October 7th," Canadian Letters
    and Images Project, https://www.
    canadianletters.ca/content
    /document-48558.

31 "Life of Diabetic Dog Prolonged," *Gazette*,
    March 23, 1922, 8, newspapers.com.

32 "Doctors Hear Lecture on Insulin
    Treatment," *Toronto Daily Star*, December
    29, 1922, 22, ProQuest Historical
    Newspapers.

33 Gilchrist, Best, and Banting,
    "Observations With Insulin," 4.

34 "Soldier Patients Laud Work of Insulin
    Clinics," *Toronto Daily Star*, March 24,
    1923, 2, ProQuest Historical Newspapers.

35 "Dietetics," Report of the Work of
    the Department of Soldiers' Civil
    Re-establishment, for the Year Ending
    December 31, 1924, https://archive.org
    /details/1925v61i4p18_1764/page/n21
    /mode/2up?q=diabetic.

36 Gilchrist, Best, and Banting,
    "Observations With Insulin," 6.

37 Ogden Besserer service record, Personnel
    Records of the First World War, Library
    and Archives Canada, RG 150, accession
    1992-93/166, box 699-4, 41824, https:
    //www.bac-lac.gc.ca/eng/discover
    /military-heritage/first-world-war
    /personnel-records/Pages/item.aspx
    ?IdNumber=41824. Unless otherwise
    noted, all quotations regarding Besserer
    are taken from this source.

38 Ogden Besserer pension record, provided by Veterans Affairs Canada. Unless otherwise noted, the quotations in the next few paragraphs are taken from this source.

39 "Late L.O. Besserer," *Ottawa Citizen*, September 26, 1922, 9, newspapers.com.

40 Quoted in Henry B.M. Best, *Margaret and Charley: The Personal Story of Dr. Charles Best, the Co-Discoverer of Insulin* (Toronto: Dundurn Group, 2003), 72.

41 "Fifty Rochesterians Saved from Death by Diabetes Through Application of Remedy Perfected by Men at Toronto University," *Democrat Chronicle*, June 4, 1923, 1, https://insulin.library.utoronto.ca/islandora/object/insulin%3AC10048_0001.

42 "Banting 'Ace Co-ordinator' of Research—MacKenzie," *Toronto Daily Star*, February 25, 1941, 4, https://insulin.library.utoronto.ca/islandora/object/insulin%3AC10155_0001.

43 Banting, "The Story of the Discovery of Insulin," W10027_0218, https://insulin.library.utoronto.ca/islandora/object/insulin%3AW10027_0218.

44 Joe Gilchrist pension record, provided by Veterans Affairs Canada. Unless otherwise noted quotations in this paragraph come from this source.

45 "Dr. Joseph A. Gilchrist: CAMC Member During First War," *Globe and Mail*, September 27, 1951, 2, ProQuest Historical Newspapers.

The Last Post

1 "Heroine's Health Breaks," *Globe*, August 18, 1936, 4, ProQuest Historical Newspapers.

2 "Earl Haig, chatting with Ojibway Indian [sic]," City of Toronto Archives, fonds 1266, item 5865, https://gencat.eloquent-systems.com/city-of-toronto-archives-m-permalink.html?key=282414.

3 Com. W.S. Dobbs, "Hospital Revisited," *The Fragment* 1, no. 1 (March 1926): 5–6, War Amps.

4 Percy Rimmell service record, Personnel Records of the First World War, Library and Archives Canada, RG 150, accession 1992-93/166, box 8286-24, 618560, https://www.bac-lac.gc.ca/eng/discover/military-heritage/first-world-war/personnel-records/Pages/item.aspx?IdNumber=618560. Additional information presented here about Rimmell's health is from his pension record, provided by Veterans Affairs Canada. Unless otherwise noted, all quotations regarding Rimmell are taken from these sources.

5 "Patients Enter Hospital," *Toronto Daily Star*, June 15, 1917, 7, ProQuest Historical Newspapers.

6 "'Long Battle' Continues for 2500 Army Veterans," *The Fragment* 1, no. 9 (November 1926): 7, War Amps.

7 Curley Christian service record, Personnel Records of the First World War, Library and Archives Canada, RG 150, accession 1992-93/166, box 1695-54, 100301, https://www.bac-lac.gc.ca/eng/discover/military-heritage/first-world-war/personnel-records/Pages/item.aspx?IdNumber=100301. Unless otherwise noted, all quotations regarding Curley Christian in the section below are taken from this source. Curley's scrapbook is also now at the Canadian War Museum (Scrapbook of Curley Christian, Accession No. 20160159-001, https://www.warmuseum.ca/collections/archive/3178758).

8 Calvin W. Ruck. *The Black Battalion, 1916–1920: Canada's Best Kept Military Secret* (Halifax: Nimbus Publishing Limited, 1987), 8.

9 Ruck. *The Black Battalion*.

10 "Limbless Man Who Enjoys Himself," *Bradford Observer*, August 19, 1936, 9, British Newspaper Archive.

11 "Limbless Hero," *Globe*, June 26, 1936, 11, ProQuest Historical Newspapers.

12 "War Romance Recalled by Trip," *Victoria Daily Times*, July 17, 1936, 9, newspapers.com.

13 "'Curly' Cheerful Despite Loss of Legs and Arms," *Winnipeg Evening Tribune*,

September 21, 1936, 1, UM Digital Collections.

14 "'I Know That Man,'" *Western Morning News*, July 27, 1936, 7, British Newspaper Archive.

15 "Mothers Weep as the King Greets Blind Heroes at Vimy," *Daily Mirror*, July 27, 1936, 1, British Newspaper Archive.

16 "Recall Landmarks Though Scars Fade," *Toronto Daily Star*, July 27, 1936, 7, ProQuest Historical Newspapers.

17 "Men Maimed at Historic Ridge Mourn for Comrades" and "Living Memorials of Vimy Worship at Hospital Here," *Toronto Daily Star*, July 27, 1936, 7, ProQuest Historical Newspapers.

18 "Canadian Amputee Writes US Casualty," *Calgary Albertan*, December 30, 1950, 11, newspapers.com.

19 "His Christie St. Work Makes Veterans Happy," *Globe and Mail*, June 14, 1949, 5, ProQuest Historical Newspapers.

20 "Opposition Flays Pension Schemes," *Gazette*, May 19, 1944, 9, newspapers. com; and Francesca Grosso, *The History of Sunnybrook Hospital: Battle to Greatness* (Toronto: Dundurn, 2014), 24.

21 B. Ryding, "Life at Christie Street," *The Christie Street Incision*, Sunnybrook Archives, https://www.communitystories .ca/v1/pm_v2.php?id=record_detail&fl =0&lg=English&ex=780&hs=0&rd =216049.

22 "Citizenship in Action," *Globe and Mail*, August 16, 1944, 6, ProQuest Historical Newspapers; and "Positive Abandonment of Christie St. Hospital Promised by

Mackenzie," *Globe and Mail*, September 11, 1944, 1, ProQuest Historical Newspapers.

23 Mary Tremblay, "The Right to the Best Medical Care," *Canadian Bulletin of Medical History* 15, no. 1 (Spring 1998): 7, https://www.utpjournals.press/doi/pdf /10.3138/cbmh.15.1.3.

24 "The Shameful Truth," *Globe and Mail*, September 4, 1944, 6, ProQuest Historical Newspapers.

25 Francis J Horan, "Hospitals and Noise," *Toronto Daily Star*, September 15, 1944, 6, ProQuest Historical Newspapers.

26 Judith Robinson, "No Privacy for Dying Soldier," *Globe and Mail*, August 14, 1944, 6, ProQuest Historical Newspapers.

27 "Christie Street Overhauling Criticized," *Globe and Mail*, September 4, 1944, 11, ProQuest Historical Newspapers.

28 "Positive Abandonment of Christie St. Hospital Promised by Mackenzie," *Globe and Mail*, September 11, 1944, 1, ProQuest Historical Newspapers.

29 "New Orthopedic Hospital Now Open," *The Hospital World* XV, no. 3 (March 1919): 84, https://archive.org/details /hospitalworld1516torouoft/page/84 /mode/2up.

30 C. Fred Bodsworth, "What a Hospital!" *Maclean's*, March 15, 1948, 18, https:// archive.org/details/Macleans-Magazine -1948-03-15/page/n9/mode/2up.

31 Lex Schrag, "Veterans Bid Adieu to Cranes, Trains," *Globe and Mail*, January 31, 1949, 3, ProQuest Historical Newspapers.

Index

Page references in bold indicate reproductions.

KRISTEN den HARTOG is a novelist and non-fiction writer, whose novels have won the Alberta Trade Fiction Book of the Year and been shortlisted for the Toronto Book Award and the Trillium Award. She is the co-author (with her sister Tracy Kasaboski) of two previous non-fiction books: *The Occupied Garden: A Family Memoir of War-torn Holland*, a *Globe & Mail* Top 100 selection, and *The Cowkeeper's Wish*, praised by *Canada's History* as a blend of "graceful prose" and "meticulous research on a stupendous scale." Work on these two books—intimate histories of ordinary families—sparked the writing of *The Roosting Box* and den Hartog's interest in how war changes the direction of people's lives so dramatically. Den Hartog lives in the west end of Toronto, not far from the former site of the Christie Street Hospital.

Photo by Jeff Winch